The Internet of Things and Big Data Analytics

The Internet of Things and Big Data Analytics
Integrated Platforms and Industry Use Cases

Edited by

Pethuru Raj, T. Poongodi, Balamurugan Balusamy, and Manju Khari

CRC Press
Taylor & Francis Group
Boca Raton London New York

CRC Press is an imprint of the
Taylor & Francis Group, an **Informa** business

AN AUERBACH BOOK

First edition published 2020
by CRC Press
6000 Broken Sound Parkway NW, Suite 300, Boca Raton, FL 33487-2742

and by CRC Press
2 Park Square, Milton Park, Abingdon, Oxon, OX14 4RN

© 2020 Taylor & Francis Group, LLC

CRC Press is an imprint of Taylor & Francis Group, LLC

ISBN: 978-0-367-34289-0 (hbk)
ISBN: 978-1-003-03673-9 (ebk)

Typeset in Garamond
by codeMantra

Contents

Preface

The Internet of Things (IoT) devices are resource-constrained as well as resource-intensive; interact with one another locally and remotely; and the amount of multi-structured data generated, collected, and stored is bound to grow exponentially. Another prominent trend is the integration between IoT devices with cloud-based applications, services, infrastructures, middleware solutions, and databases. Thus, the combination of IoT device data, data analytics, and cloud environments is going to be a stimulating and sparkling foundation for the next-generation knowledge-centric world. A variety of industry verticals, having understood the power of data in producing useful and usable intelligence, are consciously embracing data analytics platforms and processes to be extremely competitive in their offerings, outputs, and operations. There are big, fast, and streaming IoT data, and there are corresponding platforms for doing efficient and cost-effective big, real-time, and streaming analytics. This book examines pioneering technologies and tools emerging and evolving in order to capture, cleanse, and crunch data heaps to extricate actionable insights. This book also examines the application of machine and deep learning techniques in intelligent systems, services, and environments.

Author Biography

Dr. Pethuru Raj is working as the chief architect in the Site Reliability Engineering (SRE) division of Reliance Jio Infocomm Ltd. (RJIL), Bangalore, India. He has more than 17 years of IT industry experience and 8 years of research experience.

Dr. T. Poongodi is working as an associate professor, in School of Computing Science and Engineering, Galgotias University, Delhi-NCR, India. She has completed Ph.D. in Information Technology (Information and Communication Engineering) at Anna University, Tamil Nadu, India. Her main thrust research areas are Big Data, Internet of Things, Ad-hoc networks, Network Security and Blockchain Technology. She is pioneer researcher in the areas of Big data, Wireless network, Internet of Things and has published more than 25 papers in various international journals. She has presented papers at National/International Conferences, published book chapters with CRC Press, IGI global, Springer, Elsevier, Wiley, De-Gruyter and edited books with CRC, IET, and Wiley.

Dr. Balamurugan Balusamy completed his Ph.D. at Vellore Institute of Technology (VIT) University, Vellore, and is currently working as a professor in Galgotias University, Greater Noida, Uttar Pradesh, India. He has 15 years of teaching experience in the field of computer science. His areas of interest lie in the fields of Internet of Things, big data, and networking. He has published more than 100 papers in international journals and contributed book chapters.

Dr. Manju Khari completed her Ph.D. at National Institute of Technology (NIT), Patna, and is currently working as an assistant professor in Ambedkar Institute of Advanced Communication Technologies & Research, Delhi. She has 13 years of teaching experience in the field of computer science. Her interest lies in the fields of Internet of Things, big data, and networking. She has published more than 25 papers in international journals and contributed book chapters.

Contributors

K. P. Arjun
School of Computing Science and
  Engineering
Galgotias University
Greater Noida, Uttar Pradesh, India

Rohan Bali
School of Computing Science and
  Engineering
Galgotias University
Greater Noida, Uttar Pradesh, India

Balamurugan Balusamy
School of Computing Science and
  Engineering
Galgotias University
Greater Noida, Uttar Pradesh, India

T. Lucia Agnes Beena
Department of Information
  Technology
St. Josephs College
Tiruchirappalli, Tamil Nadu, India

C. Deepa
Department of Computer Science
PSG College of Arts and Science
Coimbatore, Tamil Nadu, India

E. P. Ephzibah
School of Information Technology &
  Engineering
Vellore Institute of Technology
Vellore, Tamil Nadu, India

R. Indrakumari
School of Computing Science and
  Engineering
Galgotias University
Greater Noida, Uttar Pradesh, India

S. Karthikeyan
School of Computing Science and
  Engineering
Galgotias University
Greater Noida, Uttar Pradesh, India

Parmeet Kaur
Department of Computer Science
Jaypee Institute of Information
  Technology
Noida, India

Firoz Khan
Higher College of Technology
Abu Dhabi, United Arab Emirates

Rajalakshmi Krishnamurthi
Department of Computer Science
Jaypee Institute of Information
    Technology
Noida, India

Ambeshwar Kumar
School of Computing
SASTRA Deemed to Be University
Thanjavur, Tamil Nadu, India

M. R. Manu
Computer Science Teacher
Ministry of Education,
    United Arab Emirates

G. Nalini Priya
Department of Information
    Technology
Saveetha Engineering College
Chennai, Tamil Nadu, India

K. Padmavathi
Department of Computer Science
PSG College of Arts and Science
Coimbatore, Tamil Nadu, India

Rizwan Patan
Department of Computer Science and
    Engineering
Velagapudi Ramakrishna Siddhartha
    Engineering College
Vijayawada, Andhra Pradesh, India

T. Poongodi
School of Computing Science and
    Engineering
Galgotias University
Greater Noida, Uttar Pradesh, India

P. Prabhakaran
Department of Computer Science
PSG College of Arts and Science
Coimbatore, Tamil Nadu, India

V. Pradeep Kumar
Department of Computer Science and
    Engineering
Koneru Lakshmaiah Education
    Foundation
Vaddeswaram, Andhra Pradesh,
    India

Kolla Bhanu Prakash
Department of Computer Science and
    Engineering
Koneru Lakshmaiah Education
    Foundation
Vaddeswaram, Andhra Pradesh,
    India

M. Rajasekhara Babu
School of Computer Science and
    Engineering
Vellore Institute of Technology
Vellore, Tamil Nadu, India

Manikandan Ramachandran
School of Computing
SASTRA Deemed to Be University
Thanjavur, Tamil Nadu, India

L. S. S. Reddy
Department of Computer Science and
    Engineering
Koneru Lakshmaiah Education
    Foundation
Vaddeswaram, Andhra Pradesh,
    India

K. Sampath Kumar
School of Computing Science and
    Engineering
Galgotias University
Greater Noida, Uttar Pradesh, India

Prabha Selvaraj
School of Computer Science and
    Engineering
VIT-AP Amaravathi, Andhra Pradesh,
    India

Abhishek Singh
School of Computing Science and
    Engineering
Galgotias University
Greater Noida, Uttar Pradesh, India

S. Sree Dharinya
School of Information Technology &
    Engineering
Vellore Institute of Technology
Vellore, Tamil Nadu, India

S. Sreeji
School of Computing Science and
    Engineering
Galgotias University
Greater Noida, Uttar Pradesh, India

N. M. Sreenarayanan
School of Computing Science and
    Engineering
Galgotias University
Greater Noida, Uttar Pradesh, India

R. Sujatha
School of Information Technology &
    Engineering
Vellore Institute of Technology
Vellore, Tamil Nadu, India

D. Sumathi
School of Computer Science and
    Engineering
VIT-AP Amaravathi, Andhra Pradesh,
    India

C. Thaventhiran
School of Computing
SASTRA Deemed to Be University
Thanjavur, Tamil Nadu, India

K. Thirunavukkarasu
School of Computing Science and
    Engineering
Galgotias University
Greater Noida, Uttar Pradesh, India

R. Viswanathan
School of Computing Science and
    Engineering
Galgotias University
Greater Noida, Uttar Pradesh, India

Chapter 1

Taxonomy of Big Data and Analytics Solutions for Internet of Things

S. Karthikeyan, Balamurugan
Balusamy, and T. Poongodi
Galgotias University

Firoz Khan
Higher College of Technology

Contents

1.1 Introduction

Internet of Things (IoT) is the combination of wireless sensor network, cloud computing, user interface, as the role of wireless network is to sense the data alone, where the sensors are connected to cloud server for storing the recorded data. User interface such as mobile or web application is used to receive the IoT data from the cloud. IoT application can be pointed to various fields such as healthcare, farming, industry, transportation and so on. it can be applied from household things to military bases, the sensors and the application will be changed as per the needs of the people, if an individual needs to alert any suspicious activities in his/her home, then the individual should fix a motion sensor in the home, it alerts the user if any new motions are detected in home, it can be fine-tuned and can be called as smart home (Atzori et al. 2010).

IoT came into existence around 1999 and helped humans in many places to reduce their work. They were used for basic needs such as household devices and then they replaced manpower in large numbers with small sensors, global system for mobile communications (GSM), and few servers. The next terminology is the "big data". As the IoT has evolved from wireless sensor networks and cloud computing, the IoT provides big data and handles large volumes of data that are produced by the IoT sensors or the actuators. The data can be structured, unstructured, or semi-structured depending upon the sensors that are used for the specific applications. The reason IoT generates big data is the traditional databases find it difficult to manage the unstructured as well as a huge volume of data. The generation of sensor data is continuous as the role of IoT is to alert or monitor the environment. The sensors record the data 24/7 and send a notification as the user has programmed it already in the environment (Atzori et al. 2010).

IoT generates large volumes of big data continuously from the sensors, and the recorded data are stored on cloud server, as the cloud services such as platform, software, infrastructure can be provided as per the need of the user and the requirements. In general, big data analytics is used to analyze the data and then take a decision based on the need of the user.

1.1.1 IoT Emergence

Pervasive computing, ubiquitous computing, wireless sensor network emerged from the Internet of Things around 1970s.The term "IoT" was originally coined by Kevin Ashton while working at Procter & Gamble. As the Internet was a hot topic in the late 1990s, Kevin Ashton, who was doing supply chain optimization, tried to combine two technologies: Internet and radio frequency identification (RFID). He called his presentation as "Internet of Things" (Al-Fuqaha et al. 2015).

IoT works on the principles and protocols of sensors, the Internet, cloud, and users. These components form the big picture of the IoT. The sensors or the actuators are connected to the cloud server through the Internet; then the data can be sent to the user whenever it is needed (Al-Fuqaha et al. 2015). The major roles of sensors are to capture the data from the environment; then it will be received by the user via cloud. For example, in smart homes, a motion sensor will be used to detect any suspicious activities around the location. It provides security to these smart homes by alerting and notifying the users irrespective of the distance between the home and the users.

1.1.2 IoT Architecture

The IoT architecture consists of three components: mainly IoT devices (sensors or actuators or any communication device), cloud server, and the user.

1.1.2.1 Three Layers of IoT

There are three main layers of IoT that have unique roles in the architecture, such as sensing of the data, transmission of the data, retrieving of the data.

The three major layers are

- Perception layer
- Network layer
- Application layer.

1.1.2.2 IoT Devices

These are the devices that record the data from the environment and then transmit the recorded data from the devices to the cloud servers through the IoT gateway. These devices are capable of transmitting a message from the sender to the receiver; there are chances where the sender and receiver can be the two ends and where both the ends can be IoT devices also.

Few familiar IoT devices are

- Smart devices
- Gateways
- Sensors
- Actuators
- Servers
- GSM (Figure 1.1).

1.1.2.3 Cloud Server

The cloud servers can store the data from the environment, and then the recorded data will be retrieved or reported to the user as per the constraints that are programmed to the IoT kit. Cloud computing offers various services such as infrastructure, software, and Platform as a Service.

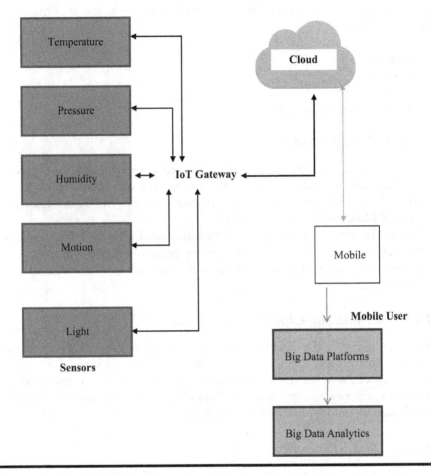

Figure 1.1   IoT architecture.

1.1.2.4 End User

The end user is the final entity who receives the message or the alert or notification from the cloud which stores the data from the IoT sensors or the actuators. If there is any delay or deletion in the received data, then the application doesn't give any value to the system.

1.1.3 IoT Challenges

The IoT generates information from sensors and the handling of that data in the cloud to make a decision displays an enormous open door for some players in all organizations and industries. Numerous organizations are sorting themselves out to concentrate on IoT and the network of their future items and administrations (Stankovic 2014):

- Security
- Storage
- Connectivity
- Bandwidth and latency.

1.1.4 IoT Opportunities

As there are numerous challenges in the IoT such as security, privacy, connectivity, storage, and reliability, it leads researchers to work on various challenges and convert them into opportunities where new methodologies and technology can be innovated (Zikopoulos and Eaton 2011).

Here, the possible opportunities that are associated with the IoT environment have been discussed such as cloud computing, privacy, security, edge computing, fog computing, integrating with human body parts such as wearables, and so on (Chen et al. 2014).

1.1.4.1 IoT and the Cloud

As the traditional local area network storage has long gone now, and IoT is the center of the Internet and cloud, the data has been recorded and stored in the cloud, where users can access or download the data as per their needs. It is estimated that in the next five to ten years, around 90% of all IoT information will be stored on cloud platforms which improve IoT data blending.

1.1.4.2 IoT and Security

IoT is all about data stored in the cloud and Internet. Even though there are many features such as easy access, cost effectiveness, sharing of resources, and so on, there are problems that arise as the data that has been stored in Internet cloud is also accessible to intruders having access to the Internet, and thereby the chances of breaching the security and accessing the servers are high (Zhou et al. 2017). From now on, around 90% of IT networks will be open to security breaches of IoT devices and this will disturb the environment. New IoT policies will be promoted by Chief Information Security Officers (CISOs) (Mahmoud et al. 2015).

1.1.4.3 IoT at the Edge

Edge computing is used to improve response time and bandwidth, by getting the computation and storage closer are to the place where it is needed. Edge computing has been implemented in major parts of IoT devices, thus enabling the users to retrieve the data faster and to increase the latency (Kim and Pathuri 2015).

1.1.4.4 IoT and Integration

As on date, around 50% of IoT devices are installed in smart homes; smart cities; and transportation, manufacturing, and many other consumer applications. It is predicted that in the next five to ten years all companies or industries would have implemented IoT in their environment.

1.1.5 IoT Applications

1.1.5.1 Real-Time Applications of IoT

Every emerging technology will have a unique application in real-time environment such as cloud computing, fog computing, artificial intelligence. IoT came into the picture to sort out the problems faced in the society (Chen et al. 2014). As its architecture is simple with a combination of Internet, sensors, cloud, and users, it is easy to apply it to any real-time problem; it enables the user or the individual to reduce the work of safeguarding entities (Lee and Lee 2015).

The applications of IoT are classified such as the following.

Consumer Applications
■ Smart homes
■ Wearables
■ Connected cars
■ Asset tracking
■ Patient monitoring in healthcare
■ Agriculture automation.

Educational Applications
■ Attendance monitoring system
■ Safety features to students
■ Anytime and anywhere learning
■ Changing boards to IoT-enabled boards.

Industrial Applications
■ Digital factory
■ Management
■ Production monitoring
■ Safety and security
■ Quality control.

The above applications are just some among *N* number of uses where IoT is used. As per the need of the society, every day one new application comes into picture.

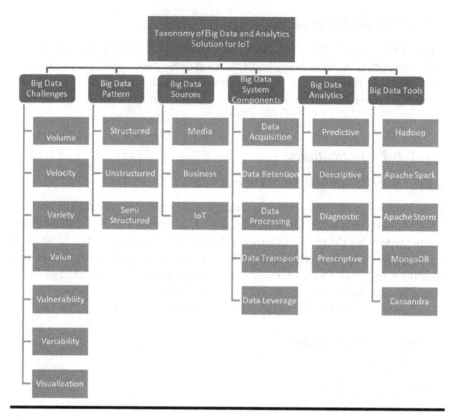

Figure 1.2 Taxonomy of big data and analytics solutions for IoT.

1.1.6 Big Data and Analytics Solutions for IoT

1.1.6.1 Big Data in IoT

The IoT and big data are closely connected as the IoT environments work on the principle of recording the data, then storing (Rialti et al. 2019), then even computing, and then retrieving it from the cloud whenever the user needs to access it (Russom 2011). The huge volume of data generated by the IoT needs the involvement of big data in IoT (Gandomi and Haider. 2015). The IoT devices include sensors, actuators, cam recorder, advanced RFID, and Bluetooth (Figure 1.2).

1.1.6.2 Big Data Challenges

There are challenges that are associated with the big data and IoT. Basically, it can be categorized into different V's of data (Jagadish et al. 2014). There are seven challenges that are associated with big data such as volume, velocity, variety, variability, vulnerability, and visualization (Labrinidis and Jagadish 2012). Here volume is the capturing

Table 1.1 Challenges of Big Data

S. No	Characteristics	Context	Example
1	Volume	Data generation in large volume	Social media generation everyday
2	Velocity	Data generation at high rate	Search results at search engine
3	Variety	Date generation in different formats	Web pages with different results
4	Value	Date generation to take decision	Predicting stock market
5	Vulnerability	Data generated with security constraints	Intruders attacking IoT data
6	Variability	Data generation with some interference	Delay in the receiving end of data
7	Visualization	Data generation with graphical representation	Tools to analyze the results

of data continuously from the environment, velocity is the high speed of sensor data that are recorded (Mikalef et al. 2018) and transferred to cloud then (Labrinidis and Jagadish 2012), variety stands for processing different types of IoT data in the cloud, vulnerability is the security of the data, and visualization is the analysis of the data for results (Marx 2013). The above challenges are familiar with big data, and it is difficult to manage the data flow in the IoT environment (Gandomi and Haider 2015).

Big data possess certain aspects that play a major role in the generation of data and speed of data (Mikalef et al. 2018):

- Volume
- Velocity
- Variety
- Value
- Vulnerability
- Variability
- Visualization (Table 1.1).

1.1.6.3 Different Patterns of Data

Data can be categorized according to the format in which it has been processed, generated, or stored. In general, traditional databases are capable of storing structured data where the schema will be defined for the database as per the needs of the individual, and it is not possible to insert some new data into the database as the schema has been fixed. New data can be inserted only after changing the schema of the database, Here big data helps to remove the issue as it can be used to generate, process, and retrieve the data in any format that the user needs.

Types of Big Data
Big data could be found in three forms:

■ Structured
■ Unstructured
■ Semi-structured.

1.1.6.3.1 Structured Data

The IoT data which can be stored, accessed, and processed in the static format is called as "structured" data. The length and the format will be static as they cannot be changed during the processing of the IoT data. The data that are stored in relational database management system (RDBMS) are structured data.

Examples of Structured Data
■ Employee list in an organization
■ Student details in a university
■ Taxpayers details in any government database
■ Library details.

1.1.6.3.2 Unstructured Data

Data with dynamic structure can be coined as unstructured data. There will not be any predefined model for these types. Unstructured data is heterogeneous data that contains many text files, multimedia. Even the organization has a huge volume of data, but the extraction of value from the data is a mammoth task as it is in an unstructured format.

Examples of Unstructured Data
■ Search results by any web pages
■ Email messages
■ Social media
■ Radar data
■ Satellite images.

1.1.6.3.3 Semi-Structured Data

Semi-structured data can contain both the structured format at one end and unstructured format at the other end. The semi-structured data can be stored in a traditional database. NoSQL (Not Only SQL) databases and object-oriented databases are considered to store semi-structured data. The database can also be called as a self-describing structure. Here the entities may belong to the structure but can have different attributes and be grouped.

Examples

DOCUMENTS STORED IN JAVASCRIPT OBJECT NOTATION

Documents stored in XML (Extensible Markup Language)

```
{
    "fruit": "Mango",
    "size": "Small",
    "color": "Yellow"
}
```

1.7 Big Data Sources

The following sources describe the list of data stored in the databases (Figure 1.3).

1.7.1 Media

Media includes social media and intuitive stages, similar to Google, Facebook, Twitter, YouTube, Instagram, just as conventional media like pictures, recordings, sounds, and webcasts that give quantitative and subjective bits of knowledge on each part of client association.

1.7.2 Business Data

The data that are captured by an organization are considered as an asset which is used for taking any crucial decisions, planning strategy, and all associated operations.

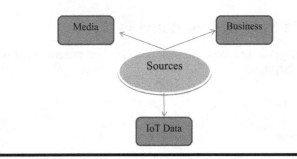

Figure 1.3 Big data sources.

1.7.2.1 Customer's Details

Name, age, mobile number, address, and all other basic details of its customers are needed for any organization for its effective running.

1.7.2.2 Transaction Details

Here the transaction details whenever a customer purchases can be noted and used for any future notifications that can be sent to the customer to increase the sale.

1.7.2.3 Interactions

Here the records such as the total number of visits by the customer; number of hits in a day; and all other interactions among the customers, stakeholders, support agents and others will be created so that on any occasion, the data can be used to take precise decisions.

1.7.3 IoT Data

Industries are using different types of sensors already, and the inclusion of the internet has led to many technological developments and reduced the workload of human beings in all aspects of the society. The IoT environment delivers intelligence using various sensors such as humidity, proximity, pressure, water quality, level, gas, IR, ultrasonic, motion detection, accelerometer, gyroscope, and optical sensors. It captures the data continuously even if there are a lot of data that are associated with multimedia such as images, videos, and so on.

The sensor data that are stored in the cloud and will increase in size can be called as big data. These sensors share the collected data with available connected devices and make it smarter for humankind, increasing functionality and effectiveness. An automated car is an example, where all the sensors collect the data from the environment and then send them the database; these data are then sent to all other vehicles.

1.8 Big Data System Components

Big data and analytics solutions usually comprise five system functions namely (Govindan et al. 2018)

1. Data acquisition
2. Data retention
3. Data transport
4. Data processing
5. Data leverage (Figure 1.4).

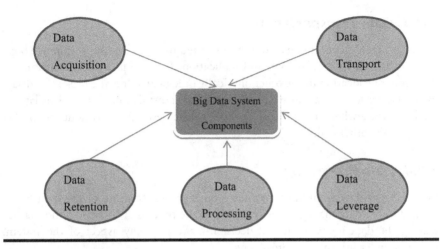

Figure 1.4 Big data system components.

1.8.1 Data Acquisition (DAQ)

It is the process of converting the physical entities into digital means, so that they can be accessed and retrieved whenever the user needs them in the future. It involves getting the data and removing the bugs or any other entities before transferring to the data warehouse. It depends on four main V's such as volume, variety, velocity, and value (Deshpande et al. 2004). It has been used in all places where data are recorded from the environment.

It does three operations such as

- Collection
- Storage
- Distribution.

1.8.2 Data Retention

It is the process in which any decisions can be taken from the available data, whenever any crucial situation occurs in industry, which is collected by the data acquisition method. Data retention policies consist of security and official or any legal worries against economics to find data formats, cryptography methods, retrieval time, and archival rules (Boyd and Crawdford 2012).

Data retention policies are the standards that are established to follow the norms of retrieving the data in the system. It makes the call of deleting any data which will be no longer required in the system and prioritizing data according to its importance.

1.8.3 Data Transportation

The data that are collected has to be transported to many servers to improve business continuity, load balancing, and replication. It is the process of transmitting data from one location to the other physically or logically. It is the reason for delaying of data or loss of data as well as the speed of transmission of data. This layer is used to ensure whether data has been sent to the destination without any packet loss from the other end.

1.8.4 Data Processing

Processing of data is another mammoth task as the structure of the data is not defined in big data management system. It is the process of collecting and manipulating the data items for useful decision-making in any aspect of the system. It comes under information processing.

The steps that are carried out are

- Collection
- Input
- Processing
- Output.

1.8.5 Data Leverage

It is the process of increasing the revenue of the organization by using the existing data in the system. In big data analytics, it uses large number of data files. As a whole, these data are huge in volume and cannot be used meaningfully, but here it can be used to predict and take any decision on any crucial situation.

There are three classifications of data leveraging:

- Automatic
- Batch
- Real-time.

1.9 Big Data Analytics Types

Big data analytics is the process of examining or finding the hidden patterns or unknown correlation from the huge volume of IoT data that are recorded by the sensors in the IoT environment. Those IoT data can be analyzed by big data analytics methods such as

1. Predictive analytics
2. Descriptive analytics

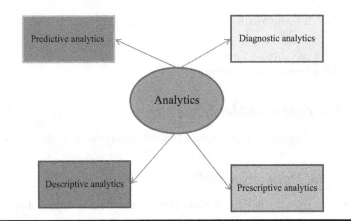

Figure 1.5 Analytics classification.

3. Diagnostic analytics
4. Prescriptive analytics (Figure 1.5).

1.9.1 Predictive Analytics

It is a method of analytics that answers the following question.

1.9.1.1 What Will Happen If ...?

It extracts the information from the available datasets, and this extraction helps us forecast the possibility that can happen in the future with risk analysis and mitigation. It is not guaranteed that all the predicted data can produce exact results; there may be a slight variation between the predicted and the future values. It is used in business as the previous customer data helps to identify the behavior and positive and negative values toward the product. It produces the probability of results for the new or the different data with the analysis of old data of the business (Waller and Fawcett 2013).

Predictive analysis uses techniques to include machine learning, statistical modeling (Duan et al. 2019), and data mining. Predictive analytics is used to analyze the increase in sales, exam results, financial services, social networking healthcare, insurance, fraud detection, pharmaceuticals, telecommunications, retail, travel, mobility, and other fields (Hazen et al. 2014). Credit scoring is the most familiar application used in predictive analytics (Waller and Fawcett 2013).

There are three different types of models such as

1. Predictive models
2. Descriptive models
3. Decision models.

There are two different analytical techniques in predictive analytics:

1. Regression techniques
2. Machine learning techniques.

1.9.2 Descriptive Analytics

It is a method of analytics that answers main questions such as the following.

1.9.2.1 What Has Happened?

It is used to answer the basic questions such as who, what, when, where, and how many to gather the information. The descriptive analytics outlines or depicts crude information and makes it something interpretable by people. It breaks down past occasions; here past occasions allude to any purpose of time that an occasion has happened, regardless of whether it is one moment back or one month prior. Descriptive analytics is valuable as it enables associations to gain from past practices and helps them in seeing how they may impact future results (Table 1.2).

For the most part, the fundamental information that gets broken down is a sum or total of a separated segment of information. Descriptive analytics is valuable in indicating things like complete stock or normal dollars spent per client.

Table 1.2 Comparisons between Analytics in Big Data

S.no	Analytics	Question	Methods	Context
1	Predictive analytics	What will happen if? What is the pattern?	Predictive modeling Statistical modeling	It predicts the future possibilities that can happen in the company
2	Descriptive analytics	What has happened? How many, when, and where?	Canned reports Ad hoc reports	It describes the events that have occurred already in the past
3	Diagnostic analytics	Why did it happen? Where must we see?	Query and drilldowns Discovery alerts	It justifies the reason for the occurrences of those events in the company
4	Prescriptive analytics	What should we do about this? What will happen if we use this?	Optimization Random testing	It suggests the solutions to overcome the past events

Associations must utilize descriptive analysis when they need to comprehend, at a total level, what is going on in their organization.

It is drafted in an easy format so that any readers who are associated with the business will be able to understand the context of the problems that are connected with sales, finance, operations, and so on. It doesn't often deal with cause and effect relationship. As a whole, descriptive analytics is mostly applied in the summary of past data. In simple terms, in the big data world, descriptive analytics gives input to advanced predictive or prescriptive analytics that supports in making any business decision.

Real-Time Examples
- Organizations' records give a past review of their financials, operations, customers, and stakeholders, sales.
- Summarizing past happenings such as sales in a specific region.
- Consolidating the total number of likes, comments, and shares in social media preferably into a table.

1.9.3 Diagnostic Analytics

It is a method of advanced analytics identifies data or information to justify the following question (Cagan 2010).

1.9.3.1 Why Did It Happen?

The ultimate objective of diagnostic analytics is to find the root cause of issues. It can be accomplished by techniques like data discovery, correlations, data mining, and drill-down. It is a method of understanding the occurrences of events and behaviors (Cagan 2010).

At this stage, historical data can be measured against other data to answer the question of why something happened. With the help of diagnostic analytics, there is a chance to drill down, discover dependencies, and distinguish patterns. Companies go for diagnostic analytics as it gives top-to-bottom insights into a particular issue. At the same time, a company ought to have detailed information at its disposal; otherwise data gathering may end up being individual for each issue and time-devouring (Cagan 2010).

1.9.3.2 Real-Time Example

Drop in website traffic of a company can lead to a decrease in the sales, and thereby revenue will also be reduced. Here diagnostic analytics finds the root cause initially, such as traffic has been reduced, and from there, it will fine-tune the problem after finding the reasons for the downside in website traffic, like software engine optimization (SEO), social marketing, email marketing, and any other factors, which are not enabling the website to reach many people. These can be done by specific strategies depending upon the need of any particular situation.

1.9.4 Prescriptive Analytics

It is a method of advanced analytics that identifies data or information to justify the following question.

1.9.4.1 What Should We Do about This?

In these analytics, both big data and artificial intelligence will come into the picture. Statistical modeling helps to assess the correlation that will show whether the hypothesis is true or false, and machine learning is used to predict the possible outcomes based on variables. Artificial intelligence suggests the solutions for any particular issue that is happening; in simple terms, it answers the *what if* questions, that is, the output for any particular input given. It uses descriptive and predictive analytics, as mathematical and computational sciences are used to extract the desired results (Bertsimas and Kallus 2014). It handles both structured (numbers, categories) and unstructured data (audio, video, images, text) and advanced analytic techniques and tools to predict and prescribe. Here the input can come from multiple sources (Gröger et al. 2014). There will not be issues with storing structured data as it can be stored in traditional database whereas storing unstructured database, it is not possible to store the data in traditional DB, to solve this issue NoSQL databases are used, it helps in making decisions. (Bertsimas and Kallus 2014).

1.10 Big Data Analytics Tools

Analytic tools are used widely to analyze the data in meaningful form among the sets of large volumes of data. Now in the market, there are many tools evolving every day to analyze the data in all forms to extract the value from the available data. It reduces the cost and time of any company as the past data can be used to take as many decisions as possible in critical situations. It is turning out to be a must for all companies because of the productivity it gives at a minimal cost. As most of the tools are open source, users can download them for free and change the modules as per the requirements of the organization.

1.10.1 Hadoop

It is a software library framework, where processing of distributed systems will be done on clusters (Vavilapalli et al. 2013). It can be extended from one to multiple machines in any environment. It is one of the most commonly used tools in big data processing in many companies for extracting the data; the hardware requirements are less as the data processing is mostly done on the cloud.

1.10.1.1 Features of Hadoop

Many features that are associated with Hadoop; few major features are listed here.

1.10.1.1.1 HDFS

It is one of the distributed file systems that run on any hardware but gives high performance and throughput by using the MapReduce algorithm. The Hadoop File System (HDFS) stores data across multiple machines by replicating the data in all other servers, in case if any data fails in primary servers. It contains two nodes:

- Name node
- Data node.

Features of HDFS
- Fault tolerance
- High reliability
- High replication
- Scalability
- Distributed storage.

1.10.1.1.2 MapReduce

It contains two tasks: map and reduce. Map gets a set of data and changes it into set of data in which the elements are broken down into Key-Value pairs. Then the reduce task takes input from the map and splits those tuples into smaller tuples and maps (Bhandarkar 2010).

Map – Splitting and Mapping
Reduce – Shuffling and Reducing

Features of MapReduce
- Local data processing
- In-built redundancy
- Independent language
- MapReduce execution framework
- Inter-process communication.

1.10.2 Apache Spark

It is an open-source and cluster computing framework. It is designed for fast computation and works on the concept of MapReduce. It has memory cluster computing which increases the processing speed of application.

Features of Spark
- Speed
- Advanced analytics
- Swift processing
- Dynamic in nature
- In-memory computation
- Reusability
- Fault tolerance
- Supports multiple languages like Java, R, Scala, and Python.

1.10.3 Apache Storm

It is a free and open source real-time distributed real-time computation system written in Java and Clojure. It is leading to real-time data analytics.

Features of Storm
- Robust and user friendly
- Real-time stream processing
- Fault tolerance
- Flexible
- Reliable
- Operational intelligence.

1.10.4 NoSQL Databases

In 1970s, Flat File Systems were used to store the data, but the problem is there is no standardization in the storage. It is a non-relational database or non-SQL database. It works on the mechanism apart from the tabular relations model for storing data. Preferably it is used to store real-time web applications and big data (Han et al. 2011).

Databases can be classified into three types:

1. RDBMS
2. Online analytical processing (OLAP)
3. NoSQL.

Features of NoSQL
- Performance is high.
- Used as a familiar query language.
- Less downtime.
- Scalability is easy.
- Flexible.

1.10.5 Cassandra

Here the data will be stored on many servers more than one replication factor so that the data will be available at all points of time without any downtime (Lakshman and Malik 2010).

Features of Cassandra
- Fast writing
- Replication
- Schema-free
- Transaction support
- Application programming interface
- Schema-free
- Flexible data storage.

1.10.6 RapidMiner

It is an environment for data mining and machine learning (ML). It can be applied in both research and real-world data mining tasks (Hofmann et al. 2013).

Applications
- Multimedia mining
- Text mining
- Feature engineering
- Datastream mining
- Distributed data mining.

1.11 Conclusion

In this chapter, components of IoT devices, such as sensors, cloud servers, IoT gateway and physical devices, which are used in transmission of the data from the environment to the network, have been discussed. This chapter discusses big data analytics where data are generated continuously. Here the challenges in the generation of big data are classified, and different patterns of IoT data have been categorized. Media, business, and IoT are the major sources of big data generation. Big data system components such as data acquisition, data retention, data processing, data transport, data leverage are explained. Predictive, prescriptive, diagnostic, and descriptive analytics are used to take an optimal decision. Tools are also used in storing the data according to the format.

References

Al-Fuqaha, Ala, Mohsen Guizani, Mehdi Mohammadi, Mohammed Aledhari, and Moussa Ayyash. "Internet of Things: A survey on enabling technologies, protocols, and applications." *IEEE Communications Surveys & Tutorials* 17, no. 4 (2015): 2347–2376.

Atzori, Luigi, Antonio Iera, and Giacomo Morabito. "The Internet of Things: A survey." *Computer Networks* 54, no. 15 (2010): 2787–2805.

Bertsimas, Dimitris, and Nathan Kallus. "From predictive to prescriptive analytics." arXiv preprint:1402.5481 (2014).

Bhandarkar, Milind. "MapReduce programming with apache Hadoop." In *2010 IEEE International Symposium on Parallel & Distributed Processing (IPDPS)*, pp. 1–1. IEEE, Atlanta, GA, 2010.

Boyd, Danah, and Kate Crawford. "Critical questions for big data: Provocations for a cultural, technological, and scholarly phenomenon." *Information, Communication & Society* 15, no. 5 (2012): 662–679.

Cagan, Christopher L. "Method and apparatus for advanced mortgage diagnostic analytics." U.S. Patent 7,853,518, issued December 14, 2010.

Chen, Shanzhi, Hui Xu, Dake Liu, Bo Hu, and Hucheng Wang. "A vision of IoT: Applications, challenges, and opportunities with China perspective." *IEEE Internet of Things Journal* 1, no. 4 (2014): 349–359.

Deshpande, Amol, Carlos Guestrin, Samuel R. Madden, Joseph M. Hellerstein, and Wei Hong. "Model-driven data acquisition in sensor networks." In *Proceedings of the Thirtieth International Conference on Very Large Data Bases*, Vol. 30, pp. 588–599. VLDB Endowment, Toronto, Canada, 2004.

Duan, Yanqing, John S. Edwards, and Yogesh K. Dwivedi. "Artificial intelligence for decision making in the era of big data – Evolution, challenges and research agenda." *International Journal of Information Management* 48 (2019): 63–71.

Gandomi, Amir, and Murtaza Haider. "Beyond the hype: Big data concepts, methods, and analytics." *International Journal of Information Management* 35, no. 2 (2015): 137–144.

Govindan, Kannan, T. C. Edwin Cheng, Nishikant Mishra, and Nagesh Shukla. "Big data analytics and application for logistics and supply chain management." *Transportation Research Part E: Logistics and Transportation Review* 114 (2018): 343–349.

Gröger, Christoph, Holger Schwarz, and Bernhard Mitschang. "Prescriptive analytics for recommendation-based business process optimization." In *International Conference on Business Information Systems*, pp. 25–37. Springer, Cham, 2014.

Han, Jing, E. Haihong, Guan Le, and Jian Du. "Survey on NoSQL database." In *2011 6th International Conference on Pervasive Computing and Applications*, pp. 363–366. IEEE, Port Elizabeth, South Africa, 2011.

Hazen, Benjamin T., Christopher A. Boone, Jeremy D. Ezell, and L. Allison Jones-Farmer. "Data quality for data science, predictive analytics, and big data in supply chain management: An introduction to the problem and suggestions for research and applications." *International Journal of Production Economics* 154 (2014): 72–80.

Hofmann, Markus, and Ralf Klinkenberg, eds. *RapidMiner: Data Mining Use Cases and Business Analytics Applications*. Boca Raton, CRC Press, 2013.

Jagadish, Hosagrahar V., Johannes Gehrke, Alexandros Labrinidis, Yannis Papakonstantinou, Jignesh M. Patel, Raghu Ramakrishnan, and Cyrus Shahabi. "Big data and its technical challenges." *Communications of the ACM* 57, no. 7 (2014): 86–94.

Kim, Ryan Yong, and Venkata Subba Rao Pathuri. "Setup of multiple IOT devices." U.S. Patent 9,210,192, issued December 8, 2015.

Labrinidis, Alexandros, and Hosagrahar V. Jagadish. "Challenges and opportunities with big data." *Proceedings of the VLDB Endowment* 5, no. 12 (2012): 2032–2033.

Lakshman, Avinash, and Prashant Malik. "Cassandra: A decentralized structured storage system." *ACM SIGOPS Operating Systems Review* 44, no. 2 (2010): 35–40.

Lee, In, and Kyoochun Lee. "The Internet of Things (IoT): Applications, investments, and challenges for enterprises." *Business Horizons* 58, no. 4 (2015): 431–440.

Mahmoud, Rwan, Tasneem Yousuf, Fadi Aloul, and Imran Zualkernan. "Internet of Things (IoT) security: Current status, challenges and prospective measures." In *2015 10th International Conference for Internet Technology and Secured Transactions (ICITST)*, pp. 336–341. IEEE, 2015.

Marx, Vivien. "Biology: The big challenges of big data." *Nature* 498 (2013): 255–260.

Mikalef, Patrick, Ilias O. Pappas, John Krogstie, and Michail Giannakos. "Big data analytics capabilities: A systematic literature review and research agenda." *Information Systems and e-Business Management* 16, no. 3 (2018): 547–578.

Rialti, Riccardo, Giacomo Marzi, Cristiano Ciappei, and Donatella Busso. "Big data and dynamic capabilities: A bibliometric analysis and systematic literature review." *Management Decision* 57, no. 8, (2019): 2052-2068.

Russom, Philip. "Big data analytics." *TDWI Best Practices Report, Fourth Quarter* 19, no. 4 (2011): 1–34.

Stankovic, John A. "Research directions for the Internet of Things." *IEEE Internet of Things Journal* 1, no. 1 (2014): 3–9.

Vavilapalli, V.K., Murthy, A.C., Douglas, C., Agarwal, S., Konar, M., Evans, R., Graves, T., Lowe, J., Shah, H., Seth, S. and Saha, B. "Apache Hadoop yarn: Yet another resource negotiator." In *Proceedings of the 4th Annual Symposium on Cloud Computing*, p. 5. ACM, Santa Clara, California, 2013.

Waller, Matthew A., and Stanley E. Fawcett. "Data science, predictive analytics, and big data: A revolution that will transform supply chain design and management." *Journal of Business Logistics* 34, no. 2 (2013): 77–84.

Zhou, Jun, Zhenfu Cao, Xiaolei Dong, and Athanasios V. Vasilakos. "Security and privacy for cloud-based IoT: Challenges." *IEEE Communications Magazine* 55, no. 1 (2017): 26–33.

Zikopoulos, Paul, and Chris Eaton. *Understanding Big Data: Analytics for Enterprise Class Hadoop and Streaming Data*. McGraw-Hill Osborne Media, Emeryville, 2011.

Chapter 2

Big Data Preparation and Exploration

T. Poongodi, M. R. Manu, R. Indrakumari,
and Balamurugan Balusamy

Galgotias University

Contents

Nowadays, the most tedious thing is to get accurate and precise data. So when it comes to huge amount of data, it is difficult to segregate them. The above-mentioned problems are solved by big data technology. The methodology of data preparation is an effective tool for decision-making and capturing of genuine data. Query processing and streaming of social network data can be efficiently processed by data preprocessing mechanism. The ensemble analysis of large sets of data is associated with different techniques involved in big data analysis. In the medical field, the authenticity of data is crucial. Every report that to be processed and analyzed should be accurate and genuine so the data preparation is an essential need for the big data processing.

2.1 Understanding Original Data Analysis

The lack of original data and understanding of the processing of current data was a real threat in medical big data processing. The major factor is the ability to understand whether the data to be segregated has to be categorized for privacy and authenticity. The originality of data is crucial, and for segregating it, plenty of information should be collected. Following are some information to be considered [1].

1. The foremost thing is to answer for all relevant question raised in suspect ability of data.
2. Accuracy of medical data in all aspects should be evaluated.
3. The decision-making based on the information should be precise and unambiguous (Figure 2.1).

There are certain steps to be followed for understanding original data analysis. They are described below.

(i) Designing of Questions and Problems
   Data should be understood by designing various questionnaires and problems to be answered and solved. The framed questions should be clear

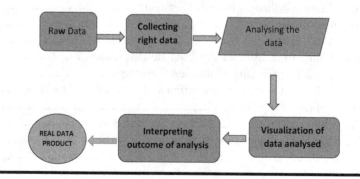

Figure 2.1   Understanding process of raw data.

and concise. The questions can be of querying or non-querying type depending on the information and scenario. The main constraint are the data should be measurable and the unit of measurement should be judgable. For example, a medical diagnosis of a patient having asthma problem shows a real scenario of querying. Sometimes the disease occurs due to food intake or by some habitual behaviors. The genetic behavior also becomes a factor for it or environmental disorders also a reason, so a real query should be asked with the chances and relevance of the data. But a question like how long asthma can be sustained with above factor is an ambiguity because all the above parameters cannot perfectly be chances for it or a constant reason for the genetic background can have a chance of getting cured by ageing. These parameters can be measurable and precise. So for each query to be answered, a large set of data has to be collected and organized.

(ii) Collection of Data

Data collection is a huge task for designing a questioner. The data collected has to be well organized and informative. The primary task is to collect existing available data before collecting new data. On the basis of existing data, missing data and parameters should be measured. The observation of the data is a very critical task for the formation of genuine data. Getting data is not a big task, but acquiring the right data is very important.

(iii) Analysis of the Data

After getting the right data, a deeper data analysis should be done. The data should be sorted in a particular order and filtered based on observable parameters to be analyzed. On the basis of overall data, the maximum, minimum, and standard deviation should be analyzed and evaluated. Any relevant tools can be used for the data analysis and for getting an accurate result from the analyzed dataset. The fluctuation of the result depends on the analysis of data. A perfect analysis provides accurate and precise results; imperfection can lead to a failure of the whole process.

(iv) Interpretation of Outcome from Analysis

The result can be altered by any mismatch in any of the above steps. The result of interpretation of outcome from analysis only depends on whether the hypothesis assumed is true or false. Rejection or failure should also be considered rather than accepting an uninterrupted data analysis.

2.2 Benefits of Big Data Pre-Processing

Big data have grown massively and been evaluated and processed in the recent years. The problems faced by traditional database systems are remedied by big data processing. Ensuring the high quality of data and cleaning of data are major tasks. Here are some fascinating benefits of big data pre-processing.

(i) Noise Filtering

In this technological era, it's very difficult to get data without noise. Most part of data processing involves the problem of missing data and outlier data management. The noise in digital data is due to the padded or unwanted bits embedded with the data in digital form. There are different methods for removal of noise from ordinary data, but in case of big data, it's a difficult task. A large amount of data need to be analyzed to reproduce the high quality of data. Big data need to be processed efficiently and accurately within prescribed time limit. But the alteration of this type of data is called as noise in big data. The imperfection of data can be effected by different factors like distribution of unmanaged data, transmission, and integration of data. Intelligent decision-making of big data can be influenced by the noise barrier effected by the above factors. The futuristic techniques in big data have the limitation of imperfection occurring during data processing. Big data can be transformed to a new form which has less noise, and this form is referred to as smart data. There are different methods for smart data processing. Here processing is a solution to noise problems in big data analysis which intense the formation of Smart data are as follows. Apache Spark framework is used to eliminate the noisy information from the clustered data. The two main methods are described in the following [1].

(a) Univariate Ensemble Method

The Univariate Ensemble method uses a single classifier for distinguishing and filtering the actual data with an outlier. It uses Random Forest algorithm for classification in different division of training set and undergo decision-making for analysis. The method also consists of a cross-validated committee filter which manipulates the data through a partition based on homogenous sections [1]. Each section in the tree undergoes voting mechanism in which the misclassified instance for the particular section is eliminated in such a way that each section iterates and results in noise-free information. It also involves a prediction mechanism for noise filtering (Figure 2.2).

Figure 2.2 illustrates the process of retrieval of smart data. There are some decision-making processes to iterate the data again and again for getting smart data. The partitioning method will analyze each part of the data units for accuracy and for making the validation process simple. The final product of this analysis will produce smart data which will be noise free and precise.

(b) Multivariate Ensemble Method

Figure 2.2 illustrates the process of retrieval of smart data. There are some decision-making processes to iterate the data again and again for getting smart data. The Multivariate Ensemble method uses multivariate Random Forest algorithm with gradient-boosted machine [3]. The multivariate algorithm uses a prediction mechanism with multiple

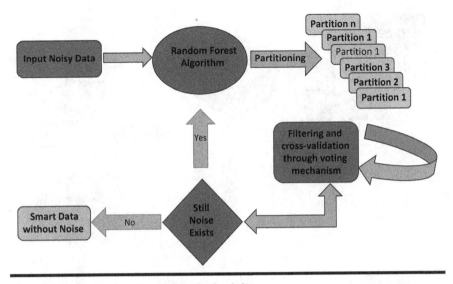

Figure 2.2   Univariate Ensemble Method diagram.

response data instead of a single data for noise filtering. The analysis involves the time factor of data as well as its clustering property. The splitting process or partitioning process will undergo regressive tree partition. The boosting will yield high performance since it can eliminate the errors or residual errors of the previous iteration. A better result will be obtained by this methodology since it involves parallel processing of a large amount of data. It is more complex than the Univariate Ensemble Method, so for processing of a single data, it yields better performance and poor time utilization.

Figure 2.3 shows a variant behavior [4] which involves partitioning of data followed by the gradient-boosting method for avoiding the residual errors so that prediction power will be improved and accuracy will be increased. The voting process will improve the precision iterates till noise-free data is obtained to form a set of smart data. As mentioned earlier, it is suitable for an ensemble of noisy data to be filtered in parallel (Figure 2.3).

(ii) Agile Big Data

The agile capability of big data analysis [5] helps in overcoming the unpredictable changes and handling large amount of information. The scalability of data can be attained through agility. The main purpose is to adapt to new changes in the methodology and framework. So for that, it involves distributed systems with a cloud computing platform for iteratively processing the data. Data transformation can be done through this agile property of big data pre-processing. It also involves joint ownership where there will be

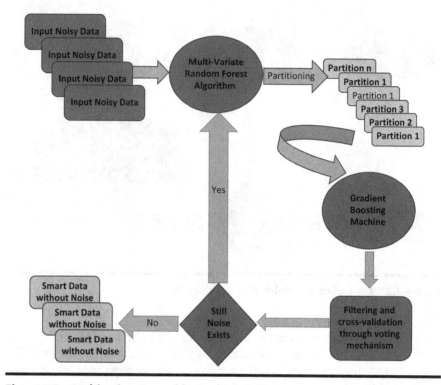

Figure 2.3 Multivariate Ensemble Method diagram.

interaction between different organizations and business partners. The joint ownership will help to improve the validation process and data migration very quickly and accurately. The agile business lab will comprise a variety of stakeholders like business and IT experts.

(a) Understanding Agile Data

The main feature of agile data is its digital transformation and migration management. In different domains, the data as well as its features will vary. This process involves the identification of data through its characteristics and activities. It will increase the quality of services and reduce the cost and reliability of data.

(b) Benefits of Agile Data

The main advantage of agile data [5] is the clarity of information. In business, enterprises will frequently change their framework and processes, so they need to manage the data to adapt to the new environment. So this capability can be easily achieved through agile data. The agile management team will make decisions in every crucial situation. The integration and transformation of data in a new platform will be reconsidered by this agile team before processing. These data contain mostly transactional data which can automate the process with higher operational efficiency. Some other benefits include the focus toward real-time results, feature engineering, better validation, and machine learning capability. The achievement of target metrics in data exploration and cleaning processes will be quite simple with agile data. The changes in scope and requirements because of different partners can be processed by this agile data methodology.

(c) Agile Data Processing

Agile processing [6] involves a set of data partners such as IT companies, business organizations, and marketing firms. In agile processing data is captured from different applications, processed for extraction, and then driven to data structuring for end user needs. Data can be categorized as snapshots and modular components. The snapshots involve information for transmission and consumption. The modular components can be processed faster by splitting them into different smaller units which involves real-time transmission of data. After structuring, data is transformed to be published for end user consumption (Figure 2.4).

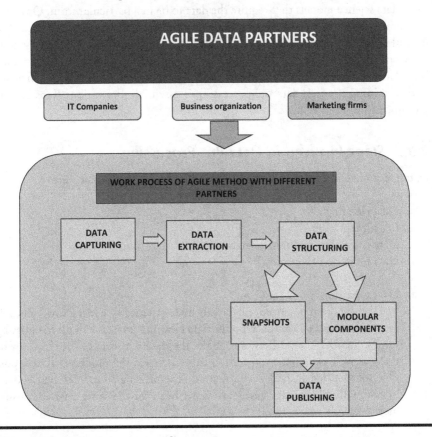

Figure 2.4 Agile data process diagram.

2.3 Data Pre-Processing and Data Wrangling Techniques for IoT

A more fascinating feature of data analytics in data science is the data pre-processing technique. Data from sources can be structured, unstructured, or semi-structured. The data extracted is unable for analysis, so data preparation is essential. The data from IoT devices undergo the data preparation process through two techniques:

- Data pre-processing
- Data wrangling.

2.3.1 Data Pre-Processing

Data pre-processing [8] is an important step in data preparation. It is a process of converting the raw data into clean data. The raw data is not suitable for analysis. It undergoes different iterative processes. Data pre-processing is mainly needed in some data science models that require the data to be in a particular form. Ordinary data processing cannot process data in a prescribed form. So pre-processing will be helpful for the processing incompatible data. The dataset will be processed by more than one machine learning algorithm, so pre-processing will be useful for that. Raw data are more noisy and have lower quality. In order to improve the efficiency of data mining process, data pre-processing is essential. The various steps in data pre-processing are as follows.

2.3.2 Steps Involved in Data Pre-Processing

Data pre-processing methods without feedback involve four major steps:

a. Data cleaning
b. Data integration
c. Data discretization/transformation
d. Data reduction (Figure 2.5).

(a) Data Cleaning

The data that is sent for analysis is inconsistent [8], has missing values, is incomplete, and has outliers. So the data cleaning process will fill the missing values, identify the outliers, and make the data consistent. The data can be noisy as well as unsynchronized, so this data cleaning process will be a possible solution for all faulty information. The missing values can be removed by manually filling data, using attribute mean for the same class, and using most probable values to fill the gap.

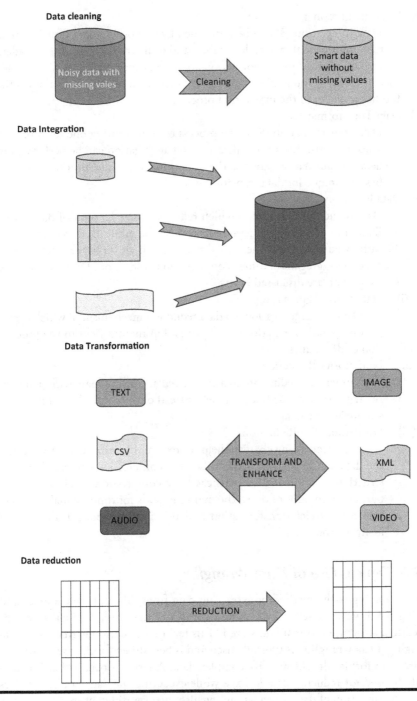

Figure 2.5   Data pre-processing diagram.

(b) Data Integration

Data integration [8] can be performed by combining data from multiple sources, multiple databases, data cubes, and ordinary flat files. The metadata in the data sources gives information about data that can be used for avoidance of errors in integration. The redundancy or duplication of values is the another problem in the integration process.

(c) Data Transformation

Data transformation [8] is the process of transforming one form of data into another form. Data normalization and aggregation can be performed in the data transformation process. The smoothing and generalization process is the best technique for data transformation.

(d) Data Reduction

Data reduction is a process which reduces a huge amount of data into a small amount of data. Data representation can be minimized so as to reduce the entire volume of data. There are different methods for data reduction such as data cube aggregation, dimension reduction, and so on. Different types of data reduction are discussed below.

(i) Data Cube Aggregation

Data cube aggregation is a data reduction mechanism in which aggregation operation is performed. Aggregation mainly yield to the production of data cubes.

(ii) Numerosity Reduction

Numerosity reduction involves the replacement of data with parametric, regression, or log linear model. Instead of the whole data unit, it uses a model of the data.

(iii) Dimensionality Reduction

The encoding mechanism helps to reduce the size of data. Sometimes the data can be lossy or lossless. Lossless compression can enable reconstruction of original data, whereas lossy compression involves loss of a particular amount of data. The main methods for dimensionality reduction are wavelet transformation and principal component analysis for analyzing outliers.

2.3.3 Typical Use of Data Wrangling

Data wrangling is the method of extracting data from different data sources and sorting them with the help of different algorithms. The resulting data is decomposed to a structured format and stored. This technique is also referred to as data munging. Data wrangling is typically used and is best suited for time series data of a particular format. It will simplify complex data. Another aspect is that it is particularly used for reducing data leakage while executing the data. It also involves the cross-validation of data. Data wrangling also involves different steps:

(i) Discovering and Structuring of Data

The discovery and structuring of data require the understanding of data. There are different criteria for data manipulation. The data needs to be restructured in a manner suitable for any analytical process.

(ii) Cleaning and Enriching

The cleaning process yields high-quality data, and the undefined values are altered and reformatted. Then the cleaned data undergo enriching. It involves deciding whether the data can be combined with some arguments or not. From the resulting data, a new form of data can be derived.

(iii) Validating and Publishing

The validation process depends on the genuineness of data. It involves repeating the analysis and distribution processes. After all analysis and processing, the data is published for end users. The data published will be more accurate and less susceptible to noise and errors. The main use of publishing data is it helps end users to get an overview of the previous steps performed by studying the documentation.

2.3.4 Data Wrangling versus ETL

Data wrangling is used to analyze data of any form from different sources, whereas ETL (extract, transform, and load) can handle only structured data. Data wrangling focuses on processing and reducing complex data into a simpler form. The main aim of ETL is to extract, transform, and load data into central enterprise for business analysis (Figure 2.6).

2.3.5 Data Wrangling versus Data Pre-Processing

Data pre-processing is a step before data wrangling. The cleaning and aggregation are done in the same manner for both. Data pre-processing is performed before the iterative steps in any analysis model, but the data wrangling is performed in between iterative processes. It performs feature engineering process compared to data pre-processing.

2.3.6 Major Challenges in Data Cleansing

Data cleansing plays an important role in the decision-making process. It helps to improve the quality of data. The problems will be more complex if the data are heterogeneous, so in these cases, the cleansing the data is better. It detects the errors and removes major errors and inconsistencies in data. It involves the mapping process for transformed data. The major challenges involve data quality and data heterogeneity. Both can be rectified by this data cleansing method.

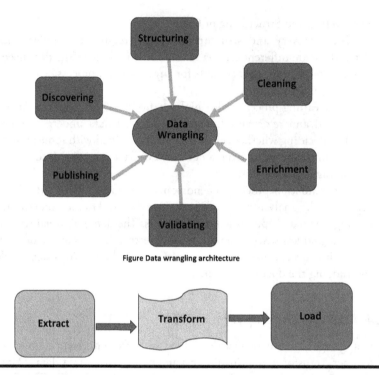

Figure Data wrangling architecture

Figure 2.6   ETL process diagram.

2.4 Challenges in Big Data Processing

Big data processing is an evolving discipline, and the sizes of databases are growing exponentially and are beyond the capabilities and capacities of traditional database management systems. A static structure is not suitable for efficient storage of files and big data databases. Gartner has identified four significant challenges: increasing speed, volume of data, variability of data, and types of data structures. In addition, value is also considered and plays a vital role in big data for efficient decision-making. Moreover, there is an increase in big data challenges and opportunities that has a major impact on science, business, government, etc.

Analytics: Big data analytics depends on heterogeneous resources which triggers consumer-based companies to analyze and understand the needs and behaviors of the customers. The lack of appropriate analytical technologies for big data needs attention and valuable insight into it. The flexible and scalable real-time big data analytics platform requires mining the relevant information from a large amount of data retrieved from heterogeneous devices. The platforms should be developed by considering the various ways to employ technologies and analyze behavioral patterns in order to enrich the operational efficiency, thus enabling the company to become successful.

Privacy: Maintaining the privacy of customers is a major concern in this enterprise era, and big data deals with personal information that users do not like to reveal. Hence, a novel methods and technologies have to be identified where customers can dynamically verify the data privacy according to the regulations defined in the service-level agreements. Without ensuring customers' privacy, it is not possible to obtain the complete information from or about the customers; thereby it leads to inefficient decision-making.

Integration: It involves merging of data from multiple sources that are maintained using various technologies in order to provide a unified framework. The data which is gathered can be un-structured, semi-structured, or structured. Integrating the different types of data is highly challenging in combining heterogeneous applications. Hence, efficient data integration mechanisms are important to obtain enriched information from raw data. The challenging issues such as overlapping of identical data, increased scalability and performance, and real-time data access are closely associated with the big data integration process.

Robust and Scalable Computing: The big data in cloud aggregates multiple different workloads and various performance goals. Processing big data architectures requires a distributed parallel processing capability to handle intrinsic I/O or CPU limitations. Subsequently, it requires more resource utilization, which in turn brings challenges in executing different jobs such as completing the disparate workloads in a cost-effective manner. The frequently occurring system failures should also be addressed while operating large systems.

As the amount of data increases rapidly in several domains, obtaining efficiency in data processing is highly challenging. Understanding, utilizing, and providing quality service in big data are perceived as upcoming challenges. Big data processing involves four steps such as data collection, pre-processing, storage, and analysis. Data quality is a significant factor in all these stages, and big data is supported by number of statistical analysis tools. A variety of analytical tools are required to manage algorithms and provide a reliable decision. Moreover, the reliability of the data source can be assured if the data quality is high. The prediction systems and the recommendation systems are the recent successful applications in big data processing.

Data quality significantly involves usability, availability, relevance, and reliability. Usability refers to the measure of whether the available data is useful and satisfies user requirements. Availability refers to the degree of access level to the available information, and it is categorized into accessibility and timeliness. Relevance refers to the degree of correlation between the existing data content and the user expectations. Reliability relies on the trust level of data that includes consistency, accuracy, and integrity (Table 2.1)

Some of the researchers have commented on the challenges of big data. In [19], Jacek concentrates on the issues regarding data quality at the time of the data collection process. The issues of data collection are analyzed by comparing the statistical survey and big data technologies. The obstacles faced in achieving quality

Table 2.1 Big Data Quality Features

Dimension	Elements
Usability	Credibility
Availability	Accessibility, timeliness
Relevance	Fitness
Reliability	Consistency, completeness, accuracy, integrity

data in big data is discussed. Chen et al. [20] compare the differences in data because of incomplete data normalization, bias weighting, improper data preprocessing, data linearization or non-linearization, loss of information discretization, etc. Li [21] reviews the complete status of data storage and management; the issues are analyzed and presented with solutions.

Issues in big data during data collection, pre-processing, storage, and analysis have to be considered. The massive amount of data poses many technical challenges in all the following steps. Several issues occur in all the phases and are discussed below.

(1) Data Collection
  (a) The recall rate is low, and less amount of data collection happens in this phase because it is very difficult to obtain the complete data due to improper network connectivity. The quality of data is highly dependent on the built-in search engine in the social network platform. The data loss is more, the gathered amount of data is low, subsequently the recall rate is too low, and finally the data which is collected may not be sufficient for analysis.
  (b) Data sparseness refers to the sparseness of score matrix of the user object that indicates that the interaction between the user and the items is sparse. In this case, the ratio of the items chosen by the user is very low in the entire project space, and the predictive performance of different recommended strategies is greatly reduced. Moreover, the available dataset is too sparse, and the accuracy would be reduced which in turn leads to the overfitting problem.
(2) Data Pre-Processing
  Noisy data is about data anomalies or data loss in the data retrieved from the prediction or recommendation system. The raw data may also be noisy because it is collected from heterogeneous sources, and it may have different unpredictable quality levels in terms of noise, consistency, redundancy, etc. Some abnormal data may arise during the data collection process, and the

online process may generate bogus data. In addition, hardware and software problems may cause noisy data which in turn leads to abnormalities in the obtained results.

(a) Incomplete data makes sense that gathered data in a certain amount of time is not adequate to reflect various issues. For instance, the data regarding a year's earthquake can be retrieved from several social media such as microblogs, twitter, etc. in order to make some predictions. Incomplete collection of statistical data about the severely affected remote areas causes incomplete and missing data in further data analysis.

(3) Data Storage

(a) Limitations in Storage Technology: The massive amount of data; storage standards; and complex and different forms such as structured, semi-structured, and unstructured data have resulted in higher requirements and challenges in big data. Big data storage needs a unified storage framework, and still there are some limitations in the present big data storage technologies.

(b) Data timeliness refers to the data content that is related to time, and it requires real-time analysis of the browsing history of the user. An accurate recommendation should also be provided for the corresponding content, and it requires high response speed. If there is any delay in the response, then it leads to expired content or invalid recommendation. For instance, the exact time requirement is vital in weather prediction, and if it could be known the next day, the prediction results are completely worthless.

2.4.1 Data Analysis

(a) *Accuracy*: The main objective of data analysis is to identify and predict the relationship between data accurately. Several analysis algorithms have been developed in order to provide effective response for the ever-growing data. Applications such as stock market, healthcare, and weather forecasting are considered as unstable areas where the real-time big data system should capture the data accurately for each variable in order to adjust the prediction in real time.

(b) *Scalability*: The conventional recommendation algorithms are not adequate to handle massive user history logs, and it is difficult to compute, analyze, and extract data with the rapid growth of the number of users and goods. The basic recommendation algorithm is time consuming, and subsequently, scalability is worse with the multi-dimensional user data. The complexity of this algorithm is also growing day by day, and the performance is getting poorer with the increase in the number of products and users.

2.4.2 Countermeasures for Big-Data-Related Issues

2.4.2.1 Increasing Collection Coverage

The built-in-search [16] and meta-search approaches [17] can be combined together to increase the coverage of the data collection to obtain more information. Moreover, these approaches are suitable for most of the social networks. The technique based on page ranking [18] integrates social information and the user's interaction data in the recommendation algorithm. The FP-Growth association rule mining algorithm [19] improves accuracy and the prediction coverage by correlating the business data available in the social network. The prediction coverage is reasonably improved in this system, and the coverage increases more than 95% in each category.

2.4.2.2 Dimension Reduction and Processing Algorithms

The dimension reduction technology alleviates the sparseness problem efficiently. The most relevant approaches are singular value decomposition and principal component analysis (PCA) [20] that are based on merging the original "d" features into "k" new features and the mapping of data from "d"- to "k"-dimensional spaces. Some default scoring can improve the resolution of similarity. The algorithms are best suited to handle sparse data such as transfer similarity, iterative optimization, diffusion, etc.

1. The database table structure and the real scenario can be merged to filter the abnormal data such as numerical exception, null check, type anomalies, etc. At the time of pre-processing, the noisy data can be removed by re-evaluating items to achieve an accuracy higher than the recommended value.

   Clustering algorithm helps in solving the problem of incomplete relational data by focusing on the dissimilarity. The fuzzy c-means and genetic algorithms based on nearest neighbor information solve missing attributes or data incompleteness [21]. The dataset can be categorized into complete and incomplete datasets, and the affinity propagation clustering algorithm is incorporated to cluster the available dataset. Based on the similarity measure, incomplete data is categorized separately in the corresponding cluster.

2. Cloud storage [16] is implemented through grid technologies, clustering applications, or distributed file systems. With the online storage services, storage device type, capacity, data availability, and location need not be considered. The hierarchical storage management strategy simplifies the storage resource management.

3. Spark platform introduces a memory-based computing model [17] and Resilient Distributed Datasets (RDD) data model [18]. A context algorithm in the spark platform is proposed to solve predictive timeliness. The algorithm combines cooperative filtering and real-time message transceiver to deal with

filtering the situation and real-time data flow that improves timeliness and accuracy of the algorithm.

4. An association rule mining algorithm was proposed to improve Bayesian classifier by merging the relevant attributes, and it reduces the number of attributes [19]. A neural-network-based prediction model and the big scale mining architecture are developed using big data processing and cloud service technology [20]. The mentioned scheme significantly improves the prediction accuracy in big data processing.

5. To solve the scalability issue, several clustering algorithms are established in order to improve the recommendation accuracy. K-means clustering algorithm [21] with improved distance measurement and selection method is proposed. Two other clustering algorithms namely Trust Aware Clustering Collaborative Filtering (TRACCF) and Project-Based Fuzzy Clustering Collaborative Filtering (IFCCF) are proposed. Initially, the data is preprocessed by PCA, and then it is improved with K-means along with fusion genetic algorithm.

2.5 Opportunities of Big Data

The emergence of big data analytics has made its impression in the growth of healthcare by providing tools to collect, manage, analyze, and incorporate huge volumes of heterogeneous, structured, and unstructured data generated by healthcare system. In these days, big data analytics is aiding the process of disease exploration and care delivery. Big data is defined by three major characteristics called the "3V's": volume, variety, and velocity [22,23]. Recently the 3V's have been extended to variability and veracity [24,25] and are thus now identified as "5V's". Big data is extending to many fields of science including agriculture [26], health [27], and Internet with *social networking* [28]. Healthcare is the main example of how the 5 V's (velocity, variety, volume, variability, and veracity) [29] work. McKinsey Global Institute recommended that if the concept of big data is used effectively and creatively, then the U.S. government can create more than $300 billion in value every year [30]. In human body, several organs are interconnected with each other, thereby producing potential markers for clinical assessment. Thus, diagnosing and envisaging diseases needs an aggregated approach which should involve both structured and unstructured clinical and non-clinical data.

2.5.1 Big Data in Biomedical Image Processing

Big data in healthcare deals with consequential big and complex datasets which are hard to analyze with the existing tools [31]. In healthcare systems, data are generated from various heterogeneous sources like clinical data, hospitals operations, laboratory, patients' symptoms uploaded from distant sensors, and pharmaceutical data [32]. Medical imaging provides vital data regarding anatomy and organ function to analyze the state of diseases. Big data in healthcare is used to solve many clinical and operational issues. The application of big data analytics in predictive modeling, population health, and quality measurement is advancing rapidly. Predictive modeling is used to prevent fraudulent actions using historical data and statistical techniques to predict future results. Predictive modeling is used to predict which patient is most likely get benefits from care management. Care management is a plan which is used to prevent hospitalization for patients having chronic conditions like pulmonary disorder, asthma, and diabetics. Big data offers incredible opportunities for measurement and quality in healthcare. Electronic Medical Record (EMR) data is used to study the effectiveness of a drug. Personalized medical treatment protocols are identified by mining huge volumes of clinical databases. In this chapter, the opportunities of big data in biomedical image processing and genomics are considered and discussed briefly.

Figure 2.7 shows the big data workflow for biomedical image processing. Managing data involves organizing, administering, and processing huge volumes of structured and unstructured data.

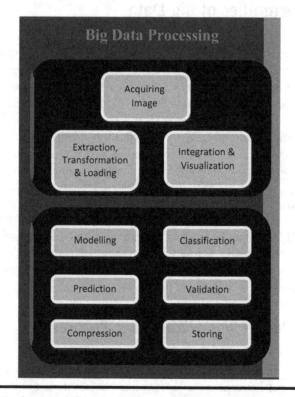

Figure 2.7   Big data workflow for biomedical *image processing*.

Image Acquisition: In biomedical imaging, an image can be captured using *magnetic resonance imaging, computed tomography, molecular imaging*, X-ray, *photo-acoustic imaging, ultra sound, positron emission tomography-computed tomography* (PET-CT). These methodologies acquire high-definition and large-size medical images, especially images of internal parts of the human body. The image captured is then transferred to a big data database for processing.

ETL: ETL is responsible for the background operation in the big data database. Primarily the data are extracted from the source that can be a legacy system file of any format, on-line transaction processing (OLTP), documents, web pages, or even data coming in a streaming fashion. After the data is being extracted, it is sent to a special area called the Data Staging Area (DSA), where transformation and cleansing of the data occur. Cleansing is the process that eliminates noise using filter on acquired images.

Integration and Visualization: In this step, the images are clustered automatically in the database. Users can preview the image before analyzing it (Figure 2.7).

Modelling: In this step, computational algorithms and mathematical models are used to format images which are easy to understand. Depending upon the application, the user can model the image if necessary. For instance, a 2D image can be modeled as 3D image to facilitate its manipulation.

Classification: The major concern in image processing is classification; pattern recognition is an example [33]. In machine learning, classification identifies to which set the current population belongs to. The process of classification is based on their type of learning. It is classified into three major categories namely *supervised learning, semi-supervised learning*, and *unsupervised learning*. Predictive modeling is an example for supervised learning [34]. Feature extraction is an example for unsupervised learning. Semi-supervised learning is a hybrid between supervised and unsupervised learning, which is suitable for scenarios where the outcome is missing for certain subjects.

Prediction: Deep convolutional neural network (CNN) is currently used to automate the diagnosis process from patient information as the CNN provides more accurate results when compared to other technologies [35].

Validation: Validation is a process of checking the quality and accuracy of the data. Validation of data ensures that the data is complete, unique, and consistent. It is performed by calculating the specificity and sensitivity of data [36]:

$$\text{Specificity} = \text{True negative/negative,}$$

$$\text{Sensitivity} = \text{True positive/positive,}$$

where *true negative* represents the correctly predicted benign symptoms, *true positive* represents the correctly predicted symptoms from the image, *positive* represents the total number of symptoms shown, and *negative* represents number of benign symptoms.

Compression: The compression technique is a data reduction process which permits the taming of the complexity of big data management tasks. Reducing the data size gives less expensive and faster analytical computations.

Storing: NoSQL (Not Only SQL) appeared in 2009 and is the commonly used database for big data. Cloud computing technology is used to store data which allows on-demand provisioning of resources with a pay-as-you-go model. Cloud computing technology accommodates the virtualization technique which uses a single *hardware resource* to host many independent *virtual machines*.

2.5.2 Big Data Opportunity for Genome

Genome analysis accommodates microarray concepts which are used in the treatment of major and complex diseases [37]. The sequencing techniques in genomics are intrinsically a big data issue as the human genome consists of 30,000–35,000 genes [38]. Modern DNA sequencing technology provides potential benefits in the fields of diagnostics and early detection of genetic predisposition. Many genome sequencers are available in the market which are capable of producing petabytes of

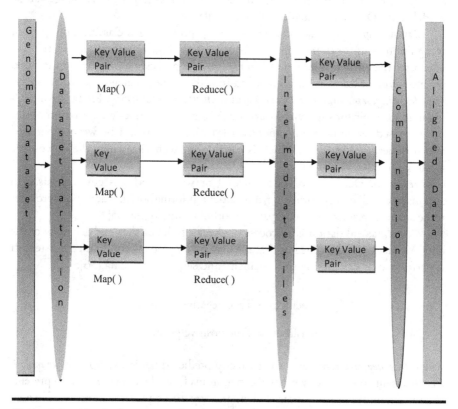

Figure 2.8   MapReduce operation for mapping individual genes.

sequence data, and they can be extended to exabytes of data. Hadoop is an excellent platform for complex genomic workflow which renders meaningful analysis. Hadoop's real time capabilities analyze and accommodate huge volumes of data. Hadoop has parallel computing option to facilitate faster sequencing. With the help of MapReduce function, a large number of genes can be mapped. The extension of Hadoop includes Hadoop-BAM and Cloudburst. Hadoop-BAM is an influencing data management tool with the MapReduce function of Hadoop which uses binary alignment works for complex activities like genotyping. Cloudburst is another technology release in the year 2009. It is very efficient in comparing genome sequences and mapping individual genes (Figure 2.8).

References

1. García-Gil, D., Luengo, J., Salvador, G., et al. (2017). Enabling smart data: Noise filtering in big data classification. *Information Sciences*. doi:10.1016/j.ins.2018.12.002
2. Chen, J., Li, K., Tang, Z., et al. (2017). A parallel random forest algorithm for big data in a spark cloud computing environment. *IEEE Transactions on Parallel and Distributed Systems*, 28(4): 919–933. doi:10.1109/TPDS.2016.2603511
3. Verbaeten, S. and Assche, A. (2003). Ensemble methods for noise elimination in classification problems. In *4th International Workshop on Multiple Classifier Systems, vol. 2709 of Lecture Notes on Computer Science*, Springer, Berlin.
4. Segal, M. and Xiao, Y. (2011). *Multivariate Random Forests*, Vol. 1, John Wiley & Sons, Inc.
5. Grady, N. W., Payne, J. A. and Parker, H. (2017). Agile big data analytics: AnalyticsOps for data science. In *2017 IEEE International Conference on Big Data (Big Data)*, Boston, MA, pp. 2331–2339. doi:10.1109/BigData.2017.8258187
6. Hwang, J., Huang, Y., Vukovic, M., et al. (2015). Cloud transformation analytics services: A case study of cloud fitness validation for server migration, In *2015 IEEE International Conference on Services Computing*, New York, NY, pp. 387–394. doi:10.1109/SCC.2015.60
7. Maślankowski, J. (2014). Data quality issues concerning statistical data gathering supported by big data technology. *Communications in Computer & Information Science*, 424(1): 92–101.
8. Chen, T. and Honda, K. (2015). Solving data preprocessing problems in existing location-aware systems. *Journal of Ambient Intelligence & Humanized Computing*, 1–7.
9. Li, J., Xu, Z., Jiang. Y., et al. (2014). The overview of big data storage and management. *IEEE, International Conference on Cognitive Informatics and Cognitive Computing, Icci*cc*. IEEE, pp. 510–513.
10. Zhong, Z., Liu, Z., Yun, H. U., et al. (2016). Efficient multi-event monitoring using built-in search engines. *Frontiers of Computer Science*, 10(2): 1–11.
11. Cheng, R. G. and Ming, L. I. (2008). Metasearch based on source search engine's link optimization. *Journal of Chongqing Normal University*.
12. Jiang, F. and Wang, Z. (2010). Pagerank-based collaborative filtering recommendation. In *International Conference on Information Computing and Applications*, Springer-Verlag, Berlin, pp. 597–604.

13. Zhang, T.-Q. (2014). *Study on integrated e-commerce recommendation system based on association rules and user preference degree.* Beijing University of Posts and Telecommunications.

14. Tsuge, S., Shishibori, M., Kuroiwa, S., et al. (2001). Dimensionality reduction using non-negative matrix factorization for information retrieval. In *IEEE International Conference on Systems, Man, and Cybernetics*, IEEE, Vol. 2, pp. 960–965.

15. Li, D., Gu, H. and Zhang, L. (2013). A hybrid genetic algorithm–fuzzy c-means approach for incomplete data clustering based on nearest-neighbor intervals. *Soft Computing*, 17(10): 1787–1796.

16. Zeng, W., Zhao, Y., Ou, K., et al. (2009). Research on cloud storage architecture and key technologies. In *International Conference on Interaction Sciences: Information Technology, Culture and Human 2009*, Seoul, Korea, 24–26 November, DBLP, pp. 1044–1048.

17. Paul, S. and Bhunia, S. (2014). Application of memory-based computing. In *Computing with Memory for Energy-Efficient Robust Systems*, Springer, New York, NY, pp. 47–50.

18. Zaharia, M., Chowdhury, M., Das, T., et al. (2012). Resilient distributed datasets: A fault-tolerant abstraction for in-memory cluster computing. In *Usenix Conference on Networked Systems Design and Implementation*, USENIX Association, Berkeley, CA, p. 2.

19. Gong, C. and Lu, J. (2016). The research of real-time recommendation system on spark. *Electronic Test*.

20. Yang, F., Xiao-Yan, A. I, Zhang, Y. H., et al. (2016). New mining architecture and prediction model for big data. *Electronic Design Engineering*.

21. Ghazanfar, M. A. and Prügel-Bennett, A. (2014). Leveraging clustering approaches to solve the gray-sheep users problem in recommender systems. *Expert Systems with Applications*, 41(7): 3261–3275.

22. Belle, A., Thiagarajan, R., Soroushmehr, S., et al. (2015). Big data analytics in healthcare. *BioMed Research International*, 10: 1–16.

23. Luo, J., Wu, M., Gopukumar, D., et al. (2016). Big data application in biomedical research and health care: A literature review. *Biomedical Informatics Insights*, 8: BII. S31559.

24. Viceconti, M., Hunter, P. and Hose, R. (2015). Big data, big knowledge: Big data for personalized healthcare. *IEEE Journal of Biomedical and Health Informatics*, 19(4), 1209–1215.

25. Yang, A., Troup, M. and Ho, J. (2017). Scalability and validation of big data bioinformatics software. *Computational and Structural Biotechnology Journal*, 15: 379–386.

26. Wolfert, S., Ge, L., Verdouw, C., et al. (2017). Big data in smart farming – A review. *Agricultural Systems*, 153: 69–80.

27. Andreu-Perez, J., Poon, C., Merrifield, R., et al. (2015). Big data for health. *IEEE Journal of Biomedical and Health Informatics*, 19(4): 1193–1208.

28. Pääkkönen, P. and Pakkala, D. (2015). Reference architecture and classification of technologies, products and services for big data systems. *Big Data Research*, 2(4): 166–186.

29. Emmert-Streib, F., Yli-Harja, O. and Dehmer, M. (2018). Data analytics applications for streaming data from social media: What to predict? *Frontiers in Big Data*, 1: 2.

30. Manyika, J., Chui, M., Brown, B., et al. (2011). *Big Data: The Next Frontier for Innovation, Competition, and Productivity*, McKinsey Global Institute, New York, NY.
31. Wang, J., Qiu, M. and Guo, B. (2017). Enabling real-time information service on telehealth system over cloud-based big data platform. *Journal of Systems Architecture*, 72: 69–79.
32. Oussous, A., Benjelloun, F., AitLahcen, A., et al. (2018). Big data technologies: A survey. *Journal of King Saud University – Computer and Information Sciences*, 30(4): 431–448.
33. Weiss, S. M. and Kapouleas, L. (1989). An empirical comparison of pattern recognition neural nets and machine learning classification methods. In *Proceedings of the Eleventh International Joint Conference on Artificial Intelligence*, pp. 781–787.
34. Jiang, F., Jiang, Y., Zhi, H., et al. (2017). Artificial intelligence in healthcare: past, present and future. *Stroke and Vascular Neurology*, 2(4): 230–243.
35. Acharya, U., Oh, S., Hagiwara, Y., et al. (2018). Deep convolutional neural network for the automated detection and diagnosis of seizure using EEG signals. *Computers in Biology and Medicine*, 100: 270–278.
36. Esteva, A., Kuprel, B., Novoa, R., et al. (2017). Dermatologist-level classification of skin cancer with deep neural networks. *Nature*, 542(7639): 115–118.
37. Koboldt, D. C., Steinberg, K. M., Larson, D. E., et al. (2013). The next-generation sequencing revolution and its impact on genomics. *Cell*, 155(1): 27–38.
38. Drmanac, R., Sparks, A. B., Callow, M. J., et al. (2010). Human genome sequencing using unchained base reads on self-assembling DNA nanoarrays. *Science*, 327(5961): 78–81.
39. Genome sequencing and assembly. *Next-Generation Sequencing and Sequence Data Analysis*, 77–83 (2015).

Chapter 3

Emerging IoT-Big Data Platform Oriented Technologies

K. P. Arjun, N. M. Sreenarayanan,
K. Sampath Kumar, and R. Viswanathan

Galgotias University

Contents

3.1 Introduction

IoT-big data systems (IoTBDSs) enabling technologies are combinations of different technologies. Internet of Things (IoT) and big data are the trending technologies nowadays [1]. IoT and big data evolved independently, but now it's time to combine them to derive the advantages of both.

IoT is about connected components that can be located anywhere; they will communicate via the Internet. The connected components are referred to as "Things"; each thing is identified by its own IP (Internet protocol) address. These connected components communicate with the environment and transfer data over the Internet the data without human intervention. The transferred data are used for taking decisions and interacting with the environment.

"Big data" is a term representing a huge amount of data; the data can be structured, semi-structured, or unstructured and are used for analyzing insight from the big data. Big data is used in medicine, weather forecasting, business, education, logistics, etc. [2].

As per a current report, there are nearly 4 trillion GB of data now through connected components, and also not surprisingly the number of connected components has also increased in the world. These connected components will collect, transfer, process, and analyze data in real time. The role of big data in IoT and business extension is that they can be used to perform different kinds of analyses of past and present data. According to the business, the data size varies; we need new real-time tools to analyze and find the insight of data.

This chapter discusses about various technologies like ubiquitous computing and cloud computing which support IoT and big data [3]. Next we look at the importance of real-time analytics and latest tools that are used for real-time analytics and their features. The two leading technologies, machine learning and deep learning, and their roles in IoT-BDSs are explained. We also discuss about different commodity sensors available in the market and their specifications. Finally we conclude and discuss future applications of IoT-BDSs.

3.2 Ubiquitous Wireless Communication

The concept of ubiquitous computing is vast; computing can occur anytime and anywhere. Compared with normal desktop computing, ubiquitous computing is performed anywhere, anytime, and in any format [4]. The computational nodes are computers, which can be available in any forms like laptops, tablets, and terminals. Terminals are the devices that can perform half computing like ATM, refrigerators, etc. The other supporting technologies that contribute highly in this computing scenario include the Internet, operating systems, sensors, microprocessors, microcontrollers, and new input/output technologies.

The concept of ubiquitous computing is very simple and clear. This technology connects small computers and communicates with the devices to perform small activities in life to serve humans. The challenge of ubiquitous computing is how to make this technology simple and user friendly by focusing more on user interface design, human instructional models, etc. [5].

In Figure 3.1, three basic forms for ubiquitous computing devices are proposed: tabs, pads, and boards. These devices have different sizes, weights, and display sizes.

If we see Figure 3.2 about ubiquitous computing, the devices have some additional forms. These additional forms are more specific and clear with respect to the application used.

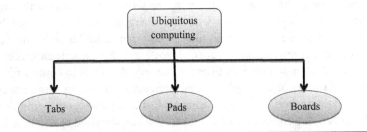

Figure 3.1 Ubiquitous computing devices.

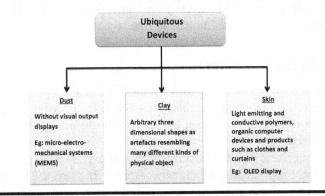

Figure 3.2 Ubiquitous computing devices with additional forms.

Actually the meaning of communication has totally changed because of the rapid changes and improvement in the technologies. The rapid changes in the technologies have improved all areas like personal life, work, industry, economy, etc. Office automation and home automation are areas affected by trending technologies. Here humans can talk or give instructions to the machines by using human voice and gestures as in human communication [6].

Ubiquitous communication has the following limitations. These will be bottlenecks to the ubiquitous technology's further improvement. The first one is the device's batteries and accumulators: devices are available lifelong to collect and process the data in real time for support the technology. The second one is human-to-machine interfaces: the whole system importantly needs human-to-machine and machine-to-machine communication. So we will focus more on creating user friendly interfaces as they are very important. The third one is the field of security – data security, storage security, and processing security – that is important to all the technology aspects.

3.2.1 Ubiquitous Computing

Ubiquitous computing uses wireless technologies to enable communication among all the connected devices. The word "ubiquitous" means present, appearing, or found everywhere, this meaning applies to the term "ubiquitous computing" also. Ubiquitous technologies combine with the emerging technology called IoT. IoT uses connected devices that communicate with each other for collecting real-time data in the form of text, audios, images, videos, etc. Likewise ubiquitous computing has additional computational abilities for connected devices to communicate with each other via wires or wirelessly [7]. IoT systems are automated and are available anywhere and anytime in the environment. But ubiquitous computing deals with only the underlying communication technologies either wired or wireless. There are many good examples of connected devices with strong communication backbones. We combine IoT with pervasive computing by interconnecting the communication network with various Wi-Fi access points and radio frequency identification (RFID), cellular, and other communication systems.

3.2.1.1 Ubiquitous Architecture

The proposed technology of ubiquitous computing has mainly three layers [8]. Figure 3.3 represents ubiquitous computing's whole task divided into three layers. These layers are the task management layer, environment management layer, and environment layer.

In this architecture, REST API and UPnP both over TCP/IP stack help data exchange between applications and master controller. The next level of communication between master controller and slave controller is by using ZigBee mesh networks. Finally communication exchange between slave controller and end device is

Layer 1	Applications
Layer 2	Master and Slave Controller
Layer 3	Devices

Figure 3.3 **Components of ubiquitous computing.**

achieved by an electronic board called Arduino microcontroller [9]. A slave controller is an electronic circuit that connects to physical devices to enable them to receive and process the commands. Overall the microcontroller manages data collection, processing, and production of final results technologically.

Ubiquitous architecture provides many advantages over connected technologies that impact our daily life. The advantages are invisible or totally out of sight of the technology embedded in our smart environment. Devices interact with social and natural these controls by humans. Correct decision making at critical situations.

Figure 3.4 shows the basic computing facilities of ubiquitous computing. The basic architecture of ubiquitous computing consists of the following components:

- Pervasive devices
- Software
- Communication connectivity.

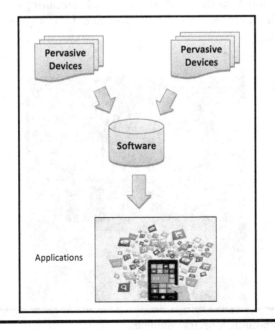

Figure 3.4 **Basic architecture of ubiquitous computing.**

Pervasive devices share all the collected information with software-equipped hardware. This communication happens with the help of wired or wireless network connectivity. This collected information is processed in software-based systems that produce the result to users. Pervasive devices are tabs, mobiles, sensors, cameras, etc. Communication connectivity is embedded with ubiquitous computing for achieving communication. Examples of communication technologies are Bluetooth, Wi-Fi, and ZigBee.

3.2.1.2 Communication Technologies

Rapid growth of any technology depends on the communication technologies used. All technologies directly or indirectly support communication technologies. So communication technologies are the vital part of each and every technology. Factors affecting the rapid growth of communication technologies are bandwidth, global connectivity, information access, new methods for information exchange, etc. Figure 3.5 shows the schematic diagram of communication technologies.

3.2.1.3 Applications

We discussed the revolutionary computing technology called ubiquitous computing. This technology interacts with computers, connected devices, nature, and people. Hundreds to thousands of connected computing devices and sensors provide new functionalities to the services and have a great impact on the applications [6].

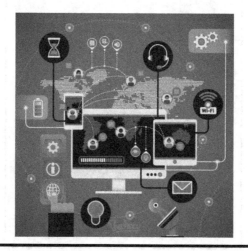

Figure 3.5 Communication technologies.

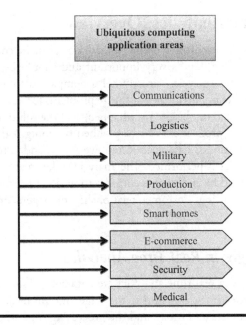

Figure 3.6   Application of ubiquitous computing.

The main application areas in Figure 3.6 are communications, logistics, motor traffic, military, production, smart homes, e-commerce, security, and medical technology.

The contribution of ubiquitous computing technology in communication is data, the fuel of the all technologies. Without communication, data or information transfer is not possible. Data may be available in different forms like text, images, audio, and videos. The data transfer may be between small distances or between two geographical locations. Ubiquitous technology provides cross-platform communication between different applications.

A logistics application deals with import and export of the raw materials or product. Here the area ubiquitous computing provides automation among all activities in logistics, from the live tracking of goods or products to their successful delivery. Here the gap between IT control systems and physical movement is very close [7]. The automobile field needs a lot of support from humans for service and assistance. Here communication and data exchange inside of the machine and between vehicles is needed to reduce the accidents and traffic. In the next area, the military, a large amount of secret data needs to transferred from machine to machine and machine to humans. Here also ubiquitous computing provides invisible, embedded, secure communication connections. In each and every stage of product development, continuous monitoring is required. This monitoring will be done by the ubiquitous computing technology.

3.3 Real-Time Analytics: Overview

Real-time analytics is used to find the immediate result or conclusion from the available data. Here the data is very important and should be made available in every stage. Real-time analytics directly helps companies to achieve their goals. The results will predict opportunities or future problems for a business [8]. All risky situations may be sorted out before they happen, and the solution may be found in advance. All business profit ideas can be grabbed by doing real-time analytics on current data. In a business, data is collected every day, added to the data history, and real-time analytics is performed. The analytics takes place either online or on a dedicated server used by the business organization. Real-time analytics is applied in real-time credit scoring, customer relationship management, fraud detection, business profit, etc.

3.3.1 Challenges in Real-Time Analytics

The main challenges in real-time analytics are data collection, i.e., getting authenticated and valid real-time data; storing the huge amount of data that we can use for real-time analytics; data format; and the processing time when we give a query to our system.

A main challenge in real-time analytics is to process huge amounts of data, data from history or present data, and produce the result in limited time. There are many online and offline real-time analytics tools available in the market; the question is is about the processing power of that particular tool, amount of data storage, and result visualization.

The time required for producing the final result is one of the challenges [9]. We load huge amount of data into our real-time analytics system and wait long for the result; that result can't acceptable for a critical problem. The amount of data may be in the range of terabytes because we process all the business data up to the current date. These amounts of data need to be processed, the result needs to be produced in the form of graph or figure, and also the analyst may ask different questions in the form of queries, and the real-time tools must give detailed answers to the queries within an acceptable amount of time.

Data form or structure is the one of the main challenges in real time analytics of a large amount of data. Data can be collected directly from the environment in real time and processed with minimum involvement of the user to get an automated report. The format of data is dependent on the organization, or the data may be of any form, i.e., structured, semi-structured, or unstructured. The collected data is stored in an analytical storage in an optimized format and processed, and the output is visualized. Figure 3.7 shows the analytics block diagram of Microsoft – one of the leading IT companies.

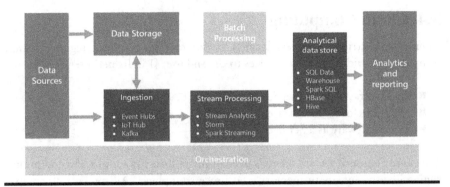

Figure 3.7   Microsoft real-time analytics block diagram.

3.3.2 Real-Time Analytics Platforms

Platforms are the smallest unit of software that will run to get a certain output. The output may be known or unknown to the user. A platform is usually a combination of hardware and software; they work together to give a certain output. Even browser software is a part of it when we do online analytics. We use a browser to access the online analytical tools hosted on one server or more than one server (cloud). Popular tools and their brief descriptions are discussed in the following [10].

Apache Storm is one of the tools we use for real-time analytics. It's a distributed processing system. The Storm usually uses a programming language to query to Apache Storm. Apache Storm is written in the language called Clojure which is one of the examples of LISP (list processing) and is like a functional programming language. Apache Spark is a common and fast large-data processing tool. It supports multiple programming languages and application programming interfaces (APIs) like Java, Scala, and Python. The main features of Oracle Streams analytics are responsive customer relationship, real-time billing, and improving efficiency through analysis of big data [11]. Oracle Streams analytics is a powerful tool, and other technologies in Oracle Streams analytics are Java, Spring, SQL, Hadoop, NoSQL, etc. Apache Flink is another real-time analytics tool. Features of Flink are high-flexibility streaming windows for continuous streaming and batch processing in one system. Flink is integrated with many other open source data processing tools. Another product of Apache is Apache Kafka. Its main features are reliability, scalability, high performance, and durability.

There are plenty of real-time analytics tools available in the market [12]. Each tool is compared with the others, and the tools are improved for wide language support, low latency in processing, high-speed batch processing system, etc.

3.4 Cloud Computing

Clouds are distributed servers located at different geographical regions. Cloud computing provides different services to the end user [13]. Its main services are

- IaaS (Infrastructure as a Service)
- PaaS (Platform as a Service)
- SaaS (Software as a Service).

The cloud computing technology is overcoming all the limitations of a computing engine like storage, main memory, and processing power. All the leading companies have started researching on cloud computing and giving services to the users. The main features of cloud computing are the following:

- Resource pooling
- On-demand service
- Easy maintenance
- Availability
- Economical feasibility
- measured service and so on.

The cloud computing is an inevitable technology nowadays because of the large number of advantages and features that directly provide benefits to the users.

3.4.1 Cloud Computing Era

The technology started with client–server architecture. Clients request and accept service from the server. The duty of the server is to process the request from client and respond back to the client. At that time, storing data in a CPU was very expensive. Then the concept of centralized and distributed computing was introduced. All the leading IT companies started their own cloud and made them available to users on the basis of on-demand resource provisioning [14].

The first cloud was implemented by Salesforce and a simple website made available through cloud. Then Amazon introduced their Elastic Compute Cloud (EC2). After that Google and Microsoft started working on cloud. The results of this were Google search engine with Web 2.0 and Google app introduced by Google and Microsoft Azure introduced by Microsoft. Nowadays the usage and applications are increasing day by day. All the desktop applications now run online with the help of the Internet.

3.4.2 Relationship between IoT and Cloud

IoT is about connected components communicating through Internet technologies for collecting and sending real-time data. The whole world can communicate by using physical objects in an intelligent fashion. Every day each physical device collects information in the range of gigabytes (GBs) to terabytes (TBs) depending on what application we employ in the technology. Cloud was introduced for removing the bottlenecks of the devices. All the services are available on user demand [15]. two emerging technologies IoT and cloud can be merged to experience the advantages of both these technologies. IoT is about connected devices collecting real-time data anywhere with the physical system fixed. But these connected devices have the disadvantages of limited storage memory and processing capacity. By merging cloud computing with IoT, we have overcome all types of limitations in network, memory, processing, etc. [16].

3.4.3 Relationship between Big Data and Cloud

Big data is a huge amount of data that can't be handled by traditional systems and software. The size of big is not defined anywhere, but we can say that the size of data which can't handle using traditional systems or software data [17].

The relationship between big data and cloud is that cloud provides all the services related to communication, storage, management, and processing. Big data is a huge amount of data, and new-era software can only manage this amount of data. Management involves not only storing; it begins from data collection, data manipulation, storage, processing, and production of final results. The leading companies have already started big-data-oriented cloud services. Amazon Redshift is an example for data warehousing. It performs big data analytics using traditional business intelligence tools in a cost-effective manner [18]. The next Amazon big data service is Amazon Elastic MapReduce (EMR). It offers Hadoop-based cloud services. Amazon EMR also supports most popular open source tools, including Apache Spark, HBase, Presto, and Flink. Microsoft Azure's big data service is called HDInsight. This also supports open source big data tools Hadoop, Spark, Hive, LLAP, Kafka, Storm, HBase and R like Amazon EMR. Another service of Microsoft Azure is Data Lake Analytics. It works based on the YARN technology. Google's BigQuery is a user friendly service. It's also called "serverless" cloud service because of its automatically configuring and managing infrastructure. And many more cloud-based big data services are offered by leading companies. Cloud computing and big data are two technologies, but both are dependent on each other.

3.4.4 Convergence of IoT, Big Data, and Cloud Computing

We have seen these three independent technologies separately [19]. These technologies can independently work with each other. The only technology common to IoT and big data is cloud computing. Each of these three technologies IoT, big data, and cloud computing have some bottlenecks. So another technology leverage each other to overcome these limitations. These three technologies can be combined for a wide range of applications.

Cloud computing and big data play an intrinsic role in between them. But IoT devices provide the data [20–22]. Figure 3.8 shows how the three independent technologies are interconnected.

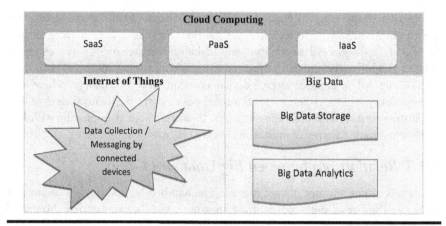

Figure 3.8 Combined block diagram of cloud, IoT, and big data.

IoT connects devices and sensors that communicate with each other through the Internet. Big data refers to a huge amount of data that can't be processed by using traditional software. Cloud computing overcomes all the limitations by using digital world. Cloud computing provides unlimited data storage area for storing data generated by IoT connected devices and provides unlimited processing capacity for big data coming from IoT devices. According to a recent survey by International Data Cooperation (IDC), within five years, 90% of IoT data will be hosted by cloud platforms. This huge amount of data is fed to big data systems for processing [23–24].

Converging these three technologies is a new area to explore and work. The main advantage of converging these three technologies is that the limitations of each of these technologies can be overcome. All three together give rise to a new technology era of decision support systems. This will provide new opportunities and a wide range of applications. This will create new job opportunities in the new IT era [25].

Figure 3.8 represents the block diagram of the technology of cloud, IoT, and big data combined. Here cloud computing acts as a caretaker of both IoT and big data. Cloud technology communicates with the other two technologies and does whatever they require. In the case of IoT, mainly storage and communication services are required from cloud. But for big data, storage capacity and processing power are required from cloud [26].

3.5 Machine Learning

Machine learning is the ability of a system or machine to change the outcomes of a scenario or situation according to the information it possesses. To put it simply, machine learning is all about final conclusion and analysis.

3.5.1 Introduction to Machine Learning with Big Data and IoT

Applications of machine learning [27] are increasing day by day with different platforms. Expeditious improvements in software, hardware, and communication areas are providing versatility of technologies and applications in various platforms. Machine learning [27] is the ability of a system or machine to change the outcomes of a scenario or situation according to the information it possesses. IoT [28] is the combination of interconnected devices, networks, digital systems, biometric devices, etc. And they can communicate with each other over networks without human interference.

The recent technology of interconnected peripherals extends its communication to real-world applications and cyberworld; as a result, the volume of data increases, and they generate big data. Now the systems need to deal with this data and perform intelligent processing on the information generated from the raw data and finally estimate the conclusion with the help of machine learning techniques.

3.5.2 Evaluation of Machine Learning Models

Machine learning extends its applications each and every day with high-performance systems. But machine learning models should generate accurate results and prediction in order to develop the use of such applications in real time. The training model is the key factor of machine learning applications, and how the model treats unseen data and how it generates predictions is very important. This issue can be rectified by the close evaluation of machine learning projects. Following are the methods used in evaluating a machine learning model for new, previously unseen data:

1. Holdout
2. Cross-validation.

Both methods use a case set (unseen data) to evaluate the system. Data used in training is not recommended because these test cases provide an accurate prediction.

3.5.2.1 Holdout

The meaning of holdout test is to check a model, i.e., how the model works on a dataset different than that used for training. It will provide an unbiased estimate of performance evaluation. In this method, the dataset is divided into three subclasses:

1. *Training Set*: Subset of dataset to build the model
2. *Validation Set*: Subset of dataset to assess the model's performance. It provides platforms for model tuning and choosing a suitable model
3. *Test Set (Unseen Data)*: Also a subset of dataset to assess the prediction performance of the model.

Advantages of Holdout

1. High speed
2. Simple design
3. Flexibility.

However the techniques provide model evaluation according to the dataset used for test cases. It may provide different results since difference in the dataset and training set can evaluate the model performance accurately.

3.5.2.2 Cross-Validation

This technique partitions the original dataset into training sets, which are used to train the model, and uses a different dataset to evaluate the model.

"k-fold cross-validation" is the common cross-validation technique. Here the dataset is divided into k equal-sized sample sets called folds. The k is the user-defined value probably 5 or 10 according to the model. The working principle is as follows: the process is repeated k times; each time $(k-1)$ sample sets are used to train the model, and the remaining set is used to test or validate the model. Finally the average of k turns is calculated, and the model performance is evaluated. For example, a five-fold cross-validation divides the dataset into approximately five equal-sized sets and selects one set for testing and the other four sets for training. This process will be repeated five times, and each time the testing set may vary.

This technique using all dataset for testing exactly once, but all data being used for training as well as testing. After k turns, the model is trained and tested by all datasets, so it can evaluate the system generally and does not depend only on a single dataset. Cross-changing the datasets for testing provides accurate results and also reduces bias and variance.

3.5.3 Machine Learning and Big Data Applications

The most powerful and exciting technologies in real-world applications are machine learning [27] and AI. Machine learning techniques drastically change computer applications and make them more humanlike. Big data deals with a large volume of data, and it helps and improves the machine learning [27] process by providing a huge amount of data. Devices with large volumes of data can perform more accurately and predict results more precisely.

3.5.3.1 Machine Learning Applications

Applications of machine learning [27] will cover all the domains of computer science and embedded systems. In each domain, machine learning can be of different nature and can perform various methodologies based on the nature of domain and application. Machine learning has lots of aspects to deal with large amounts of data. In today's life, in each and every area, machine learning uses its features to provide information and helps in future prediction.

Applications of machine learning include the following.

1. Virtual Personal Assistants

    Virtual Personal Assistants provide relevant information according to the queries asked over voice. Alexa, Siri, Google are examples of Virtual Personal Assistants. You can ask questions like "What is the temperature today?" "What is my schedule for next two days?" For answering, it uses your related queries and receives information from other devices. You can also give instructions to assistants like "set alarm for 5 AM tomorrow" and set some reminders also.

    Virtual Personal Assistants are integrated into different domains, for example,
    – Amazon Echo and Google Home (smart speakers)
    – Samsung Bixby on Samsung S8 (smartphones)
    – Google Allo (mobile apps).
2. Self-Driving Cars

    This is one of the finest applications of machine learning. They will analyze the current situation and traffic, and according to the data, they drive well through the roads without a human's physical presence.
3. Dynamic Pricing

    Setting the price of things and services according to the demand is named as dynamic pricing, for example, flight tickets, movie tickets, cab fare, etc. By the use of machine learning, dynamic pricing fixes the cab fare in crowded areas, flight charge in festival season, etc.
4. Google Translate

    Google neural machine translator works on different languages and dictionaries for accurate translation. It uses Natural Language Processing to translate from one language to another. Also it uses some techniques like Chunking, Named Entity Recognition (NER), and Part-of-speech (POS) Tagging.
5. Traffic Alerts (Maps)

    Google Maps provides efficient route identification with traffic assistance. It functions by analyzing people currently using the app and historical data of that route. Users use maps, so it provides location, information about speed and time, route in which vehicles are traveling. By using this huge volume of data, Google Maps provides effective traffic alerts.
6. Search Engine Result Refining

    Search engines like Google and Bing use complex machine learning to rank the pages, and based on ranks, they provide the search result. If you open the first five results and stay on those results for long, then search engine assumes that these results are more accurate. Similarly if you open a result and close it rapidly, then it assumes this result as not being accurate. In this way, complex algorithms work in the back end and provide more accurate results.

3.5.3.2 Big Data Applications

In a fraction of a second, the volume of digital data increases without any restriction. Experts say that after few years, "Data Tsunami" may occur because of the high population of data. The world generates a huge amount of data every microsecond through media including social media, medical field, research, education sector, entertainment fields, sports, etc.

Big data is a huge amount of unprocessed data with high complexity. So, the processing methods are also highly complex and time consuming. Big data is used to predict or make an accurate decision by analyzing huge amounts of previous sets of data.

Applications of big data include the following.

1. Social Media Analytics

   The rapid advancement of social media has generated large amounts of verity data through different channels. Similarly various activities and methods like IBM's Cognos Consumer Insights are developed to analyze social media activities. They can analyze users' activities in social media and can advertise the products according to the response of users. By using these insights, companies can change their pricing and can provide offers to attract customers. Companies can change their strategies toward the digital market based on how customers respond to the advertisement and by analyzing sales information.

2. Medical field

   It is one of the most relevant areas where big data plays an important role.
   - Big data can reduce unwanted diagnosis by analyzing previous results.
   - It helps to predict epidemic outbreaks.
   - It can easily identify diseases in earlier stages.
   - Doctors can provide treatments according to previous evidence.
   - It helps in medical researches and new medicine productions.

3. Media and entertainment sector

   Nowadays people are using many applications through mobile phones and other smart devices, and most of them are using social medias; these are the main sources of data generation. Some of the benefits of big data analysis in media sector are as follows:
   - Predicting users' interests and providing suggestions
   - Optimized media streams and on-demand media access
   - Receiving insights from users
   - Identification of an effective advertisement platform.

4. Weather prediction

Weather sensors and satellites are deployed around the world. They collect and analyze large amounts of data for predictions in the following areas:
- global warming
- natural disaster pattern
- predicting weather conditions and cyclones and their behavior
- analyzing global weather changes.

5. IoT

IoT devices extract large amounts of data and is used by various companies and government. Big data analytics provide more useful information from the data accumulated in IoT devices like sensors and cameras

3.6 Deep Learning

Deep learning can provide valuable information by extracting complex and high-level data using various learning algorithms. Also it helps by providing insights into the future as well as in decision-making. Most of the businesses are now benefiting from the advantages of deep learning methods for better marketing.

3.6.1 Applying Deep Learning into Big Data

Big data and deep learning [29] are two major areas of data science. Many organizations collect huge amounts of data for various activities. Many companies also analyze big data for business analytics and decision-making. Deep learning techniques extract complex data and convert them into valuable information by various learning and extracting techniques. Supervised and unsupervised learning methods extract massive volume of data and generate huge amounts of digital information.

The importance of deep learning [29] in big data analytics includes semantic indexing, conducting discriminative tasks, and semantic tagging. Deep learning technologies need to be efficient in the areas of data streaming, multi-dimensional data, and data scalability.

3.6.1.1 Semantic Indexing

Extracting information from the data is associated with data analytics. Efficient storage structures and fast retrieval of data are the major problems in big data because the data is a large amount of text, image, video, audio, animation, etc. Semantic indexing provides effective techniques in knowledge discovery and data comprehension, so search engines work quickly and efficiently.

3.6.1.2 Performing Discriminative Tasks

By performing discriminative tasks in big data analytics, deep learning [29] algorithms can extract non-linear datasets. They can also perform discriminative tasks on linear datasets. This method has two advantages:

1. It extracts information with deep learning [29], providing non-linearity to the data. So the it is more closely associated to AI.
2. Linear analytics models on extracted data are more efficient.

3.6.1.3 Semantic Multimedia Tagging

Learning algorithms helps in semantic tagging. Semantic tagging enables image segmentation and annotation of various scenes. Deep learning techniques can also be used for action-scene identification and video data tagging. It will help to extract valuable features to perform discriminative tasks in multimedia.

3.6.2 Deep Learning Algorithms

Deep learning algorithms use neural networks for data analysis and data extraction. In each layer of a neural network, data is extracted, and a simplified dataset is passed to the next layer. Different layers extracts different features from the data and finally provide valuable information. Deep layers have more powerful features to extract data compared with upper layers. The ability to analyze a large volume of features makes deep learning [29] more powerful and efficient. Like the human brain, it can define AI functions to process data and generate patterns for decision-making. Following are the major deep learning networks:

1. Backpropagation
2. Feedforward Neural Networks (FNN)
3. Convolutional Neural Networks (CNN)
4. Recurrent Neural Networks (RNN)
5. Generation of image descriptions
6. Recursive Neural Network
7. AutoEncoders
8. Max Pooling

3.6.3 Deep Learning Applications in IoT – Foundational Services

In this computer era, the amount of data generated each day is unpredictable, because each device accumulates a large volume of data. In IoT [28], a large number of sensing devices collect or generate huge sets of data for many applications. Depending on the nature of applications, data is extracted in different ways, and the nature of data being sensed by the devices is also different. Applying various learning algorithms to such big data can generate valuable information, predict future insights, and quicken decision making [29–31]. For example, in the case of satellite data, satellites revolve around the earth and accumulate a large amount of data using various sensors and cameras. Then various deep learning algorithms are applied to satellite data to predict the weather and help in development of maps, communication, networks, media activities, geographical pictures, and more. Similarly in medical field, microdevices collect data on various human biological activities and convert them into medical information by the use of deep learning methods.

References

1. Mario Frustaci et al., "Evaluating critical security issues of the IoT world: Present and future challenges." *IEEE Internet of Things Journal* 5.4 (2017): 2483–2495.
2. Rishad Shafik et al., "Real-power computing." *IEEE Transactions on Computers* 67.10 (2018): 1445–1461.
3. Payam Barnaghi et al., "Semantics for the Internet of Things: Early progress and back to the future." *International Journal on Semantic Web and Information Systems (IJSWIS)* 8.1 (2012): 1–21.
4. Shancang Li et al., "The Internet of Things: A security point of view." *Internet Research* 26.2 (2016): 337–359.
5. Luís Ferreira et al., "A cloud and ubiquitous architecture for effective environmental sensing and monitoring." *Procedia Computer Science* 64 (2015): 1256–1262.
6. Zhiwei Yan et al., "Is DNS ready for ubiquitous Internet of Things?" *IEEE Access* 7 (2019): 28835–28846
7. Lathies Bhasker T., "Pervasive computing issues, challenges and applications." *International Journal of Engineering and Computer Science* 2.12 (2013): 3337–3339.
8. Vishal Meshram et al., "A survey on ubiquitous computing." *ICTACT Journal on Soft Computing* 6.2 (2016): 1130–1135.
9. Sriram Karthik Badam et al., "Vistrates: A component model for ubiquitous analytics." *IEEE Transactions on Visualization and Computer Graphics* 25.1 (2018): 586–596.
10. Waman Radhakrishna Parulekar, "Ubiquitous computing architecture, applications and challenges." *International Journal on Future Revolution in Computer Science & Communication Engineering* 4.4 (2018): 694–696.
11. Hiro Gabriel Cerqueira Ferreira et al., "A ubiquitous communication architecture integrating transparent UPnP and REST APIs." *International Journal of Embedded Systems* (2018): 188-197.
12. Nicoleta Tantalaki, "A review on Big Data real-time stream processing and its scheduling techniques." *International Journal of Parallel Emergent and Distributed Systems* (2019).
13. K. Jayanth Kumar et al., "Big Data real time analytics: Applications and tools." *The International Journal of Innovative Research in Science, Engineering and Technology* (2017).
14. Muhammad Habibur Rehman et al., "The role of Big Data analytics in industrial Internet of Things." *Future Generation Computer Systems* 99 (2019): 247–259.

15. Alessio Botta et al., "Integration of cloud computing and Internet of Things: A survey." *Future Generation Computer Systems* 56 (2016): 684–700.
16. Sonali Chandel et al., "Enterprise cloud: Its growth & security challenges in China." In *2018 5th IEEE International Conference on Cyber Security and Cloud Computing (CSCloud)/2018 4th IEEE International Conference on Edge Computing and Scalable Cloud (EdgeCom)*, Shangai, China, 22–24 June 2018, pp. 144–152. IEEE, 2018.
17. Mohammad Aazam et al., "Cloud of things: Integrating Internet of Things and cloud computing and the issues involved." In *Proceedings of 2014 11th International Bhurban Conference on Applied Sciences & Technology (IBCAST)*, Islamabad, Pakistan, 14–18 January 2014, pp. 414–419. IEEE, 2014..
18. Kim Thuat Nguyen et al., "Survey on secure communication protocols for the Internet of Things." *Ad Hoc Networks* 32 (2015): 17–31.
19. Panagiotis I. Radoglou Grammatikis, "Securing the Internet of Things: Challenges, threats and solutions." *Internet of Things* 5 (2019): 41–70.
20. Cai Hongming et al., "IoT-based Big Data storage systems in cloud computing: Perspectives and challenges." *IEEE Internet of Things* 4.1 (2016): 75–87.
21. Jasmine Zakir et al., "Big Data analytics." *Issues in Information Systems* 16.2 (2015): 81–90.
22. Meng Xiaofeng et al., "Big Data management: Concepts, techniques and challenges." *Journal of Computer Research and Development* 1.98 (2013): 146–169.
23. Evgeniy Yur'evich Gorodov et al., "Analytical review of data visualization methods in application to Big Data." *Journal of Electrical and Computer Engineering* 2013 (2013): 969458:1–969458:7.
24. Rakesh Kumar et al., "Apache Hadoop, NoSQL and NewSQL solutions of Big Data." *International Journal of Advance Foundation and Research in Science & Engineering* 1.6 (2014): 28–36.
25. Chang Liu et al., "External integrity verification for outsourced Big Data in cloud and IoT: A big picture." *Future Generation Computer Systems* 49 (2015): 58–67.
26. Geethapriya Thamilarasu et al., "Towards deep-learning-driven intrusion detection for the Internet of Things, security and privacy in Internet of Things." Sensors 19.9 (2019): 1977.
27. Kai Hwang et al., *Big-Data Analytics for Cloud, IoT and Cognitive Computing*, Wiley, 2017.
28. Jon Kepa Gerrikagoitia et al., "Making sense of manufacturing data." Working paper, April 2016.
29. Pedro M. Domingos, "A few useful things to know about machine learning." *Communications of the ACM* 55.10 (2012): 78–87.
30. Sundresan Perumal et al., "Internet of Things (IoT) digital forensic investigation model: Top-down forensic approach methodology." In *2015 Fifth International Conference on Digital Information Processing and Communications (ICDIPC)*. IEEE, 2015.
31. Yann LeCun et al., "Deep learning." *Nature* 521.7553 (2015): 436.

Chapter 4

Big Data System based IoT Enabling Technologies: Ubiquitous Wireless Communication, Real-Time Analytics, Machine Learning, Deep Learning, Commodity Sensors

Manikandan Ramachandran
SASTRA Deemed University

Rizwan Patan
Velagapudi Ramakrishna Siddhartha Engineering College

M. Rajasekhara Babu
Vellore Institute of Technology

Ambeshwar Kumar
SASTRA Deemed University

C. Thaventhiran

SASTRA Deemed University

Contents

4.1 Internet of Things

The Internet of Things, or IoT, involves a computing concept or devices that are said to be interrelated with each other. The IoT mainly consists of digital machines, things or devices, and animals or human beings, possessing unique handlers or identifiers (UIDs) without the requirement of human-to-human or human-to-computer interaction. A "thing" in the IoT here either refers to an elderly patient with a pressure monitoring device implanted, a domestic animal possessing sensors, or any object that is allocated with an IP address and is capable of transferring data over a network. Over time, due to the advancement in the areas of applications (such as smart home, healthcare, transportation, vehicle monitoring, and surveillance), certain challenges of IoT enabling technologies have become widespread. Figure 4.1 shows the schematic representation of IoT.

As illustrated in the figure, IoT represents the Internet-able nature of modern physical devices, vehicles, *connected devices*, or smart devices. Hence, IoT devices possess sensors and software that makes data acquisition and data exchange between users or devices through the Internet possible. Besides, the objects involved in IoT

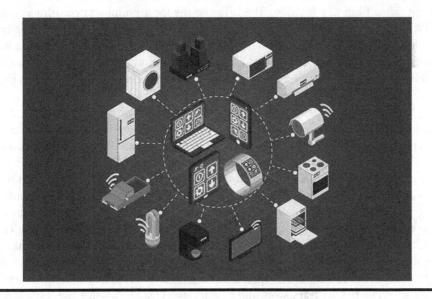

Figure 4.1   IoT.

are said to be easily controlled in a remote manner with the objective of allowing direct integration with a computer, therefore resulting in economic advantages and user efficiency. Different thoughts have emerged as far as IoT is concerned. Some people think about IoT being connected in terms of computers, tablets, and smartphones. But IoT portrays a world where just about anything is said to be connected and communicated in an intelligent manner. On the contrary, the physical world is predicted to become one of the biggest information systems with the evolution of the IoT. For example, an IoT shopping application easily tracks the location of devices to analyze a person's shopping preference, habits, and so on. Apart from this, a shopping app would link to a smart fridge that analyzes the past consumption of the user in deciding which food is required and hence sends the grocery list to the person's smart phone in a smart manner. In other words, a smart fridge automatically orders the products without the interaction or intervention of a human.

On a comprehensive scale, the IoT is found to be applicable to several things, like transportation networks and smart cities, that assist in minimizing waste and enhance the efficiency for several things involving energy usage and also helps in understanding and improving how we work and live. However, the reality in IoT remains in that it ensures endless opportunities and connections. Many of the opportunities can impact or influence today's environment; hence but the door is also open to many challenges.

With advancement in the field of both wireless technologies and networks, a remote network cannot be perceived without its interrelationship with other networks. Ubiquitous wireless communication (UWC) systems involve different types of wireless heterogeneous networks to achieve intercommunication with any device at any time from any location. The IoT, one the most prominent constituents of UWC necessitates the embedding of computational potential between devices in multiple systems. Besides, an IoT network produces enormous amounts of data in heterogeneous formats, and the applications of big data analytics have increased rapidly in the past few years leading to the next generation of intelligence for big data analytics.

Machine learning proves to be a mandatory tool for big data, as the volume, the variety, and the velocity are frequently improvising the potentialities of typical data analytics. Progress in machine learning is often stimulated through achievements in distinct sub-areas, as it possesses the potentiality to enable intelligent sensors to assimilate data without the need to accurately program the details. Deep learning is a contemporary blooming branch of machine learning that increases the learning performance via multiple layers of processing. This chapter aims to address the concerns about IoT devices, their interrelations, and services they may offer, including an efficient analysis of big data produced by IoT with machine learning techniques and models that will enable IoT to develop and become part and parcel of everyday life. Hence, this chapter first starts with the fundamentals of IoT and then describes the IoT framework and its working. A list of real-time applications of IoT is provided. Certain challenges involved in IoT deployment are also discussed.

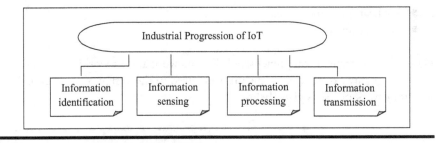

Figure 4.2 Industrial progression of IoT.

4.1.1 Fundamentals of IoT

In the current era, we are encompassed by plenty of IoT-enabled devices that emit data and communicate through heterogeneous devices uninterruptedly. Moving ahead, in this chapter, the fundamentals required for constructing an IoT application is presented. IoT being a homogenous application employs present-day information technologies, comprising several technical areas, including sensor technology, processing of information, securitizing the information, and communication between users. The four parts of industrial progression of IoT are shown in Figure 4.2.

As shown in the figure, the four parts are identification of the information, information sensing, processing of information, and transmission of the same. Besides, the three elements involved in IoT are sensing of the devices or terminal, network connection, and background evaluation. Among these three, sensing is the basic element. On the other hand, the overall structure of IoT comprises two subsystems: the radio frequency identification (RFID) and information network system. RFID includes a tag and reader and obtains the signal and then sends the signal or packet to the middleware of the information network system via the Internet. The names of objects or things are obtained via Object Naming Service (ONS), whereas the information pertaining to a product is obtained via Electronic Product Code (EPC) interfaces. Therefore, IoT combines several physical product information services based on the setting up of the Internet.

4.1.2 IoT Framework and Its Working

IoT framework comprises several layers of technologies with the potentiality of assisting IoT. It represents how several technologies associate with each other and transmits the extensibility, interchangeability, and arrangement of IOT distributions in discrete settings. The comprehensive framework of IoT is comprises four layers:

- Sensing layer
- Network layer

■ Application support layer
■ Application layer.

Figure 4.3 illustrates a comprehensive IoT framework and its working.

An elaborate explanation of the units involved in the design of the comprehensive framework of IoT is given below.

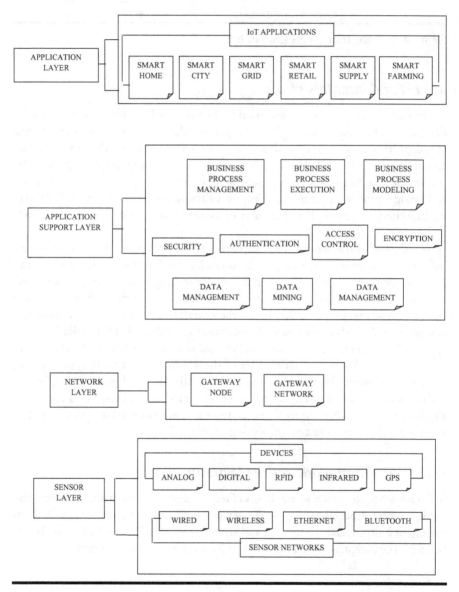

Figure 4.3 Comprehensive framework of IoT.

4.1.2.1 Sensing Layer

This is the first and foremost layer of IoT and is composed of smart objects that are heavily integrated with sensors. This layer [1] performs the task of acquiring information pertaining to physical devices. The sensors have the potentiality to interconnect with the physical and digital worlds making it possible to collect and process real-time information gathered from real-time applications. As an object does not have the ability to communicate with other objects, to the process of exchanging information is performed via sensors or through RFID using a gateway in the communication sublayer. Besides, the devices forming the sensing layer also extend to the network layer and then exchange information through the gateway.

Different types of sensors for different purposes exist in the market. The sensors have the capability to obtain measurements pertaining to temperature, quality of air, speed with which a vehicle or node traverses, humidity level, pressure level, electricity, and so on. In certain cases, a sensor with different memory capacities also has the potentiality to record a number of measurements. Besides, a sensor also records the physical characteristics and transforms them into signals that are inferred by an instrument. According to their distinctive purpose, sensors are classified as body sensors, environmental sensors, home appliance sensors, and so on. Most commonly, the sensors in IoT are found to be highly connected to the sensor gateways via a local area network (LAN) customarily, Ethernet, Wi-Fi connections like ZigBee, Bluetooth, and so on. On the other hand, for sensors that do not necessitate connectivity to sensor aggregators, their relatedness to backend servers is administered via a wide area network (WAN) such as the General Packet Radio Service (GPRS). Finally, the sensors using sensing devices with comparatively less power and low data transfer rate form wireless sensor networks (WSNs). With this primary advantage, WSNs are achieving vogue as they can entertain far more sensor nodes while possessing sufficient battery life and covering large areas.

4.1.2.2 Network Layer

As mentioned above, huge amounts of data are assimilated by these sensors, and this necessitates a powerful and effective wired or wireless network framework as a transport channel. The network layer comprises different types of wireless or cable gateway, network access, encouraging both single-way and two-way transmission modes, route identification and controlling sensing layer data, and finally controlling the information. In the current scenario, networks are highly suited for applications involving machine-to-machine (M2M) communication. However, with wider range of services involving IoT, to name a few, services involving high speed transaction, applications involving context aware area, heterogeneous networks with numerous technologies and required to work with each other. These networks are heavily designed for various applications suited for private, public, or hybrid models and are therefore constructed to handle the requirements pertaining to communication involving waiting time and high/low frequencies. Various gateways and gateway networks involved in the design of framework are illustrated in Figure 4.3.

4.1.2.3 Application Support Layer

The application support layer performs the task of processing information via analytics, security controls, and device administration. One of the foremost characteristics of this layer is its business and process rule engines. In this layer, the IoT systems establish connections among objects which information in the context of events such as identifying current location and gathering information about the data traffic. The event involved in the application support layer is encapsulating the sensory data periodically. On the other hand, certain events include immediate response, like acting in case of crisis while acquiring patient's health conditions. Therefore, for both post-processing and immediate response, the rule engines in the application support layer reinforce the management of decision logics. Depending on the condition, both interactive process and automated process are triggered with the objective of empowering a more flexible IoT system.

Besides, different analytics tools are utilized to obtain pertinent information from a large amount of raw data and to organize them at a much quicker rate. For example, analytics such as in-memory analytics empower huge data volumes that are cached in random access memory (RAM) instead of storing them in the physical disks. By using appropriate in-memory analytics, data query time is minimized and the decision-making process is improved. On the other hand, streaming analytics is considered widely as data in motion and is very much needed in a real-time scenario so that the decision-making is carried out in an effective and efficient manner.

One of the aspects of application support layer is data management. Here, data management refers to the capability to supervise flow of information. With data management in the application support layer, information is said to be accessed, integrated, and controlled. Therefore, higher layer applications are said to be safeguarded from the requirement to process irrelevant data and minimize the risk of disclosure of privacy of data. On the other hand, data management preserves the most relevant data; data filtering techniques like data anonymization, data integration, and data synchronization are also utilized to hide the details of the information while providing only relevant information suited for specific applications. Finally, with the aid of data abstraction, information is said to be extracted with the objective of providing a customary business view of data to achieve considerable swiftness and reused across domains.

Apart from the above-mentioned analytics, anonymization, security is administered throughout the IoT architecture starting from the sensor layer to the application layer. By securitizing the data, system hacking is said to be prevented, preventing the information being accessed by an unauthorized person, hence minimizing the likelihood of risks. The application layer involves reinforcing the sublayer and different types of practical IoT applications. Reinforcing the sublayer bestows IoT with extensive services and abilities, based on the different types of applications in IoT field, along with industrial applications and applications based on customer needs.

4.1.2.4 Application Layer

Finally, the IoT application layer includes smart environments in applications such as construction, healthcare, agriculture, home, production, supply chain management, trade and tourism, environment and energy management, and so on.

4.1.3 Real-Time Applications of IoT

IoT applications are prospering in all industries and markets. The IoT has developed rapidly in several industries and markets. It bridges all groups of users, from those who are trying to minimize the consumption of energy and save energy for their daily chores to large industries that are in need of boosting their business performances. IoT has not only manifested convenient in accessing critical applications in several industries, but also has heightened the abstraction of advanced automation. Let's interpret the potentialities of IoT in several industries and look at how the real-time application of IoT is influencing industries. Some of the real-time applications of IoT are

- Smart homes
- Energy applications
- Healthcare applications
- Education
- Environmental monitoring applications
- Manufacturing applications
- Transportation
- Online shopping
- Inflight services
- Data analytics
- City-wide traffic monitoring system
- Industrial automation
- Agriculture.

4.1.4 Challenges Involved in IoT Deployment

Though IoT provides a magnificent set of advantages, it also presents a significant set of challenges. Amongst them, meeting customer expectations is one of the major concerns; easing the method by which the security has to be addressed, keeping the IoT hardware in an updated fashion, addressing connectivity issues, waiting for governmental regulations are some of the major concerns. Here is a list of some of its major issues.

4.1.4.1 Security

IoT creates an ecosystem of interconnected devices communicating over networks. With a larger number of drawbacks blocking the security of IoT devices, ensuring end-to-end security in an IoT environment is found to be a paramount task. This is because of the reason that the concept behind the design of networking appliances and other objects is found to be in the inception stage, and also during a product's design stage, security is not a major concern. In addition, as IoT is a budding market, several product producers and constructors are more focused in getting their products to market quickly, rather than securing the products in the initial stage. However, with the deployment of IoT, little control is said to be achieved despite several security measures involved. This results in the security being compromised when exposed to different types of attacks.

4.1.4.2 Privacy

With a higher sophistication of IoT involved, substantial personal data of the user in great detail are provided without the user's active participation. With the objects and things in the IoT environment performing data transmission in an autonomous manner, the working is also designed in conjunction with other objects and things for effective communication. Hence, interoperability for IoT is considered to be a highly essential factor so that networked elements or the objects work together in a smooth manner. However, data transmission between the objects or things does not result in any other privacy issues by itself. Privacy is said to be a major concern when the data transmission is said to occur between the endpoints; therefore, sensitive information should be protected. But the concept of networking objects is relatively new, specifically in terms of comprehensive association and autonomous data transfer that are fundamental and central to the IoT. However, due to the ease of access, a lot of users do online monetary transactions by providing lots and lots of valuable information about themselves. Hence, unknowingly lots and lots of information are said to be floating, raising both privacy and security concerns.

4.1.4.3 Software Complexity

Some users or organizations using IoT also find IoT systems highly complicated in terms of several aspects like design, deployment, and maintenance specified with their use of numerous technologies. The IoT has led to a technological revolution that provides higher effectiveness and improved productivity rate in the current equipment framework. Moreover, with the advantage of cloud-based IT technologies and potentialities, the execution of real-time data analysis enables self-governed decision-making and provides prospects for elite services and revenue streams. However, it can be a complicated, fragmented, and potentially fraught transformation, especially for those operating in industrial sectors, where traditional equipment and existing infrastructure cannot be replaced quickly or cost effectively.

4.1.4.4 Flexibility

Though many users or industrial establishments using IoT are highly bothered about the flexibility of an IoT system to integrate easily with another, they also have the concern of finding themselves in an environment of various contrasting or distinctive systems. Though found to be highly flexible, several IoT devices fail to ensure transparency. The processes are therefore not known to the users who are therefore left to assume the behavior of the devices.

4.1.4.5 Compliance

IoT, like any other technology in the domain of business, must obey the rules and regulations involved. However, as the design of IoT is highly complicated, complexity in terms of design or cost makes the subject of compliance seem demanding when several consider conventional software compliance a battle.

4.1.4.6 Unforeseeable Response

The higher the volume of devices deployed using IoT in several areas, the most unforeseeable is its behavior. Though it is said to be well designed in certain areas, there is no guarantee that it will react in the same manner in other areas. Also, with more similarities found in the devices, employing the same connection technology and components is highly vulnerable, because with a defect found in one device or sensor, the system is said to be compromised.

4.2 Big Data Analytics

Big data analytics investigates huge amounts of data to extract the patterns that are considered to be hidden, identify the correlations between the hidden patterns, and so on. With the advent of and improvement in technology, data are said to be analyzed in an effective manner via big data analytics. In other words, it helps organizations and establishments to use the valuable data and acquire new opportunities with the identified data. Hence, a smarter business with higher profit rate is said to be achieved by making both the seller and buyer happy. In this chapter, we first define data science and big data. Then, the technologies involved in big data are described followed by an explanation on the applications of big data in several domains. Finally, the opportunities and issues related to big data analytics are discussed.

4.2.1 Data Science and Big Data

Data science deals with both structured and unstructured data. In other words, it is referred to as the field that deals with everything related to data. It starts from data cleansing and proceeds to data preparation and finally data analysis. Figure 4.4 shows the three crucial regions of data science.

As illustrated in this figure, data science [2] is simply referred to as the integration of statistics, mathematics, and logical programming in situations involving problem-solving; capturing data; and the potentiality to view things in a different manner. However, big data refers to huge data volumes that are not said to be processed in an effective manner using the conventional form of processing that exists in the market.

4.2.2 Technologies Involved in Big Data

Big data analytics [3] involves the combination of different materials and methods in processing. The technology is made effective by the collective use of these materials and methods by organizations to gain relevant results for strategic management and implementation in a timely and precise manner. Several organizations consider different technologies involving big data for their success, which heavily depends on the organizations using it and the type of service they provide. However, the nine most prevailing technologies involved in big data used by competing organizations are

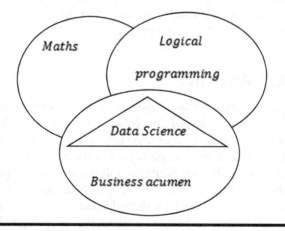

Figure 4.4   Structure of data science.

- Data pre-processing
- Data virtualization
- Data integration
- Data quality management
- In-memory storage
- Predictive analysis
- Knowledge discovery tools
- Stream analytics
- Distributed storage.

4.2.3 Applications of Big Data

As per the strategy followed in business market, industries missing the opportunities related to big data are said to miss innovation, competition, and productivity. In other words, the tools and technologies involved in big data [4] aid in assisting industries to transform huge amounts of data in a swift manner, therefore assisting them to improve production efficiency. Hence, the applications related to big data are found to create a new era in all aspects of life and in all sectors. Figure 4.5 shows examples of big data applications in different industries.

As illustrated in the figure, the applications of big data range from banking, to insurance, to education and media, to healthcare and transportation. Hence, the big data is found to be of profound significance and is widely applied in various sectors.

4.2.4 Opportunities and Issues in Big Data Analytics

With the evolution of human civilization, data collection and perceiving critical information are the two foremost things to be considered. From prehistoric data storage to the present-day sophisticated technologies of Hadoop and MapReduce, different methods and materials have been used for storing and analyzing data. However, several opportunities and issues in big data analytics have to be handled in a proper manner for productive results.

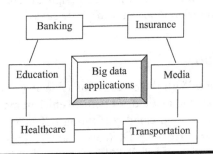

Figure 4.5 Big data applications.

4.2.4.1 Advantages of Big Data Analytics

Some of the advantages of big data analytics are

- Lower cost
- Newer business opportunities
- Application in all sectors of organizations
- Efficient decision-making in a competitive market
- Applicability to both unstructured and semi-structured data.

4.2.4.2 Issues in Big Data Analytics

Some of the issues of concern in big data analytics are as follows:

- Hadoop is harder to understand.
- Rise of unstructured and semi-structured data.
- Dealing with scalability.
- Validating and securing big data.
- As big data are said to be created in a swift manner, organizations also need to respond to them in a swift manner.

4.3 Wireless Communication and IoT

One of the crucial segments of the IoT framework is a wireless communication system. The wireless communication system acts as a platform for two-way communication between the users, specifically for collecting data or information and supervising delivery of messages in a continuous manner with less human intervention. Hence, it is said to be applied to different IoT applications. Some of the IoT applications with wireless communication system are essential industries, such as power grids and oil fields, and chores involved in routine life in smart cities. This chapter introduces wireless communication and IoT. In this chapter, first the design and architecture of wireless communication are described. We then discuss modern ubiquitous wireless communication with IoT design structure. Finally, the implementation of communication models for IoT is discussed.

4.3.1 Introduction

IoT is a new movement. With the objective of achieving a ubiquitous computing system, several materials and methods work in an efficient manner in the IoT. Some of them are RFID, WSN, and cloud computing (CC). Among all the technologies and methods, these three – RFID, WSN, and CC – play a prospective role in the IoT. With the inception of IoT, WSN is considered to be its most salient area. The main goal of IoT is to construct a worldwide network with the aid of all the probable objects. Besides, WSN is considered to be the most truly aiding technology that lets a user understand and achieve the real objective of IoT. The main idea behind wireless communication [5] and IoT is to associate the sensing layer and network layer in the IoT.

4.3.2 Architecture of Wireless Communication

Figure 4.6 shows the architecture of wireless communication. As illustrated in the figure, two different types of nodes are present, and they are in two different colors for differentiation, with blue-colored nodes representing the normal nodes and violet-colored nodes representing the nodes being detected as the sink nodes *SN* for performing a specific task. With the sensor being detected, nodes in the neighboring area are said to be connected with each other in a wireless mode for better communication.

Finally, the sink node obtains the data or the data packet from the closest neighboring node. This therefore forms the basis of a self-sufficient network in WSN.

4.3.3 Modern Ubiquitous Wireless Communication with IoT

The ubiquitous wireless communication is also referred to as pervasive communication. It is the dissemination of communications framework and wireless technologies throughout the environment to enable ceaseless connectivity. Amongst them, one of the most distinguished elements of pervasive communication is the IoT. It involves the embedding of computational potentialities into everyday objects throughout the environment, with which they are connected to each other. Ubiquitous networking refers to the integration of both wired and wireless technologies that underpin communication between several objects involved. On the other hand, ubiquitous networks in home/industry environments are extending the model of connectivity to all types of objects or things that are found to be heavily in use to construct both home and industrial network services. This type of technology in both home and industry uses either thing-to-thing or thing-to-gateway connections for accessing the IoT. In this way, the data are said to be stored for future use and for accessing varied services, such as remote home sensors, remote industry sensors, etc. Broadband access and progress in ubiquitous computing have encouraged the progress of power line communication providing homogeneous

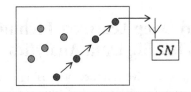

Figure 4.6   Architecture of WSN.

services via an authentic and strong system of the open system interconnection (OSI) model.

4.3.4 Implementation of Communication Models for IoT

While the idea of incorporating computers, sensors, and networks to observe and supervise devices has been around for decades, the recent convergence of crucial inclinations is unfolding in the current reality for the IoT. The main objective of IoT therefore is to provide a fully interconnected "smart" world, with cordial and good correlations between objects. With this, the communication models for IoT are given below.

■ *Device-to-Device Communication Model*: In device-to-device (D2D) communication model, communication is said to take place between two devices directly, instead of happening through an application server. D2D communication is used for local services, where users' data is transmitted directly between the users without the aid of any network based on proximity service. Next, D2D model is used where emergency communication is concerned, in case of different natural disasters like hurricanes and earthquakes. This is because of the reason that the conventional communication network does not work due to the damage caused by the network. Hence, an ad-hoc network is said to be established through D2D. Finally, when IoT enhancement integrates with IoT, a precisely interconnected wireless network is said to be created. An example of D2D-based IoT is the communication between one vehicle and another in the Internet of Vehicles (IoV).

■ *Device-to-Cloud Communication Model*: Here, communication is said to take place between a device and cloud. Here, the IoT device is said to be connected via Internet cloud service for exchanging or transferring data and control messages.

■ *Device-to-Gateway Communication Model*: In device-to-gateway communication model, communication is said to take place between a device and the gateway node. Here, an application software acts as the intermediate between the device and the cloud server.

■ *Back-End Data Sharing Communication Model*: In this model, data is shared between objects via a back-end server.

4.4 Machine and Deep Learning Techniques for Wireless IoT Big Data Analytics

In the age of the IoT, an extensive number of sensing devices acquire or generate a lot of sensory data at a definite period of time for a broad range of applications. Based on the applicability of the application, these objects result in big data streams. Applying data analytics over such big data streams to identify and explore new types of information, forecast upcoming perceptions, and make decisions accordingly in a fair manner is considered to be a crucial process. This makes IoT a notable prototype for both home and industrial applications and is therefore found to be of higher value resulting in technology that improves the quality of life. This section is an overview of using a class of advanced machine learning techniques [6], namely deep learning, to smoothen the analytics and learning in the IoT area. In this chapter, a brief review of machine and deep learning for IoT is presented. Besides, the applications of IoT with big data analytics in wireless mode are also explained.

4.4.1 Introduction to Machine and Deep Learning

4.4.1.1 Design Considerations in Machine Learning

One of the applications of artificial intelligence is machine learning. Machine learning provides systems the potentiality to learn from activity or objects in an automatic manner and upgrade from the current state without being exceptionally programmed. On the other hand, machine learning [7] concentrates on the design and development of computer programs with the objective of accessing the data and learning from them. The learning process starts with the observations for the purpose of observing the patterns in data and therefore ensuring decisions in a better manner in the near future according to the circumstances provided by the user. The main objective in the design of machine learning remains in allowing the computers learn in an automatic manner without the involvement of humans and make actions accordingly. Figure 4.7 shows the schematic representation of machine learning using a flower as an object.

As illustrated in the figure, with an image as input, the machine learning model initially performs manual feature extraction. Manual extraction of features results in a considerable amount of time being consumed and therefore involves computational complexity. Following feature extraction by human beings, classification of whether the given flower represents a rose, lotus, or sunflower is performed. Here, classification is performed via machine learning.

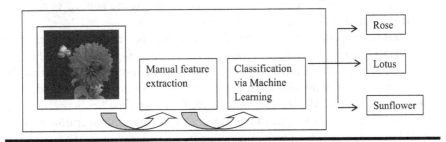

Figure 4.7   Schematic diagram of machine learning model.

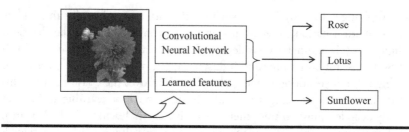

Figure 4.8 Schematic diagram of deep neural network.

4.4.1.2 Design Considerations of Deep Learning

Deep learning on the other hand is a subgroup of machine learning. Deep learning is similar to machine learning with the only difference being the capabilities with which it is said to be performed. Conventional machine learning methods are progressive but require a certain direction. But with deep learning methods [8], the algorithms decide on whether the prediction involved in deep learning is correct or not. The basic structure of deep learning method is designed in such a manner that it draws conclusions regarding the objects of resultant prediction just like a human being. In order to achieve this objective, deep learning utilizes a layered structure of algorithms referred to as the artificial neural network (ANN), analogous to the neural network of the human brain. This makes deep learning more effective than conventional machine learning methods. Figure 4.8 shows the schematic representation of deep learning using a flower as an object.

As illustrated in the figure, features are not extracted manually; rather features are learned by applying the convolutional neural network. With the learned features and by applying deep neural network, the images are classified.

4.4.2 Machine and Deep Learning Methods

Machine learning uses the following four methods.

- *Supervised Machine Learning Method*: Here, past events or occurrences are observed using labeled examples. These past events are applied to the new data to predict the future course of action or events.
- *Unsupervised Machine Learning Method*: In unsupervised machine learning method, the information to be used is neither classified nor labeled. Here, a hidden structure is described from unlabeled data; however, it is said that the correct output is not obtained. Only inferences are said to be obtained.
- *Semi-Supervised Machine Learning Method*: This method lies between supervised machine learning method and unsupervised machine learning method. Here, only a small amount of labeled data and a large amount of unlabeled data are observed.

■ *Reinforcement Machine Learning Method*: This is a learning method that communicates with the environment resulting in actions and identifies the presence of errors. One of the most pertinent characteristics of this method is learning by trial and error.

Besides the machine learning methods given above, some of the deep learning methods are listed below:

■ Convolutional neural network
■ Recurrent neural network
■ Long short-term memory
■ Autoencoders
■ Sparse autoencoders
■ Stacked autoencoder
■ Backpropagation
■ Stochastic gradient descent
■ Learning rate decay.

4.4.3 Utilization of Learning Methods for IoT Big Data Analysis

Compared to conventional machine learning methods, deep learning methods have gained popularity in the recent years. Though ANNs have gained popularity in the past decades, it is difficult to apply them if the number of layers is increased. Besides, with higher computational complexity involved in the implementation of feedforward neural networks, the implementation process is found to be cumbersome. With these limitations involving computational complexity and more data, deep learning techniques have gained from progressions in efficient training algorithms of deep networks.

4.4.4 Applications of IoT with Big Data Analytics in Wireless Mode

The demands of big data and analytics in IoT have aggressively improved over the years and have thus resulted in dramatic advancements in decision-making processes. Due to this, the need and demand for applying data analytics to big data in IoT have expanded as well, thereby altering the way data collection, storage, and analysis are being made. Besides, big data and analytics have higher prospects for acquiring information in a meaningful form from the data collected by sensor devices. The widespread need for big data and IoT interprets the functional and nonfunctional descriptions for data analytics. Some of the applications of IoT with big data analytics in wireless mode are given below.

4.4.4.1 Smart Cities

In the recent future, approximately 70% of the world's population is expected to reside in cities. To accommodate the new demand, rise in the number of cities with the increase in the population (i.e., huge data) residing in these cities, municipalities around the globe are turning toward IoT [9] to improve their services, cut costs, and increase the awareness for a safer and greener environment. With big data analytics, these are said to be done by implementing efficient water supply via smart meters that have the potentiality to improve leak detection and also ensuring consumers have real-time access to information pertaining to consumption. Next, IoT in smart cities can pave the way toward providing solutions for congestion-free traffic. These are to be handled by fixing smart signals, by alerting drivers before a possible accident, and suggesting diversions accordingly. Finally, energy-efficient buildings are also the focus nowadays with the objective of minimizing the emission of carbon monoxide.

4.4.4.2 Transport Sector

IoT big data have even made swift changes in the transportation sector. In the current era, the field of transportation has also evolved as a blooming sector with the availability of automatic cars with sensors and road traffic signals to sense the traffic and make changes in an automatic manner. Besides, several sensors fixed in the vehicle even provide information pertaining to the ongoing status of the vehicle, so that any congestion is intimated to the users in a consistent manner.

4.4.4.3 Weather Forecasting

There are several applications of IoT in environmental monitoring. Some of them include protection of environment, continuous monitoring of weather, and monitoring of water safety. In all the above-mentioned applications, the purpose of sensors lies in detecting and measuring environmental changes on a regular basis. Through several sensors, big data on pollution in air and water are said to be easily collected via repeated sampling. This assists in averting considerable pollution and associated calamities. The applications of IoT big data permit operations to reduce human involvement in farming system analysis and regularly monitor the same. With the introduction of IoT big data in the field of air and water pollution, the systems possess the potentiality to recognize changes in irrigation, soil analysis, and environment accordingly. This enables us to avert considerable contamination and related calamities. In the area of weather monitoring, though strong and advanced systems in the present day permit deep monitoring, they do not support widely used instruments like radar and satellites. However, with the introduction of IoT, big data technologies in the area of weather monitoring support fine-grained data and provide better accuracy and flexibility. By efficient and effective weather monitoring, early detection and response to calamities and prevention of loss of life and property are said to be assured.

4.4.4.4 Agriculture

In the field of agriculture, the advent of Internet and several things connected together paves way for both IoT and big data. With the inception of big data in the field of agriculture, involving information regarding soil type, irrigation type, crops to be cultivated, and IoT involved, precision in farming is said to be achieved by introducing smart instruments to measure the drones for field monitoring, water management, soil monitoring, and process monitoring. Besides, livestock monitoring is said to be performed deliberately by using cow monitoring solutions, installing feasibility of rancher for cattle location, and so on.

4.4.4.5 Healthcare

IoT appliances have been advantageous in health and wellness applications. To monitor the health condition of a patient continuously, several wearable devices have found a profound place in the industry. With the introduction of IoT, health applications [10] have been made available for the elderly and patients with critical health conditions. In the current era, with huge amounts of data (i.e., big data) regarding the patient to be analyzed, IoT sensors are utilized to monitor and record the readings of a patient's health conditions pertaining to blood pressure, sugar level, temperature, and so on and transmit warnings in case any abnormal indicators are said to be identified. Figure 4.9 shows the block diagram of IoT in a

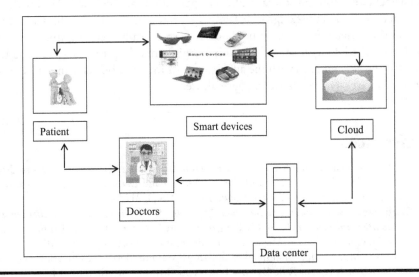

Figure 4.9   Block diagram of smart healthcare.

healthcare system. There are a number of applications of IoT in the healthcare sector. With the introduction of IoT in the healthcare applications [11], patients' lives and living conditions are said to be improved. This is said to be achieved via smart medical sensors to monitor different body parameters such as breathing, blood pressure, and sugar level pertaining to different patients (i.e., big data). Pressure monitoring and several other fitness monitoring sensors have resulted in the increase in the frequency of health monitoring.

With this, elderly patients have the potentiality of monitoring their own health frequently. Besides, even before the condition of a patient who arrives at the hospital is found to be critical, the hospital authorities have the technology to diagnose and start the treatment immediately.

4.5 Conclusion

In this chapter, ongoing research work on the IoT platform that allows a network of devices that communicate, analyze, and process information in a collaborative manner is presented. The IoT network generates huge amounts of data in several forms and formats that are stored and processed in cloud using different materials and methods, and this chapter provides its framework and working to understand certain issues concerning IoT devices, their interconnectedness, and services they may offer, including an efficient, effective, and secure analysis of the data. Besides, this chapter also provides challenges faced by IoT due to the large volume of data (i.e., big data) involved in wireless communication. Apart from the challenges faced, the design of modern ubiquitous wireless communication with IoT and its implementation to fit in several real-time applications are included. Also, with the big data involved in the design of IoT for wireless communication, to fit in real-time applications, machine learning methods and, specifically, deep learning methods with a detailed comparison of machine learning and deep learning are included. Finally, the chapter ends with the applications of IoT with big data analytics in the areas of smart city, transport, and agriculture.

References

1. Huang-Chen Lee and Kai-Hsiang Ke, "Monitoring of Large-Area IoT Sensors Using a LoRa Wireless Mesh Network System: Design and Evaluation", *IEEE Transactions on Instrumentation and Measurement*, Vol. 67, No. 9, 2177–2187, 2018.
2. Soenke Ziesche, *Innovative Big Data Approaches for Capturing and Analyzing Data to Monitor and Achieve the SDGs*. Bangkok: United Nations, ESCAP, Economics and Social Commission for Asia and the Pacific East and North-East Asia Office.
3. Dewan Md. Farid, Mohammad Abdullah Al-Mamun, Bernard Manderick, and Ann Now, "An Adaptive Rule-Based Classifier for Mining Big Biological Data", *Expert Systems with Applications*, Vol. 64, 305–316, 2016.

4. Nilanjan Dey, Aboul Ella Hassanein, Chintan Bhatt, and Amira S. Ashour, *Internet of Things and Big Data Analytics Toward Next-Generation Intelligence*. Vol. 30. Berlin: Springer.

5. Neetesh Kumar and Deo Prakash Vidyarthi, "A Green Routing Algorithm for IoT-Enabled Software Defined Wireless Sensor Network", *IEEE Sensors Journal*, Vol. 18, No. 22, 9449–9460, 2018.

6. Feras A. Batarseh and Eyad Abdel Latif, "Assessing the Quality of Service Using Big Data Analytics with Application to Healthcare", *Big Data Research*, Vol. 4, 13–24, 2015.

7. Mohammad Saeid Mahdavinejad, Mohammadreza Rezvan, Mohammadamin Barekatain, Peyman Adibi, Payam Barnaghi, and Amit P. Sheth, "Machine Learning for Internet of Things Data Aanalysis: A Survey", *Digital Communications and Networks*, Vol. 4, No. 3, 161–175, 2017.

8. Mehdi Mohammadi, Ala Al-Fuqaha, Sameh Sorour, and Mohsen Guizani, "Deep Learning for IoT Big Data and Streaming Analytics: A Survey", *IEEE Communications Surveys & Tutorials*, Vol. 20, No. 4, 2923–2960, 2018.

9. Zaheer Khan, Ashiq Anjum, Kamran Soomro, and Muhammad Atif Tahir, "Towards Cloud Based Big Data Analytics for Smart Future Cities", *Journal of Cloud Computing*, Vol. 4, No. 1, 1–11, 2015.

10. Maruf Pasha and Syed Muhammad Waqas Shah, "Framework for E-Health Systems in IoT-Based Environments", *Wireless Communications and Mobile Computing*, Vol. 2018, 11, 2018.

11. David Windridge and Miroslaw Bober, "A Kernel-Based Framework for Medical Big-Data Analytics". In: *Interactive Knowledge Discovery and Data Mining in Biomedical Informatics: State-of-the-Art and Future Challenges*. Lecture Notes in Computer Science, 8401. Springer, pp. 197–208, 2014.

Chapter 5

Distinctive Attributes of Big Data Platform and Big Data Analytics Software for IoT

Rohan Bali, Abhishek Singh, and
Balamurugan Balusamy
Galgotias University

G. Nalini Priya
Saveetha Engineering College

Contents

5.1 Introduction

The major need today is the ability for computer engineers and statisticians to deal with big data and big data analytics. The rate at which both structured and unstructured data are growing is exponential; thus comes the role of big data analytics. Effective analysis of data is a major contributor to profit in business now. Further, with the advancement in data processing power, analyzing big data is a much needed task now [1]. One of the distinctive attributes of a big data platform is data ingestion. When various big data sources exist with data in numerous formats (i.e., a lot of sources with data in dozens of formats), it is often difficult for businesses to ingest information at high speed and process it expeditiously to remain competitive. From start to finish, vendors provide code programs that are tailored to specific computing environments or code applications. Once information consumption is automatic, the code will modify the method and also embody the information preparation options to structure and organize information; therefore it is often analyzed on the fly or at a later time by business intelligence (BI) and business analytics (BA) programs. Data ingestion is a process by which information is stirred from one or a lot of sources to a destination wherever it may be held on and additionally analyzed. The information can be in several formats and is available from numerous sources, as well as relational database management systems (RDBMSs), different styles of databases, S3 buckets, comma separate values (CSVs), or from streams. Since the information comes from totally different places, it must be cleaned and reworked in an efficient manner that permits you to research it in conjunction with information from different sources. Otherwise, your information is sort of a bunch of puzzle items that do not work along [2]. You can ingest information in real time, in batches, or in an effective combination of the two (this is named "lambda" architecture). After you ingest information in batches, information is processed at often regular intervals. This may be very helpful if you have processes that run on schedule, like reports that run daily at a selected time. The period-of-time consumption is helpful once the knowledge gleaned is extremely time-sensitive, like information from an influence grid that has to be monitored from moment to moment. Of course, you'll be able to additionally ingest information employing a lambda design. This approach makes an attempt to balance the advantages of batch and period-of-time modes by victimization instruction execution to supply comprehensive views of batch information and additionally victimization data processing to supply views of time-sensitive information.

Data management is also another distinctive attribute of the big data platform. Big data management is the organization, administration, and governance of huge volumes of structured and unstructured information.

The goal of big data management is to ensure a high level of information quality and accessibility for BI and big data analytics applications. Firms, government agencies, and alternative organizations use ways of big data management to assist them to deal with aggressive pools of information, generally involving several terabytes or maybe petabytes of knowledge saved in many file formats. Effective big data management helps corporations find valuable info from huge sets of unstructured information and semi-structured information from a range of sources, as well as records of decisions taken, system logs, and social media sites. Most big data environments transcend relative information bases and ancient information warehouse platforms to include technologies that are suited to processing and storing non-transnational styles of data [3]. The increasing concentration on aggregation and analyzing big data is shaping new platforms that combine the standard information warehouse with big data systems in a very logical information deposition design. As a part of the method, the platform should decide what information should be unbroken for compliance reasons, what information may be disposed of, and what information ought to be unbroken and analyzed so as to enhance current business processes or give a business with a competitive advantage. This method needs careful information classification so that, ultimately, smaller sets of information may be analyzed quickly and fruitfully.

After data ingestion and data management, the next major step is ETL (extract, transform, load). ETL is the method of gathering information from a vast variety of sources, organizing it along, and integrating it into one repository. In most firms, helpful information is inaccessible; one study discovered that a small fraction of companies either get "little tangible profit" from their information or no benefit. The info tends to be latched away in isolated silos, bequest systems, or seldom-used applications. ETL is the method of organizing that information out there by extracting information from multiple sources and making it usable for cleansing, transformation, and, eventually, business insight. Some individuals perform ETL through programs written in SQL or Java; however, there are unit tools out there that modify the method. This chapter checks out in detail ETL use cases, the benefits of victimization associate ETL tool instead of hand committal to writing, and what shoppers ought to hunt for in ETL tools.

A data warehouse is another important factor when it comes to the storage of data in an organized manner. A data warehouse may be a united repository for all the information collected by an enterprise's varied operational systems, be they physical or logical. Data storage emphasizes the capture of information from various sources for access and analysis instead of execution.

Typically, an information warehouse may be an electronic information service housed on the enterprise mainframe server or, progressively, within the cloud. Information from various online transaction processing (OLTP) applications and different sources is extracted by selection for BI activities, call support and to answer user inquiries. Data warehouses will profit organizations from IT tools and a business perspective [4]. Separating the analytical processes from the operational processes will enhance the operational systems and alter business users to access and question relevant information faster from multiple sources. Additionally, information warehouses can give information of higher quality and consistency, thereby up BI. Businesses will opt for on-premises, the cloud, or data-warehouse-as-a-service systems. On-premises information warehouses from IBM, Oracle, and Teradata provide flexibility and security; thus, IT companies will focus on their information warehouse management and configuration. Cloud-based information warehouses like Amazon Redshift, Google BigQuery, Microsoft Azure SQL information warehouse, and Snowflake alter firms to quickly scale up while eliminating initial infrastructure investments and in-progress maintenance needs.

When it comes to big data, the first thing that comes to mind is Hadoop. Hadoop is an open-source supply distributed process framework that manages processing and storage for big data applications running in clustered systems. It's in the middle of a growing scheme of big data technologies that a single unit won't be able to support advance analytics, together with prophetical analytics, data processing, and machine learning applications. Hadoop will handle varied types of structured and unstructured information, giving users a lot of flexibility for collection, processing, and analyzing information than that offered by relative information bases and data warehouses. Formally referred to as Apache Hadoop, the technology was developed as a part of an associated open supply project inside the Apache Package Foundation (APF). Business distributions of Hadoop are presently handled by four primary vendors of big data platforms: Amazon Web Services (AWS), Cloudera, Hortonworks, and MapR Technologies. Additionally, Google, Microsoft, and alternative vendors provide cloud-based managed services that are designed on high of Hadoop and connected technologies. Hadoop runs on clusters of artefactual servers and may rescale to support thousands of hardware nodes and big amounts of knowledge. It uses a distributed classification system that is designed to provide speedy information access across the nodes in a very cluster, and fault-tolerant capabilities; therefore, applications will still run even if individual nodes fail [5]. Consequently, Hadoop became a foundational information management platform for large information analytics uses when it emerged within the mid-2000s. During the development of Nutch open supply program, Hadoop was created by PC scientists Doug Cutting and Cafarella using electro-acoustic transducer and net crawler. When Google printed technical papers, particularly its Google classification system (GFS) and MapReduce programming framework in 2003 and 2004, respectively, Cutting and Cafarella changed earlier technology plans and developed a Java-based MapReduce implementation and a Google classification system. In early 2006, those parts (MapReduce, GFS) were split away from Nutch and have become a separate Apache subproject, which Cutting named Hadoop when his son's stuffed elephant. At an equivalent time, Cutting was employed by net services company Yahoo, which became the primary production user of Hadoop later in 2006. (Cafarella, then a grad student, went on to become a university academic.) Use of the Hadoop's framework increased the following few years, and three freelance Hadoop vendors were founded: Cloudera in 2008, MapR a year later, and Hortonworks as a Yahoo spin-off in 2011. Additionally, AWS launched a Hadoop cloud service known as Elastic MapReduce in 2009. That was all before Apache discharged Hadoop 1.0.0 in December 2011 by a succession of 0.x release. Hadoop is primarily used for analytics applications, and it can store different types of information, thus making appropriate massive data analytics sensitive. Massive information environments generally contain not only huge amount of same information, but also varied types of information, i.e., from structured to semi-structured and unstructured types of data like web clickstream records, net server and mobile application logs, social media posts, client emails and detector information from the Internet of Things (IoT) [6].

Analyzing the streaming data is a major task in big data analytics. Thus, we need streaming computing. ADP system, a stream computing and processing system, analyzes multiple data streams from several sources. The word "stream" in stream computing means actuation in streams of information, processing the info and streaming it back out as one flow. Stream computing uses software system algorithms that analyze the information in real time because it streams in to extend speed and accuracy while managing data handling and analysis. In 2007, IBM declared the automatic data processing system of stream, referred to as System S. This system runs on 800 microprocessors, and therefore, it permits software system applications to separate tasks in order to set up the info into a solution. ATI Technologies conjointly declared a stream computing technology that permits the graphics processing units (GPUs) in conjunction with superior, low-latency CPUs to unravel advanced procedure issues. ATI's stream computing technology springs from a category of applications that run on the GPU rather than on a CPU. S4 (Simple Scalable Streaming System) is a distributed stream processing engine inspired by the MapReduce model. We tend to design this engine to unravel real-world issues within the context of search applications that use data processing and learning algorithms. Current industrial search engines, such as Google, Bing, and Yahoo!, generally offer organic net that ends up in response to user queries, while a "cost-per-click" advertising model offers revenue [7]. The context could embody user preferences, geographic location, previous queries, previous clicks, etc. A serious computer program must solve thousands of queries per second, which can embody many ads per page. To maintain user feedback, we tend to develop S4, a low-latency, ascendible stream processing engine, with minimal overhead and support. A production setting determines measurability (i.e., the ability to feature additional servers to extend outturn with minimal effort) and high handiness (i.e., the ability to realize continuous operation with no human intervention within the presence of system failures). We think of extending the open supply Hadoop platform to support computation of unbound streams; however, we tend to quickly complete the Hadoop platform that was extremely optimized for execution. MapReduce systems operate on the data by programming the data into batch jobs. In-stream computing paradigm possesses a stream of events that flow into the system at a given rate; over that rate, we've no management. The processing system should maintain the event rate or degrade it graciously by eliminating events, which is generally referred to as load shedding. The streaming paradigm dictates a totally different design than the one employed in execution [8]. Trying to create a general platform for each batch and stream computing would lead to an extremely advanced system that will find yourself not being best for either task. The most demand for analysis is to possess a high degree of flexibility to deploy algorithms to the sphere terribly quickly. This makes it potential to check online algorithms often mismatch the live traffic.

Analyzing data is crucial for a business to gain profits. Data is wealth in today's time, which makes it very important, and hence, we have to analyze data. Data analytics and machine learning are two major aspects here. Data analytics is the method of examining knowledge sets so as to draw conclusions concerning the data they contain, progressively with the help of specialized systems and code. Knowledge analytics technologies and techniques are widely utilized in industries to alter organizations to create more-informed business choices and by scientists and researchers to verify or confute scientific models, theories, and hypotheses.

As a term, knowledge analytics preponderantly refers to an assortment of applications, from basic BI, news and online analytical process (OLAP) to numerous sorts of advanced analytics. In this sense, it's similar in nature to BA, another umbrella term for approaches to analyzing knowledge – with the distinction that the latter is headed to business uses, whereas knowledge analytics features a broader focus. The expansive read of the term is not universal, though: In some cases, individuals use knowledge analytics specifically to mean advanced analytics, treating bismuth as a separate class [9]. Knowledge analytics initiatives will facilitate businesses, increase revenues, improve operational potency, optimize selling campaigns and client service efforts, respond quickly to rising market trends, and gain a competitive edge over rivals – all with the last word goal of boosting business performance. Counting on the actual application, the information that is analyzed will contain either historical records or new information that has been processed for period analytics uses. Additionally, it will return from a mixture of internal systems and external knowledge sources. At a high level, knowledge analytics methodologies embrace exploratory data analysis (EDA), which aims to search out patterns and relationships in knowledge, and critical discourse analysis (CDA), which applies applied math techniques to see whether or not hypotheses of a few knowledge set are true or false. EDA is usually compared to detecting, whereas CDA loves the work of a choose or jury throughout a court trial – a distinction initial drawn by statistician John W. Tukey in his 1977 book exploratory knowledge analysis. Data analytics is classified into quantitative knowledge analysis and qualitative knowledge analysis. The quantitative knowledge analysis involves the analysis of numerical knowledge with quantitative variables that may be compared or measured statistically. The qualitative approach is very instructive as it focuses on understanding the contents of non-numerical knowledge like text, images, audio, and video, as well as common phrases, themes, and points of the reading. At the applying level, bismuth and news provide business executives and alternative company employees with unjust data concerning key performance indicators, business operations, customers, etc.

Today, machine learning is different in the various industries. It has been proven to be a great success for various domains. Machine learning has been boomed to a great extent; however, it has been existing for a very long time, as it isn't a new concept. Machine learning algorithms have been developed since the early 1970s. It has grown exponentially in recent times due to the computation speed now available, which was not there in the three decades back. Today, an enormous amount of structured and unstructured data also have emphasized the importance of machine learning algorithms and models [10]. The following are a few examples of the various domains in which machine learning is used:

■ *Image Analytics*: Making a clear distinction between different forms and shapes. It is successfully implemented for medical analysis and face expression analysis.

- *Object Recognition*: Making predictions with the help of datasets such as video streams (combined) and multisensory fusion for autonomous driving.
- *Security*: Certain heuristics that distill attack patterns to protect ports, networks, privacy using fingerprint analysis, etc.
- *Deep Learning*: Generating rules that are used in marketing, sales promotion, etc. for data analytics and big data handling.

5.2 Data Ingestion

Big data consumption is concerning moving information – particularly unstructured information – from wherever it's originated into a system wherever it will be kept and analyzed like Hadoop. Information consumption is also continuous or asynchronous, time period or batched or each (lambda architecture) relying upon the characteristics of the supply and therefore the destination. In several eventualities, the supply and therefore the destination might not have identical information, temporal order, format, or protocol and can need some sort of transformation or conversion to be usable by the destination system. Because the range of IoT devices grows, each volume and variance of knowledge sources – sources that currently have to be compelled to be accommodated and infrequently in real time – is increasing speedily. Nevertheless, extracting the information consumption that relies on the destination system may be a vital challenge in terms of your time and resources. Creating information consumption as economical as doable helps focus resources on huge information streaming and analysis, instead of the mundane efforts of knowledge preparation and transformation [11].

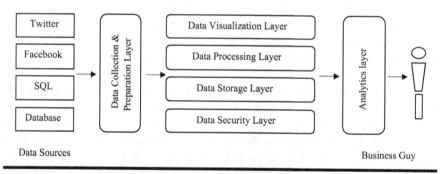

Data ingestion

5.3 Typical Issues of Knowledge Consumption

Complex, Slow, and Costly

1. Purpose-made and overengineered tools create huge information consumption complicated, time intense, and costly;

2. Writing custom scripts and mixing multiple products with amass and consumption information related to current huge information ingestion solutions take too long time and prevent on-time deciding needed of today's business surroundings;
3. Statement interfaces for existing streaming processing tools produce dependencies on developers and fetters access to information.

Security and Trust of knowledge

1. The necessity of sharing distinct bits of information is incompatible with current transport layer data security capabilities that limit access at the cluster or role level;
2. Adherence to compliance and information security rules is troublesome, complicated and clear;
3. Verification of information access and usage is troublesome and time-intensive and infrequently involves a manual method of piecing along totally different systems and reports to verify wherever data is sourced from; however, it's used, and United Nations agency has used it in the way typically.

Problems of Knowledge Consumption for IoT

1. Difficulty in equalization restricted resources of power, computing and information measure with the number of information signals being generated from huge data streaming sources;
2. Unreliable property disrupts communication outages and causes information loss;
3. Lack of security on most of the world's deployed sensors puts businesses and safety in danger.

5.4 Features Required for Data Ingestion Tools

While some corporations prefer to build their own information bodily function framework, most corporations can realize that it's easier and, betting on the answer, more cost-effective to use an information bodily function tool designed by data integration specialists. With the correct information bodily function tool, you'll extract, process, and deliver information from a large variety of information sources to your varied data repositories and analytics platforms to feed metallic element dashboards and ultimately frontline business users in less time and fewer resources of victimization.

Not all solutions are alike, of course, and finding the simplest information bodily function tool for your wants is tough [12]. Some criteria to think about using examination tools are as follows:

■ *Speed*: The power to ingest information quickly and deliver information to your targets at the rock bottom level of latency acceptable for every explicit application or state of affairs.

■ *Platform Support*: The power to attach with information stored on premises or within the cloud and handle the categories of knowledge your organization is collecting currently and should collect within the future.
■ *Scalability*: The power to scale the framework to handle giant information sets and implement quick in-memory dealing process to support high-volume data delivery.
■ *Source system impact*: The power too often accesses and extracts information from supply operational systems while not impacting their performance or ability to still execute transactions.

Other options you will wish to think about include integrated federal agency (change information capture) technology, support for playacting lightweight transformations, and easy operation.

5.5 Big Data Management

Big data management could be a broad thought that encompasses the policies, procedures, and technologies used for the gathering, storage, governance, organization, administration, and delivery of huge repositories of knowledge. It will embody information cleansing, migration, integration, and preparation to be used in news and analytics [13]. Massive information management is closely associated with the thought of data lifecycle management (DLM).

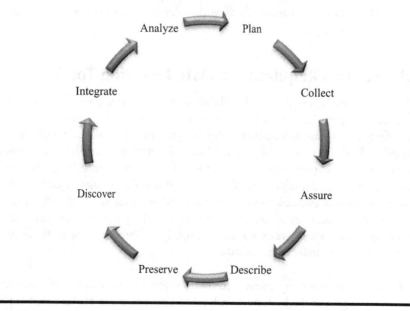

The data lifecycle

Within a typical enterprise, folks with many alternative job titles could also be concerned in massive information management. They embody a chief development officer (CDO), chief info officer (CIO), information managers, information directors, information architects, information modelers, information scientists, information warehouse managers, information warehouse analysts, business analysts, and developers.

5.6 ETL

ETL stands for "extract, transform, load" and is the common paradigm in which information from multiple systems is combined to one info, data store, or warehouse for gift storage or analytics. ETL platforms are an important part of enterprise infrastructure for many years. However, the arrival of cloud, SaaS, and large information has made Associate in Nursing explosion within the variety of recent information sources and streams, spiking demand for correspondingly additional powerful and complicated information integration. Period body process, information enrichment, the flexibility to handle billions of transactions, and support for structured or unstructured information from any supply, whether or not on-premise or within the cloud, have all become necessities for today's enterprise data integration solutions [14]. Further, these tools should be climbable, flexible, fault tolerant, and secure – all things that old-school, on-premise solutions merely cannot deliver.

5.6.1 History

ETL emerged within the seventies, once giant enterprises began to mix and store info from multiple sources with completely different information varieties, like payroll systems, sales records, and inventory systems. The requirement to integrate this information naturally followed, paving the means for the event of ETL. The data warehouse came into vogue within the 1980s. This sort of info might integrate information from multiple sources. The matter was that a lot of information warehouses needed vendor-specific ETLs [15]. Thus, it wasn't long before several enterprises complete up with multiple ETLs; none of them integrated. As time went on, the number of knowledge sources and kinds – together with the number of ETL vendors – increased dramatically. Consequently, costs bated to grade that allowed ETL to become a viable answer for the mid-market, serving to build fashionable, data-empowered businesses for firms.

5.6.2 How the ETL Method Works

Imagine a retail merchant with each brick-and-mortar businesses and online storefronts. Like several companies, the retail merchant has to analyze sales trends across its entire business. However, the backend systems for these storefronts are seemingly found to be separate. They will have completely different fields or field formats (such as day-month-year dates vs month-day-year dates). They will use systems that cannot "talk" to every alternative. This occurs often wherever ETL comes in. ETL extracts the relevant information from each system, transforms it to fulfill the format necessary for the information warehouse, and then loads it into the information warehouse.

Here's a Breakdown of the Three Phases

■ Extraction is the method of retrieving information from one or additional sources – online, brick-and-mortar businesses, gift information, salesforce information, and plenty of others. When retrieving the information, the ETL loads it into an area and prepares it for the subsequent section;

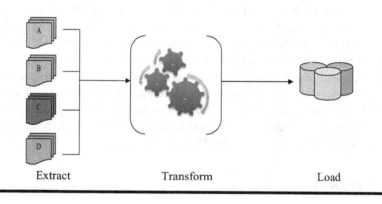

<table>
<tr><td>Extract</td><td>Transform</td><td>Load</td></tr>
</table>

ETL

■ Transformation is important to perform, which paves the means for information integration. Just like the previous example of a retail merchant with completely different channels, the transformation might involve reformatting. However, typically there are alternative forms of transformation, for instance, computation wherever currency amounts to square measure born again from U.S. bucks to Euros;

■ Loading involves success in inserting the incoming information into the target info, data store, or information warehouse.

5.6.3 ETL Challenges

While ETL could be a powerful tool for managing your information, it comes with lot of challenges. That said, a variety of headaches are relieved with correct designing. There are a number of the foremost current ETL challenges, which are discussed in the following.

5.6.3.1 Challenge #1

Scaling: There are a variety of ETL tools with the glorious capability to handle giant volumes of knowledge; however, scaling with ETL tools is difficult. Suppose your ETL tool moves information in batches. Can you be ready to move the information in batches if the dimensions of your business double? Or, if you have got to feature new information sources, some ETL tools need you to reload your information once you create an amendment, which doesn't scale over time.

5.6.3.2 Challenge #2

Remodeling Information Properly: This method is tough to urge right. Moving information into one place, obtaining victimization formats that are compatible while not loading duplicates or incompatible information varieties, corrupting the information, or just missing important information needs careful designing and testing.

5.6.3.3 Challenge #3

Handling Diversity of Knowledge Sources: The quantity of knowledge a thriving company might want to investigate continues to grow exponentially. These days, you will wish to investigate information from unstructured sources, period sources, S3 buckets, flat files, CSVs, streaming sources, etc [16]. Transportation of knowledge is difficult for these systems, but these systems are best handled in several ways: Giant volumes of RDBMS information are also best reworked in giant batches, whereas streaming sources may be best reworked unendingly.

5.6.4 Types of ETL Tools

Depending on however you would like to rework your information, and wherever you would like to rework your information, completely different tools are acceptable. For a comparative list of ETL tools, see a contemporary list of ETL tools.

- *Batch*: Execution ETL tools are designed to maneuver giant volumes of knowledge at an equivalent scheduled time, typically once network traffic is low.
- *Cloud native*: These ETL tools are hosted within the cloud, wherever you'll be able to leverage the experience and infrastructure of the seller. Additionally, they're optimized to figure with cloud-native information sources.

- *Open supply*: Open supply ETL tools are changed and shared because their style is a publically accessible, or free, and has lower value than industrial alternatives.
- *Real time*: These tools will provide information in real time rather than processing the information in giant batches. These tools are best for providing information that's streaming, or for information that's related to time-sensitive higher cognitive process (such as information from a sensing element that needs immediate action).

5.7 Data Warehouse

In computing, a data warehouse (DW or DWH), also called associate degree enterprise information warehouse (EDW), is a system used for news and information analysis and is taken into account a core part of BI. DWs are central repositories of integrated information from one or a lot of disparate sources. They store current and historical information in one single place that is used for making analytical reports for employees throughout the enterprise. The information (such as selling or sales) maintained within the warehouse is uploaded to the operational systems. The information might meet up with associate degree operational information store, and the information about cleansing for added operations ensures data quality before it's utilized in the DW for news. ETL-based information warehouse uses staging, information integration, and access layers to accommodate its key functions. The staging layer or staging information stores information extracted from each of the disparate supply data systems. The combination layer integrates the disparate information sets by remodeling the information from the staging layer usually storing this remodeled information in associate degree operational data store (ODS) information. The information integrated layer contains one more information, usually referred to as the information warehouse information, in which the information is organized into hierarchical teams – usually referred to as dimensions – and into facts and mixture of facts. The mixture of facts and dimensions is usually referred to as a star schema. The access layer helps users retrieve information. Most of the information is cleaned, remodeled, cataloged, and created accessible to be used by managers and different business professionals for data processing, OLAP, research and call support. But to retrieve and analyze information; to extract, transform, and cargo information; and to manage the information wordbook are also thought of essential parts of a knowledge deposition system [17]. Several references to information deposition use this broader context.

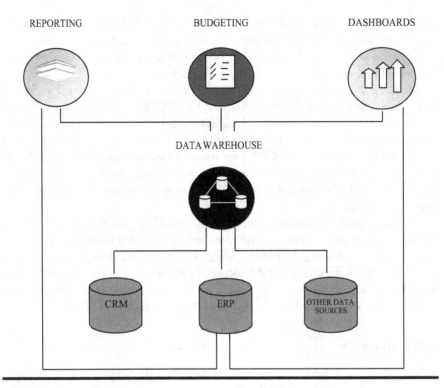

REPORTING   BUDGETING   DASHBOARDS

DATA WAREHOUSE

CRM   ERP   OTHER DATA SOURCES

Data warehouse architecture

Thus, associate degree dilated definition for information deposition includes BI tools; tools to extract, transform, and cargo information into the repository; and tools to manage and retrieve data.

5.8 Related Systems

Types of information marts embody dependent, freelance, and hybrid information marts.

OLAP is characterized by a comparatively low volume of transactions. Queries are usually terribly complicated and involve aggregations. For OLAP systems, an interval is highly effective when the system goes live. OLAP applications are widely utilized by data processing techniques. OLAP databases store aggregative, historical information in multidimensional schemas (usually star schemas). OLAP systems generally have information latency of a number of hours, as hostile information marts; in general, latency is anticipated to be nearer to one day. The OLAP approach is employed to obtain two-dimensional information from multiple sources and views. The three basic operations in OLAP area unit are roll-up (consolidation), drill-down, and slicing and dicing.

Online group action process (OLTP) is characterized by an outsized variety of short online transactions (INSERT, UPDATE, DELETE). OLTP systems emphasize in no time question process and maintaining information integrity in multi-access environments. For OLTP systems, effectiveness is measured by the number of transactions per second. OLTP information bases contain elaborate and current data. The schema accustomed to storing transactional databases are the entity model (usually 3NF). Normalization is the norm for information modeling techniques during this system.

Predictive analytics concerns finding and quantifying hidden patterns within the information victimization-complicated mathematical models, which will be accustomed to predicting future outcomes. The prognosticative analysis is completely different from OLAP. OLAP focuses on historical information analysis and is reactive in nature, whereas prognosticative analysis focuses on the longer term. These systems are also used for client relationship management (CRM).

5.8.1 Benefits

A data warehouse maintains a duplicate of data from the supply group action systems. This field quality provides the chance to:

- Integrate information from multiple sources into one information and information model. A lot of congregation of information to single information;
- Mitigate the matter of information isolation-level lock rivalry in group action process systems caused by tries to run giant, long-running, analysis queries in group action process databases;
- Integrate information from multiple supply systems, enabling a central read across the enterprise. This profit is often valuable, however significantly thus once the organization has grown up by the merger;
- Improve information quality by providing consistent codes and descriptions, drooping or maybe fixing unhealthy information;
- Present the organization's info systematically;
- Provide one common information model for all information of interest no matter the data supply;
- Restructure the information so it is smart to the business users;
- Restructure the information so it delivers glorious question performance, even for complicated analytic queries, while not impacting the operational systems;

- Add price to operational business applications, notably CRM systems;
- Make a decision-supporting queries easier to put in writing;
- Organize and elucidate repetitive information.

5.9 Hadoop

It is an open-source data platform or framework developed in Java, dedicated to storing and analyzing the big sets of unstructured knowledge. With the info exploding from digital mediums, the globe is flooded with stylish huge knowledge technologies. But Apache Hadoop was the primary one that caught this wave of innovation. Let's conclude what's Hadoop code and Hadoop system. We are going to study the whole Hadoop scheme, Hadoop applications, Hadoop Common, and Hadoop framework [18]. It allows multiple coincidental tasks to run from single to thousands of servers without delay. It consists of a distributed classification system that permits transferring knowledge and files in split seconds between totally different nodes. It provides efficiency even though a node fails.

5.9.1 History

Inspired by Google's MapReduce that splits associate degree application into little fractions to run on totally different nodes, scientists Doug Cutting and Cafarella created a platform known as Hadoop 1.0, using electro-acoustic transducer, and launched it in the year 2006 to support distribution for Nutch program. It was created and offered for the public in Gregorian calendar month 2012 by Apache code Foundation. Named once a yellow soft toy elephant of Doug Cutting's child, this technology has been unendingly revised since its launch. As a part of its revision, it launched its second Word of God Hadoop 2.3.0 on February 20, 2014, with some major changes within the design.

5.9.2 Core Hadoop Elements

There are four basic or core elements:

Hadoop Common: It's a group of common utilities and libraries that handle alternative Hadoop modules. It is certain that the hardware failures are managed by Hadoop cluster mechanically.

HDFS: HDFS could be a Hadoop-distributed classification system that stores knowledge within the sort of little memory block and distributes it across the cluster. Every knowledge is replicated multiple times to confirm knowledge handiness.

Hadoop YARN: It allocates resources that successively permit totally differ-ent users to execute varied applications without fear concerning the augmented workloads.

Hadoop MapReduce: It executes tasks in an exceedingly parallel fashion by dis-tributing it as little blocks.

Complementary Hadoop Elements

1. *Ambari*: Ambari is a web-based interface for managing, configuring, and testing huge knowledge clusters to support its elements such as HDFS, MapReduce, Hive, HCatalog, HBase, ZooKeeper, Oozie, Pig, and Sqoop. It provides a console for watching the health of the clusters and permits assess-ing the performance of bound elements such as MapReduce, Pig, and Hive in an exceedingly easy approach.
2. *Cassandra*: Associate degree open supply extremely scale-able distributed sys-tem. NoSQL is dedicated to handle large information across multiple artifact service, without any failure.
3. *Flume*: A distributed and reliable tool for effective aggregation, i.e., aggregat-ing and moving bulk of streaming knowledge into HDFS.
4. *HBase*: A non-relational distributed knowledge bases running on the large knowledge Hadoop cluster that stores a great amount of structured data. HBase acts as associate degree input for the MapReduce jobs.
5. *HCatalog*: It's a layer of table and storage management that permits the devel-opers to access and share the info.
6. *Hadoop Hive*: Hive is a knowledge warehouse infrastructure that permits accounting, querying, and analyzing of knowledge with the assistance of a query language the same as SQL.
7. *Hadoop Oozie*: A server-based system that schedules and manages the Hadoop jobs.
8. *Hadoop Pig*: A fanatical high-level platform that is liable for manipu-lating the info hold on in HDFS with the assistance of a compiler for MapReduce and a language known as Pig Latin. It permits the analysts to extract, remodel and cargo (ETL) the info while not writing the codes for MapReduce.
9. *Solr*: A extremely ascendible search tool that allows classification, central con-figuration, failovers, and recovery.
10. *Spark*: Associate degree open supply quick engine liable for Hadoop stream-ing and supporting SQL, machine learning, and process graphs.
11. *Hadoop Sqoop*: A mechanism to transfer a vast quantity of knowledge between Hadoop and structured databases.
12. *Hadoop Zookeeper*: Associate degree open supply application that configures and synchronizes the distributed systems.

5.10 Stream Computing

Digital businesses succeed by achieving larger period intimacy with their customers across each touchpoint and channel, and zilch delivers that intimacy – and speedier business insights and quicker business results – quite like stream computing. In the 21st century, stream computing is changing into the inspiration for the transformation of all customer-facing and backend business processes. Streaming is as basic to today's always-on economy as relative information architectures were to the previous era of enterprise computing. At the center of this revolution are advances in the period event process, continuous computing, in-memory information persistence, and altering information capture. Once deployed among associate degree enterprise's cloud computing infrastructure, these technologies drive a continuous feed of period information updates, discourse insights, optimized experiences, and fast results into all business processes. Over the approaching decade, information-at-rest architectures such as data warehouses, information lakes, and transactional information stores are central to enterprise information methods. In Wikibon's recent huge information analytics market update, we have a tendency to uncover many trends that time toward a brand new era within which stream computing is the foundation of most information architectures: Media and recreation could be a key vertical marketplace for stream computing, relying on backend cloud infrastructure that supports period packaging, loading, process, and artificial intelligence (AI)-driven personalization of content delivery. Stream computing is the foundation of the many new-edge applications, as well as access by mobile, embedded, and "IoT" devices, with backend infrastructure providing period device management and in-stream analytic process [19]. Enterprises increase their investments in in-memory, continuous computing, modification information capture, and alternative low-latency solutions, whereas convergence increase those investments with their huge information, at-rest environments, as well as Hadoop, NoSQL, and RDBMSs. Streaming environments are evolving to support the low-latency, application-level processing of live information in any volume, variety, frequency, format, payload, order, or pattern. Stream computing backbones are deployed to manage additional stageful, transactional workloads, execute in-stream machine learning, and handle alternative advanced musical organization situations that have so far been the province of relative databases and alternative at-rest repositories. Online transactional analytic process, information transformation, information governance, and machine learning are progressively moving toward low-latency, stageful streaming backbones.

Vendors are introducing innovative solutions that incorporate streaming platforms, ensuring that they will function a sturdy supply of truth for various applications.

Databases are deconstructed and reassembled into new approaches to handle rising necessities, particularly the necessity to handle continuous machine learning DevOps workflows and edge-facing IoT analytics.

Cloud suppliers have integrated streaming technologies into the center of their resolution portfolios for quality, IoT, serverless computing, and alternative key resolution patterns.

Enterprises are migrating additional inferencing, coaching and alternative workloads toward edge devices that use period streams of regionally noninheritable device information.

Open-source streaming environments such as Kafka, Flink, and Spark Structured Streaming have become vital enterprise big data platforms.

Batch-oriented huge information deployments are increasing thanks to additional fully period, streaming, and low-latency end-to-end environments.

5.10.1 Why Is the Streaming Process Needed?

Big data information established the worth of insights derived from process information. Such insights aren't all created equal. Some insights are very valuable shortly when it's happened with the worth diminishing with time. Stream process permits such eventualities, providing insights quicker, typically among milliseconds to seconds from the trigger.

Following are a number of the secondary reasons for the mistreatment of stream process.

Reasons 1: Some information naturally comes as an endless stream of events. To try and do execution, you would like to store it, stop information assortment at your time, and process the info. Then, you've got to try and do consequent batch to worry concerning aggregating across multiple batches. In distinction, streaming handles never-ending information streams graciously and naturally. You'll notice patterns, examine results, explore multiple levels of focus, and conjointly simply explore information from multiple streams at the same time. Streaming naturally matches with statistic information and detection patterns over time. For instance, if you're Associate in Nursing attempt to notice the length of an Internet session in a very endless stream (this can be an example of making an attempt to notify a sequence). It's terribly arduous to try and do it with batches as some session can represent two batches. Streaming will handle this simply [20].

Reason 2: Methoding lets the information build up and check out it right away, whereas stream process data are available to unfold the process over time. Therefore, streaming will work with tons of hardware in execution. Moreover, streaming conjointly permits approximate question process via systematic load shedding. Therefore, streaming fits naturally into use cases wherever approximate answers are adequate.

Reason 3: Typically, information is large and it's not even doable to store it. Streaming allows you to handle giant fireplace horse vogue information and retain solely helpful bits.

Reason 4: Finally, there are tons of streaming information on the market (e.g., client transactions, activities, web site visits), and its information is increasing with IoT use cases (all quite sensors). Streaming could be a rather more natural model to accept and program those use cases.

However, streaming is not used a tool for all use cases. One sensible rule of thumb is that if the process requires multiple passes through full information or has random access (e.g., a graph information set), then it's difficult to use streaming. One massive missing use case in streaming is machine learning algorithms to coach models. On the other hand, if the process misses the info or has a temporal neighborhood (i.e., process tends to access recent data), then it's known as decent suited streaming.

5.10.2 How to Do Stream Processing?

If you wish to make an Associate in Nursing App that handles streaming information and takes period selections, you'll either use a tool or build it yourself. The solution depends on what proportion and quality you intend to handle, what proportion you wish to scale, what proportion, responsibility, and fault tolerance you would like to have, etc.

If you wish to make the App yourself, place events in a very message broker topic (e.g., ActiveMQ, RabbitMQ, or Kafka), write a code to receive events from topics within the broker (they become your stream), and publish the results back to the broker. Such a code is named Associate in Nursing actor.

However, rather than writing them on top of the state of affairs from scratch, you'll use a stream processing framework to save lots of time. An incident stream processor helps you to write the logic for every actor, wire the actors up, and attach the perimeters to the info source(s). You'll either send events on to the stream processor or send them via a broker. An event stream processor can do the exertions by aggregating information, delivering it to every actor, ensuring they run within the right order, aggregating results, scaling if the load is high, and handling failures. Among examples are Storm, Flink, and Samza. If you prefer to make the app this fashion, please check up on various user guides. Since 2016, a brand new plan known as Streaming SQL has emerged (see article Streaming SQL a hundred and one for details) [21]. We have to decide a language that permits users to put in writing SQL like queries to question streaming information as a "Streaming SQL" language. Streaming SQL languages are increasing in number.

Projects such as WSO2 Stream Processor and SQLstream supported SQL for quite five years:

- Apache Storm additional support for Streaming SQL in 2016;
- Apache Flink additional support for Streaming SQL in 2016;
- Apache author additional support for SQL (also known as KSQL) in 2017;
- Apache Samza additional support for SQL in 2017.

With Streaming SQL languages, developers will quickly incorporate streaming queries into their Apps. By 2018, most of the stream processors support process information via a Streaming SQL language.

5.11 Data Analytics

Data analytics refers to the set of quantitative and qualitative approaches so as to derive valuable insights from information. It involves several processes that embody extracting information and categorizing it in order to find its varied patterns, relations, connections, and valuable insights. These days nearly every organization has morphed itself into an information-driven organization, which suggests they're deploying an approach so as to gather a lot of data that's associated with the shoppers, markets, and business processes. This data is then classified, maintained, and analyzed so as to create a sense of it and derive valuable insights out of it.

Understanding Big Data analytics

Though, the term "information analytics" may appear easy. Information analytics is most advanced once it's deployed for large information applications. The three most significant attributes of huge information are volume, rate, and selection.

The need for large information analytics springs from all the info that's created at unsafe speeds on the Intranet. Our digital lives can create massive information even larger due to the ever-increasing liking of people to visualize what their lives are ever-connected to the web world. It's calculable that by 2020 the additive information that can be generated will be equal to 1.7 MB each second for each individual on earth. This shows the number of information that is generated and therefore the necessity for large information analytics tools so as to create the sense of all that data. It organizes, transforms, and models the information needed for the wants so as to draw the required conclusions and distinguish patterns within the data.

5.11.1 Types of Data Analytics

Prescriptive Analytics: This sort of analytics deals with the analysis supporting the principles and suggestions in order to dictate a particular analytical path for the organization.

Predictive Analytics: This sort of analytics ensures that the trail is foreseen for the long-term course of action.

Diagnostic Analytics: It is employed for the particular purpose of discovering or crucial why a particular issue happened. This sort of analytics typically revolves around acting on a dashboard.

Descriptive Analytics: This sort of analytics supports the incoming information and therefore the mining of this information. This analytics is available with an outline supporting the info.

Descriptive	Diagnostic	Predictive	Prescriptive
What has happened?	Why did it happen?	What will happen next?	What should I do?
	Looking Back	Looking Foward	

Four types of analytics

5.11.2 *Working with Massive Data Analytics*

The subject of knowledge analytics may be a terribly immense, and therefore, the probabilities are huge. Prescriptive analytics ensures the large information analytics will shed the sunshine on the varied aspects of the business and supply you a pointy specialization in what you wish to try and do in terms of knowledge analytics. Prescriptive analytics adds heaps of import to any organization due to the specificity and terseness of this domain. We will deploy the prescriptive analytics notwithstanding the trade vertical supported constant rules and rules.

The domain of analytics will make sure that the domain of huge information is deployed for predicting this supporting information in long term. A decent example of prophetic associate lyrics is the including of analytical aspects to the sales cycle of an enterprise. It starts with the lead supply analysis, analyzing the sort of communication, the number of communications, the channels of communication together with the sentiment analysis through the heightened use of machine learning algorithms, etc to return up with an ideal prophetic analysis methodology for any enterprise. Diagnostic analytics is employed for the particular purpose of discovering or crucial why a particular course of action happened. As an associate example, you'll be able to work with diagnostic analytics so as to review a particular social media campaign for springing up with the number of mentions for a post, the number of followers, page views, reviews, fans, and such different metrics so as to diagnose why a particular issue happened [22]. Descriptive analytics is essentially used for returning the methodology of uncovering patterns that may add worth to a company. As an associate example, you'll be able to consider the credit risk assessment. It involves predicting, however, doubtless a particular client by default relies on his credit history. It takes into account the varied aspects just like the monetary performance of the client, obtaining inputs from the past monetary establishments that the person might need to be approached and different platforms just like the social media, online support with the web-based resolution. Since no organization these days will keep it while not being outdated with information, it's imperative that information analytics is an essential part of the info journey of any organization these days. Therefore, the organization supports the various kinds of information analytics. Today, progressive enterprises will really act and style an awfully sturdy path to success supported by the information that they need.

5.11.3 Tools in Data Analytics

In this section, we are going to be orienting you with the varied aspects of the massive knowledge analytics domain. Therefore herein includes a list of analytical courses that you just will take as follows:

1. *Apache Spark*: Spark could be a framework for time period knowledge analytics that is a component of the Hadoop system.
2. *Python*: This is often one in all the foremost versatile programming languages that are speedily being deployed for numerous applications as well as machine learning.
3. *SAS*: SAS is advanced analytical tool that is getting used for operating with large volumes of information and derives valuable insights.
4. *Hadoop*: It's the foremost standard huge knowledge framework that's being deployed by a number of the widest variety of organizations from around the world for creating a sense of huge knowledge.
5. *SQL*: This is often the structured command language that's used for operating with computer database management system.
6. *Tableau*: This is often the foremost standard BI tool that's deployed for information visualization and BA.
7. *Splunk*: Splunk is the tool of selection for parsing the machine-generated knowledge and deriving valuable business insights out of it.
8. *R Programming*: R is that the one range programming language that's getting used by knowledge scientists for applied math computing and graphical applications.

5.12 Machine Learning

Machine learning is the associate application of AI that has systems and has the power to mechanically learn and improve from expertise while not being expressly programmed. Machine learning focuses on the event of PC programs that may access knowledge and use it to learn for themselves. The process of learning begins with observations or knowledge, like examples, direct expertise, or instruction, so as to visualize for patterns in knowledge and build higher selections from examples that we offer in the future. The first aim is to permit the computers to learn mechanically without human intervention or help and modify actions consequently.

5.13 Supervised Learning

Supervised learning is the machine learning task that maps associate degree input to associate degree output, thereby forming, e.g., input–output pairs. It infers that a labeled coaching information consists of a group of coaching examples. In supervised learning, every example consisting of associate degree input object (typically a vector) and the desired output worth (also known as the superordinate signal) could be a try. A supervised learning algorithmic program associate degree erases the coaching information and produces an inferred performance, which might be used for mapping new examples. Associate degree optimum state of affairs can leave the algorithmic program to properly verify the category labels for unseen instances. This needs the learning algorithmic program to generalize from the training information to unseen things in an exceedingly "reasonable" method.

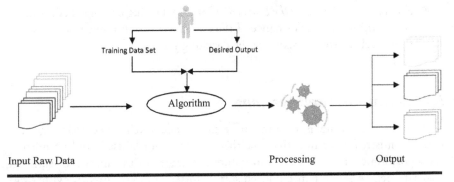

Supervised learning

The parallel task in human and psychological science is commonly noted as idea learning.

5.13.1 Steps

In order to unravel a given drawback of supervised learning, one has to perform the subsequent steps:

- *Determine the Sort of Coaching Examples*: Before doing the rest, the user ought to decide what reasonable information is to be used as a coaching setting. Just in case of handwriting analysis, as an example, this could be one written character, a complete written word, or a complete line of handwriting.
- *Gather a Coaching Set*: The coaching set is a representative of the real-world use of the program. Thus, a group of input objects is gathered and the corresponding outputs are gathered, either from human consultants or from measurements.

- *Determine the Input Feature Illustration of the Learning Algorithmic Programs*: The accuracy of the learning algorithmic programs powerfully depends on, however, the input object to delineate. Typically, the input object is reworked into a feature vector that contains a variety of options that are descriptive of the article. The number of options shouldn't be overlarge, as a result of the curse of dimensionality; however, it ought to contain enough info to accurately predict the output.
- *Determine the structure of the learning algorithmic programs and corresponding learning algorithmic program*: As an example, the engineer might like better to use support vector machines or call trees.
- *Complete the Look*: Run the learning algorithmic program on the gathered training set. Some supervised learning algorithms need the user to work out the management parameters. These parameters are also adjusted by optimizing performance on a set (called a validation set) of the coaching set, or via cross-validation.
- *Evaluate the Accuracy of the Learned to Perform*: During parameter adjustment and learning, the performance of the ensuring algorithm must be measured on a check set that's break free the coaching set.

5.13.2 Unsupervised Learning

Unsupervised learning is training of a man-made intelligence (AI) algorithmic rule mistreatment info that's neither classified nor labeled, and permitting the algorithmic rule to act on info without steerage. In unsupervised learning, associate degree AI system could cluster unsorted info consistently with similarities and variations although there are not any classes provided. AI systems of unsupervised learning are usually related to generative learning models, although they will conjointly use a retrieval-based approach (which is most frequently related to supervised learning). Chatbots, self-driving cars, automatic face recognition programs, skilled systems, and robots are among the systems that will use either supervised or unsupervised learning approach. In unsupervised learning approach, associate degree AI system is related to unlabeled and unclassified knowledge, and also, the system's algorithms act on the information without previous coaching. The output relies upon the coded algorithms. Subjecting a system to unsupervised learning is a method of testing AI. Unsupervised learning algorithms will perform a lot of advanced processing tasks than supervised learning systems. However, unsupervised learning may be unpredictable than the alternate model. Associate degree unsupervised learning AI system may, for instance, understand on its own the way to type cats from dogs; it'd conjointly add unforeseen and unwanted classes to subsume uncommon breeds, making muddle rather than order [23].

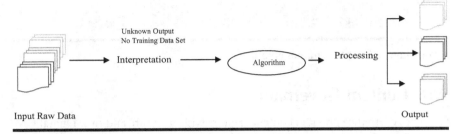

Unsupervised learning

5.14 Content Management

Content management (CM) is the method used for assortment, delivery, retrieval, governance, and overall management of data in any format. The term is often employed in relation to the administration of the digital content lifecycle, from creation to permanent storage or deletion. The content concerned could also be pictures, video, audio, and multimedia system similarly as text. CM practices and processes will vary by purpose and organization, thereby causing variations in steps or nomenclature [24].

5.15 Content Management Process

The stages of the CM lifecycle are as follows:

1. *Organization*: It is the primary stage where classes are created, taxonomies designed, and classification schemes developed.
2. *Creation*: Content is classed into the field of study classes.
3. *Storage*: Content format and storage selections are created with easy access, delivery, security and different factors attributable to the organization's desires.
4. *Workflow*: Rules are designed to maintain various roles of content while maintaining consistency with the organization's policies.
5. *Editing/Versioning*: This step involves managing multiple content versions and presentation changes.
6. *Publishing*: The stage where content is delivered to users, which might be outlined as web site guests or internal business enterprise via the computer network for workers.
7. *Removal/Archives*: The ultimate stage where content is deleted or moved to associate archive once it's sometimes accessed or obsolete.

Seven stages of content management

5.16 Content Governance

Content governance provides content creators with structure and tips. Digital CM governance will verify priorities, offer elaborate standards, assign possession for content, and supply access management. This helps to make standardized user expertise, minimize content bloat, and make internal controls. Common tools that organizations use embody content workflows, taxonomies, and magnificent guides, in conjunction with records management tools that embody audit trails for compliance.

5.16.1 Types of Digital Content Management

For almost every class of digital content, there's a corresponding tool or method for managing it.

Social Media CM: Social media CM tools are Sprout Social, Google Analytics, and BuzzSumo.

Web Content Management: Web site management is employed to make, manage, and show webpages. An online CM system could be a program that gives organizations some way to manage digital data on a web site without previous information of web programming and might embrace elements for a selected trade, like a content management application (CMA) that automates the assembly of hypertext mark-up language.

Mobile Content Management: Mobile content management (MCM) provides secure access to company information on smartphones, tablets, and alternative devices. The most elements of MCM are file storage and file sharing.

Enterprise Content Management: Associate in Nursing enterprise content management (ECM) system has elements that help enterprises to manage information effectively. Electronic warfare elements are involved in the processes such as streamlining access, eliminating bottlenecks, minimizing overhead, together with version management, routing, archiving, content governance, and security.

5.17 Content Management Systems and Tools

In addition to CM platforms for specific content varieties, there also are general content management systems (CMS) that offer machine-controlled processes for cooperative digital CM and creation. A CMS normally includes options like format management, business enterprise practicality, and therefore the ability to update content [25]. A CMS will enable a user to make a unified look and have version management; however, a drawback is that it typically will need specific coaching for content creators. A digital asset management (DAM) system is another style of CMS that manages documents, movies, and alternative wealthy media assets. A couple of samples of notable CMSs are WordPress, Joomla, and Drupal.

5.18 Data Integration

Data integration is the method of mixing data from totally different sources into one, unified read. Integration begins with the ingestion method process and includes steps such as cleansing, ETL mapping, and transformation. Knowledge integration ultimately allows analytics tools to supply effective, unjust BI. There's no universal approach to knowledge integration. However, knowledge integration solutions generally involve a couple of common components, together with a network of information sources, a master server, and shoppers accessing knowledge from the master server.

In a typical knowledge integration method, the shopper sends a letter of invitation to the master server for knowledge. The master server then intakes the required knowledge from internal and external sources. The information is extracted from the sources, then consolidated into one, cohesive knowledge set. This can be returned to the shopper to be used.

Even if an organization is receiving all the information it desires, that knowledge usually resides among a variety of separate knowledge sources. As an example, for a typical client 360 use case study, the information that has to be combined might embrace data from their CRM systems, Internet traffic, promoting operations code, client-facing applications, sales, and client success systems, and even partner information, simply to call it. Data from all of these sources usually requires a force to make analytical desires or operational actions, which will be not a tiny task for knowledge engineers or developers to bring all along.

Let's take a glance at a typical analytical use case. Although not unified knowledge, one report generally involves work on multiple accounts and multiple sites, accessing knowledge at intervals from native apps, repetition over the information, reformatting, and cleansing – all before analysis will happen.

Conducting these operations as expeditiously as attainable highlights the importance of information integration. It additionally showcases the key edges of a well-thought-out approach to knowledge integration. Workers in each department – and typically in disparate physical locations – progressively want access to the company's knowledge for shared and individual comes. IT desires a secure answer for delivering knowledge via self-service access across all lines of business [26].

Additionally, workers in nearly every department are generating and rising knowledge that the remainder of the business desires. Knowledge integration has to be cooperative and unified so as to enhance collaboration and unification across the organization. Once an organization takes measures to integrate its knowledge properly, it cuts down considerably on the time it takes to arrange and analyze that knowledge. The automation of unified views cuts out the requirement for manually gathering knowledge; associated workers now not ought to build connections from scratch whenever they have to run a report or build an application. Additionally, exploitation of the proper tools, instead of hand-coding the mixing, returns even larger (and resources overall) to the dev team.

All the time saved on these tasks will be placed to alternative, higher uses, with additional hours earmarked for analysis and execution to make a company additional productive and competitive. There's a great deal to stay with once it involves a company's knowledge resources. To manually gather knowledge, workers should grasp each location and have all necessary codes to put in before they start in order to make sure that their knowledge sets are going to be complete and correct. If an information repository is added, which worker is unaware, they're going to have associate incomplete knowledge set.

With machine-driven updates, however, reports will be run simply in real time, whenever they're required. Knowledge integration efforts really improve the worth of a business' knowledge over time. As knowledge is integrated into a centralized system, quality problems are known and necessary enhancements are enforced, which ultimately ends up in additional correct knowledge – the inspiration for quality analysis.

5.19 Data Governance

Data governance (DG) is the overall management of the provision, usability, and integrity associate degree security of information utilized in an enterprise. A sound knowledge governance program includes a body or council, an outlined set of procedures, and an idea to execute those procedures. Businesses take pleasure in knowledge governance; as a result, it ensures knowledge is consistent and trustworthy. This is often important as a lot of organizations think about knowledge to create business selections, optimize operations, produce new product and services, and improve gain.

5.19.1 Data Governance Implementation

The initial step in implementing a DG framework involves shaping the homeowners or custodians of the info cases within the enterprise. This role is known as data stewardship. Processes should then be outlined to effectively cowl; however, the info is held on, archived, insured, and guarded against mishaps, stealing, or attacks. A group of standards and procedures should be developed that defines the info is to be utilized by approved personnel. Moreover, a group of controls and audit procedures should be placed that ensures current compliance with internal information policies and external government rules, which guarantees the information is employed in an exceedingly consistent manner across multiple enterprise applications.

These groups comprise business managers, information managers, and workers; moreover, finish users are acquainted with relevant information domains among the organization. Associations dedicated to promoting best practices in such information governance processes embrace the info Governance Institute, the info Data Management Association (DAMA), and also the info Governance Professionals Organization [27].

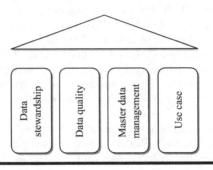

Four pillars of data governance

5.20 Data Stewardship

An essential attribute of the information steward is to be in command of varied parts of the information. The key objective of such knowledge governance is to assure knowledge quality in terms of accuracy, accessibility, consistency, completeness, and change. Teams of information stewards are generally shaped to guide actual DG implementations. These groups embody information directors, business analysts, and business personnel at home with specific aspects of knowledge among the organization. Knowledge Stewards work with people positioned within the overall knowledge lifecycle to assist knowledge use conforming to a company's knowledge governance policies.

References

1. I. Yaqoob, I.A.T. Hashem, A. Gani, S. Mokhtar, E. Ahmed, N.B. Anuar, A.V. Vasilakos, Big data: from beginning to future, *International Journal of Information Management* 36 (6) (2016) 1231–1247.
2. F.J. Riggins, S.F. Wamba, Research directions on the adoption, usage, and impact of the Internet of Things through the use of big data analytics, in: *Proceedings of 48th Hawaii International Conference on System Sciences (HICSS'15)*, Hawaii, IEEE, 2015, pp. 1531–1540.

3. https://medium.com/stream-processing/what-is-stream-processing-1eadfca11b97
4. M.R. Bashir, A.Q. Gill, Towards an IoT big data analytics framework: smart buildings systems, in: *2016 IEEE 18th International Conference on High Performance Computing and Communications; IEEE 14th International Conference on Smart City; IEEE 2nd International Conference on Data Science and Systems (HPCC/SmartCity/DSS)*, Sydney, IEEE, 2016, pp. 1325–1332.
5. C. Lee, C. Yeung, M. Cheng, Research on IoT based cyber physical system for industrial big data analytics, in: *2015 IEEE International Conference on Industrial Engineering and Engineering Management (IEEM)*, Singapore, IEEE, 2015, pp. 1855–1859.
6. www.webopedia.com/TERM/S/stream_computing.html
7. P. Rizwan, K. Suresh, M.R. Babu, Real-time smart traffic management system for smart cities by using Internet of Things and big data, in: *International Conference on Emerging Technological Trends (ICETT)*, Kollam, IEEE, 2016, pp. 1–7.
8. Q. Zhang, X. Zhang, Q. Zhang, W. Shi, H. Zhong, Firework: Big data sharing and processing in collaborative edge environment, in: *2016 Fourth IEEE Workshop on Hot Topics in Web Systems and Technologies (HotWeb)*, Washington, DC, IEEE, 2016, pp. 20–25.
9. https://searchdatamanagement.techtarget.com/definition/data-warehouse
10. M.M. Rathore, A. Ahmad, A. Paul, IoT-based smart city development using big data analytical approach, in: *IEEE International Conference on Automatica (ICA-ACCA)*, Curicó, IEEE, 2016, pp. 1–8.
11. B. Ahlgren, M. Hidell, E.C.-H. Ngai, Internet of Things for smart cities: interoperability and open data, *IEEE Internet Computing* 20 (6) (2016) 52–56.
12. www.guru99.com/data-warehousing.html
13. O.B. Sezer, E. Dogdu, M. Ozbayoglu, A. Onal, An extended it framework with semantics, big data, and analytics, in: *2016 IEEE International Conference on Big Data (Big Data)*, Washington, DC, IEEE, 2016, pp. 1849–1856.
14. B. Cheng, A. Papageorgiou, F. Cirillo, E. Kovacs, Genetics: geo-distributed edge analytics for large scale riot systems based on dynamic topology, in: *2015 IEEE 2nd World Forum on Internet of Things (WF-IoT)*, Milan, IEEE, 2015, pp. 565–570.
15. H. Wang, O.L. Osen, G. Li, W. Li, H.-N. Dai, W. Zeng, Big data and industrial Internet of Things for the maritime industry in northwestern Norway, in: *TENCON 2015-2015 IEEE Region 10 Conference*, Macao, IEEE, 2015, pp. 1–5.
16. www.quora.com/What-does-data-ingestion-mean
17. J.L. Pérez, D. Carrera, Performance characterization of the serviocity API: an IoT-as-a-service data management platform, in: *2015 IEEE First International Conference on Big Data Computing Service and Applications (BigDataService)*, Redwood City, CA, IEEE, 2015, pp. 62–71.
18. M. Villari, A. Celesti, M. Fazio, A. Puliafito, AllJoyn Lambda: an architecture for the management of smart environments in IoT, in: *2014 International Conference on Smart Computing Workshops (SMARTCOMP Workshops)*, Hong Kong, IEEE, 2014, pp. 9–14.
19. https://hortonworks.com/solutions/data-ingestion/
20. A.J. Jara, D. Genoud, Y. Bocchi, Big Data for cyber physical systems: an analysis of challenges, solutions and opportunities, in: *2014 Eighth International Conference on Innovative Mobile and Internet Services in Ubiquitous Computing (IMIS)*, Birmingham, IEEE, 2014, pp. 376–380.

21. Z. Ding, X. Gao, J. Xu, H. Wu, IoT-StatisticDB: a general statistical database cluster mechanism for big data analysis in the Internet of Things, in: *2013 IEEE International Conference on Green Computing and Communications (GreenCom), IEEE and Internet of Things (iThings/CPSCom)and IEEE Cyber, Physical and Social Computing*, Beijing, IEEE, 2013, pp. 535–543.

22. www.alooma.com/blog/what-is-data-ingestion

23. C. Vuppalapati, A. Ilapakurti, S. Kedari, The role of big data in creating sense her, an integrated approach to create next-generation mobile sensor and wearable data-driven electronic health record (EHR), in: *2016 IEEE Second International Conference on Big Data Computing Service and Applications (BigDataService)*, Oxford, IEEE, 2016, pp. 293–296.

24. A. Ahmad, M.M. Rathore, A. Paul, S. Rho, Defining human behaviors using big data analytics in social internet of things, in: *2016 IEEE 30th International Conference on Advanced Information Networking and Applications (AINA)*, Crans-Montana, IEEE, 2016, pp. 1101–1107.

25. https://intellipaat.com/blog/what-is-hadoop/

26. E. Ahmed, M.H. Rehmani, Introduction to the special section on social collaborative Internet of Things, *Computers & Electrical Engineering* 100 (58) (2017) 382–384.

27. D. Arora, K.F. Li, A. Loffler, Big data analytics for classification of network-enabled devices, in: *2016 30th International Conference on Advanced Information Networking and Applications Workshops (WAINA)*, Crans-Montana, IEEE, 2016, pp. 708–713.

Chapter 6

Big Data Architecture for IoT

V. Pradeep Kumar, Kolla Bhanu
Prakash, and L. S. S. Reddy
Koneru Lakshmaiah Education Foundation

Contents

6.1 Introduction

Internet of Things (IoT) was considered as the latest technology development in wireless sensor networks where a set of electronic sensors will communicate among themselves by reading the external environmental factors such as temperature, pressure, and speed, and send that information for further processing. All possible smart products were used all over household, and in real-time industry, this IoT technology was incorporated as part of their regular usage. This interaction of sensors for any purpose in IoT has given it a new paradigm that was defined as "The Internet of Things allows people and things to be connected anytime, anyplace, with anything and anyone, ideally using any path/network and any service" (Perera et al. 2013). The wide range of domains and application areas such as healthcare, transport, household appliances, aviation, vehicles, and environment are using electronic IoT devices at a large scale for providing efficient services for organizations and individuals.

IoT provides platforms, frameworks, and services where sensors, actuators, and other electronic devices are deployed and connected through internet for a wide range of communications for sharing information with external environment. IoT devices act as data collection devices where they sense data from external environment and transmit it for further processing through communication solutions, such as Bluetooth, Wi-Fi, ZigBee, and GSM, to a remote controlled computer-based systems for taking decision and providing services. In the IoT, there are three paradigms: internet-oriented, sensor, and knowledge (Atzori et al. 2010). The wide range of adaptations of wireless technology in IoT makes it as next evolutionary technology providing full opportunities offered by the internet technology (Hsieh et al. 2011).

IoT devices generate huge amount of data for processing, which is manageable by only through big data (Ge et al. 2018). Each component involved in IoT technology, such as temperature sensors, healthcare applications, and digital devices, generates huge amount of structured, unstructured, and semi-structured data, which results in big data. According to Ali (2016) and Hashem et al. (2015), big data was used as database tool for capturing, storing, processing, and analyzing this huge amount of data sets generated by IoT devices. In Reinsel et al. (2012), it was stated that big data technologies are used as new-generation technologies for massive volume of data of different formats for high velocity capture of data, discovery, and analysis. It was also revealed that big data is classified into three aspects, namely, data sources, analytics, and presentation of the results of analytics.

6.2 IoT with Big Data Characteristics

The seven major characteristics of big data (Thinxstream Technologies, 2018) are volume, variety, velocity, variability, veracity, validity, and volatility. IoT has specific features that map to the characteristics of big data, which are as follows.

Number of IoT Devices (*Volume*): As IoT devices were of low cost so many IoT products are involving many IoT devices for gathering the information from real-time environments and interacting among themselves to generate data for completion of their task to achieve their specific functionality.

Multiple IoT Devices (*Variability*): Many of the manufacturers are developing these IoT devices so similar task can be done on multiple IoT devices, and they even need to perform cross-boundary components interaction for generating data for generic functionality of IoT product.

Data Types (*Variety*): The multiple IoT devices generate data in different formats even they are of similar types. The data can be either structured, unstructured, or semi-structured, which can be easily managed with big data.

Data Quality/Nature (*Veracity*): The data generated in these IoT devices will be varied (Pandya et al. 2017) at different instances; sometimes they are fully functional or fail to operate and get degraded in performance because of less backup of power in device or wore out because of its end of lifetime, which lead to malfunction of device. These types of problems in IoT devices generate low quality of data, which leads to veracity that plays a very important role while performing analytics on that data.

Update Frequencies (*Velocity*): IoT devices generate data at different frequencies; some devices like temperature sensor recording temperature have less functionality so they may send data at low frequency, whereas some IoT products for creating automation of speed and break monitoring in driverless car have more functionality so they may send huge amount of data at high frequency, which needs advanced tools and technologies to manage such data, which in turn is possible with big data.

Context Data and Historical Data (*Validity and Volatility*): IoT data varies according to the environment where the data was gathered depending upon the response of IoT devices, which may be static/low frequency and dynamic/high frequency. Big data needs both current and historical data for performing better analysis of the IoT product performance.

6.3 IoT Reference Architecture

The basic building blocks of IoT reference model are sensors, actuators, communication networks, protocols for communication, and context-aware processing of events. The model needs much like big data for performing analytics and presenting that information to business environments. Figure 6.1 gives the basic architecture

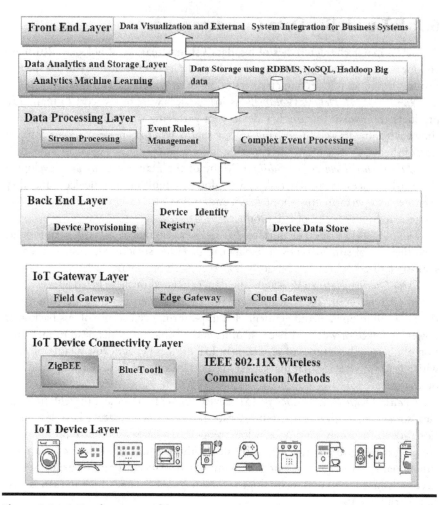

Figure 6.1 IoT reference architecture.

model of IoT, which covers all layers starting from end-end device layer communication to front end layers viewing the analyzed data for business systems. IoT device layer comprises all kinds of devices: slow, low-frequency operated devices like temperature sensor at nuclear reactor, fast and high-frequency operated devices like automated car. The next layer, device connectivity layer, specifies a set of communication protocols used by devices such as ZigBee, Wi-Fi, and Bluetooth. The IoT gateway layers connect the back end layer with IoT connectivity layers comprising latest large-scale technologies such as cloud computing and edge computing supporting IoT devices. The back end layer plays a vital role in terms of device identity generation, provisioning for utilization resources to complete their vital tasks, and holding device data for further processing in next layers. Data processing layer does stream processing, fixes rules for processing data, and even manages complex event processing in terms of reporting information to the next layers. Data analysis and storage layer uses some machine learning algorithms to analyze and predict the data generated by IoT devices. The final layer, front end layer, connects the end user or any business systems for reporting the processed data for further utilization. The front end layer deals with data visualization, and it even integrates with other system for supporting business systems.

6.3.1 Big Data Components

Big data represents the large volume of data that was not supported by traditional relational databases. It holds large data sets for analyzing with machine learning algorithms. The basic components of big data can be categorized based on their abstract layers for storing and processing business data.

Storage Systems: It was the basic component that deals with storage file systems like HDFS (Hadoop File System) to store those large data sets along with their metadata for major computation. NoSQL data stores like HBase with distributed column-oriented data support key value pair and use hash tables to store data sets.

Computation and Logic Layer: This layer involves MapReduce, Pig, etc. for dealing with computation for large data sets. MapReduce first does the processing of raw data sets mapping to key value data structure, and then, it takes care of converging them into small data sets for easy computation. Pig and Hive are two high-level languages that are built on Hadoop platform for processing huge data sets in parallel. They can be scripted for doing Map Reducer jobs.

Application Logic or Interaction: It uses Hive, Cascading, etc. for providing framework to integrate with the application environment. Hive, like SQL, is basically used for HDFS to analyze its data by interaction and then process it similar to query evaluation engine. Cascading was a framework for providing data processing Application Programming Interface (API) for big data.

Specialized Analytics Databases: Databases, e.g., Netezza or Greenplum, have the ability for scaling out and are known for a quick information ingestion and revive, which is a compulsory prerequisite for analytical models.

6.3.2 IoT Architecture Layers Mapping to Big Data Components

IoT reference architecture layers from back end layer for holding device stores until to front end layer for visualizing data purely map to big data components.

1. The large storage systems like HDFS can be used to hold the large number of IoT devices information like their identity for referring them with unique id and their integration with other IoT devices for generating information which they recorded from external environment for further processing.

2. The data processing layer needs a framework like MapReducer or Pig for easy processing of the large amount of data sets generated with large number of IoT devices. IoT devices need fast processing of data as it needs to take decision or complete within a span of seconds and provide service to external environment.

3. The data analytic storage layer of IoT reference architecture needs support of Hive or Cascading as they support with the application framework to process huge data with some application logic and provide an interaction with user environment for analyzing data.

4. Front end layer of IoT architecture specialized analytic software is to provide display information to end user or provide facility of integrating this information with other business system for further processing of IoT data.

6.4 Device Connectivity Options

A huge ecosystem of IoT device connectivity was the process where a small set of connected devices send data to other devices, applications, or servers. The IoT device connectivity needs some specific protocols to create such communication among themselves or with other components of IoT architecture layer. Here, we study the device connectivity under two categories: first, communication between IoT devices (Belem Pacheco et al. 2018) and internet and second, communication between IoT devices (Belem Pacheco et al. 2018) and gateways.

6.4.1 Communication between IoT Devices and Internet

The communication technologies for support of communication of IoT devices and internet are studied for two modes of wireless networks, i.e., infrastructure and ad hoc network. In infrastructure mode, the devices' access points with access control are necessary for communication, whereas in ad hoc network mode, there is no access control at access point for communication.

Bluetooth: A short-go interchanges innovation coordinated into most cell phones, which was a noteworthy favorable position for individual items, especially wearables. Bluetooth was outstanding to versatile clients. In any case, not very far in the past, the new noteworthy convention for IoT applications showed up Bluetooth Low Energy (BLE) (Natallia 2018) or Bluetooth Smart (Natallia 2018). This innovation is a genuine establishment for the IoT, as it is adaptable to all market developments. In addition, it was intended to decrease control utilization.

ZigBee 3.0 (Natallia 2018): A low-control, low information rate remote system utilized for the most part in modern settings. ZigBee Alliance even made the general language for the IoT – Dotdot – which makes it feasible for keen articles to work safely on any system and flawlessly see one another.

Wi-Fi: The innovation for radio remote system administration of gadgets. It offers quick information exchange and can process a lot of data. This was the most prevalent sort of availability in LAN conditions.

Cellular Technology: The premise of cell phone systems. In any case, it was likewise appropriate for the IoT applications that need working over longer separations. It can exploit cell correspondence abilities, e.g., GSM, 3G, 4G (and 5G soon). The innovation can exchange high amounts of information; however, the power utilization and the costs are high as well. Hence, it very well may be an ideal answer for tasks that send little measurement of data.

LoRaWAN (Long Range Wide Area Network) (Natallia 2018): A convention for wide zone systems. It is intended to help enormous systems (e.g., brilliant urban areas) with a great many low-control gadgets. LoRaWAN can provide minimal effort, is versatile, and can secure bidirectional correspondence in different enterprises.

Finally, Table 6.1 highlights the features of communication technologies used for IoT devices (Natallia 2018). All the above connectivity technologies are studied under different parameters so as to provide a wide range of choice for IoT device manufacturers to target certain issues of users while interacting with external environment.

6.4.2 Communication between IoT Devices and Gateway

The communication between IoT devices and gateway depends on communication protocol in which interaction with middleware components of application was made possible with message delivery.

MQTT (*Message Queue Telemetry Transport*) (Natallia 2018): A lightweight convention for sending straightforward information streams from sensors to applications and middleware. The Ability convention over TCP/IP and incorporates three segments: supporter, distributer, and dealer. The distributer gathers information and sends it to endorsers. Distributers and supporters check the approval and guarantee the security of the representative tests. MQTT suits small, cheap, low-memory, and low-power devices.

DDS (*Data Distribution Service*) (Natallia 2018): An IoT standard for ongoing, adaptable, and superior machine-to-machine correspondence. It was created with the Object Management Group (OMG). Deploy DDS both in low-impression gadgets and in the cloud.

The DDS standard has two main layers:

- Data-Centric Publish-Subscribe (DCPS) (Natallia 2018), which delivers the information to subscribers;
- Data-Local Reconstruction Layer (DLRL) (Natallia 2018), which provides an interface to DCPS functionalities.

Table 6.1 Features of Communication Technologies Used for IoT Devices

Parameters \ Technology	Bluetooth	ZigBee	Wi-Fi	Cellular	LoRaWAN
Standard	Bluetooth 4.2	ZigBee 3.0 based on IEEE 802.1 5.4	Based on IEEE 802.11	GSM/GPRS/EDGE (2G), UMTS/HSPA (3G), LTE (4G)	LoRaWAN
Frequencies	2.4 GHz	2.4 GHz	2.4 and 5 GHz bands	900/1800/1900/2100 MHz	Various
Range	50–150 m (Smart/BLE)	10–100 m	Approximately 50 m	35 km (GSM); 200 km (HSPA)	2–5 km (urban area), 15 km (suburban area)
Data rates	1 Mbps (Smart/BLE)	250 kbps	150–200 Mbps, 600 Mbps maximum	35–170 kbps (GPRS). 120–384 kbps (EDGE), 384 Kbps–2 Mbps (UMTS), 600 kbps–10 Mbps (HSPA), 3–10 Mbps (LTE)	0.3–50 kbps

Source: Natallia (2018).

AMQP (*Advanced Message Queuing Protocol*) (Natallia 2018): An application layer protocol for message-oriented middleware conditions. It was endorsed as a global standard.

The processing chain of the protocol (Natallia 2018) includes three components that follow certain rules:

1. *Exchange*: It gets messages and puts them in the queues (Natallia 2018).
2. *Message Queue*: It stores messages until they can be safely processed with the client app (Natallia 2018).
3. *Binding*: It states the relationship between the first and second components (Natallia 2018).

6.5 Device Stores

IoT device stores deal with type of data generated while measuring parameters from the external environment of the product. The wide variety of data delivered with IoT devices can be categorized into different data types based on their interaction with other IoT devices or themselves reading values for further processing for the next-level layers of IoT reference architecture. IoT devices generated data that can be divided into two extreme types of data: One can be long data files like audio visual generated with surveillance cameras, and other can be tiny log files generated for temperature sensors reading. The information/yield (I/O) profiles of every data type, as far as per using and composing, contrast so much that it isn't practical to plan a one-measure fits-all if IoT storage architecture will include the information created having those two types of data.

6.5.1 IoT Impacts on Storage

IoT device stores will impact on storage, which can be studied under two categories: (i) storage implications and (ii) data center impact.

6.5.1.1 Storage Implications

IoT brings various ramifications for data center and capacity structure. To start with, it will be basic to get the information off gadgets, which for the most part contain minimal inner capacity, and onto a verified, supported up to capacity framework. Not exclusively was this information novel, but also it tends to be entirely profitable. It could incorporate natural information that empowers the business to follow expenses, or center example information from investigation groups in the Arctic, for instance. Information from sensors and so forth contains extensive quantities of little pieces of information, and will require abnormal amounts of I/O.

A lot of this ongoing information will be put away in databases and, to be broke down accurately, should be handled and organized appropriately. For instance, a temperature increment may not be accurately connected with other information – e.g., part wear – if the information focus land in the wrong request. This suggests the requirement for quick stockpiling – positively strong state drives (SSDs) – particularly if handling is to be executed as close to continuous as could reasonably be expected. After some time, this is probably going to drive interest for the sorts of rapid, streak substitution advancements being created with various makers, e.g., Samsung's multi-stream controller innovation, which records lower control among its favorable circumstances; Intel's 3D Xpoint; and farther, attractive RAM (MRAM).

Substantial information objects, then again, require consecutive exchanges, so object stockpiling could be the most ideal approach to oversee, store, and recover this sort of information. Thus, one of the greatest changes will be the requirement for more stockpiling limit. This implies more prominent capital use, more prominent weight on the in-house data center and the cloud supplier to keep a cover on expenses, and a requirement for more stockpiling administration with IT groups. Undertakings may choose to fall back on cloud-based capacity, which is likewise where much information investigation handling could occur.

6.5.1.2 Data Center Impact

As the quantity of gadgets in organizations and homes develops into billions, the supporting foundation needs to change. Vast volumes of exchanges from substantial quantities of dispersed gadgets will extend numerous focal data center frameworks as far as possible. A great part of the traffic – crude information from the field – will be approaching. Preparing may happen in the data center, be that as it may, to stay away from separation inertness and bound to be downloaded and handled locally.

To be helpful for continuous investigation, IoT information will require low idleness among servers and capacity, so these capacities should draw nearer and, in certain occurrences, nearly converge, as with hyper-scale and hyper-met foundation. In the case of utilizing the cloud, the key was to guarantee the service level agreements (SLAs) incorporate measurements, e.g., idleness among capacity and preparing capacities. Also, in light of the fact that low inactivity was basic, we are probably going to see increasingly little data centers worked to be nearer to the information. The aftereffects of investigation might be nourished back profoundly; however, the information itself need not be nourished. This will likewise influence wide territory arrange wide area networks (WAN) transfer speed necessities.

Data center endpoint gadgets may need to change since information streams into the data center will increment – as of not long ago, the data center has for the most part been a generator of information for utilization. The volumes and sorts of information will change, as youthful advances develop, making a requirement for the data center to stay adaptable, ready to grow, and contract as required. Security keeps on being basic, with sensors regularly being genuinely uncertain, so the venture will depend on the security given by the data center or the cloud supplier. Somewhere else, the assortment and quantities of gadgets will make security challenges, as connections between them are multifaceted nature.

6.6 Device Identity

Identification of interacting components of any system is very important to ensure its correct composition and operation. In IoT system, the start of interaction happens from devices that act as the base components. These things will interact with external environment and gather physical data and initiate the process of actual task. Device identity was mostly managed with things identifier, which identifies the entity of interest of IoT application. An example of thing identifier was like **asset tracking** – where organization keeps tracks of all their assets starting from their manufactured product to any movable assets like their vehicles using radio frequency identification (RFID) tags or barcode.

6.6.1 Identity Management of IoT

Device identity plays a prominent role in identity management of IoT (Chaudhuri 2018) in performing identity and access management in IoT. Identity Access Management (IAM) can manage human-to-device, device-to-device, and/or device-to-service/system (DigiCert, Inc. 2017). IoT systems must have a strategy for overseeing device identity and perform at least some of the following functionalities:

- Providing a unique naming framework for IoT gadgets;
- Creating a life cycle for IoT gadgets;
- Developing a very much characterized procedure for enlisting the IoT gadgets;
- Designing a security framework for IoT gadgets;
- Highlighting all-around characterized verification and approval process for administrator neighborhood access to associated gadgets;
- Creating shields for securing distinctive sorts of information, and protection shields for actually recognizable data in order to make a point;
- Defining and reporting which people can get access to the distinctive sorts of information (e.g., nearby administrators, outside organizations);
- Providing rules for confirming and approving sporadically associated IoT gadgets;
- Determining techniques for performing access control to IoT gadgets.

Device identity, i.e., thing identifier, needs to undergo the following process in order to perform aforementioned activities:

1. Allocation;
2. Registration;
3. Resolution;
4. Security, privacy, and data protection;
5. Interoperability issues.

Allocation: Its purpose was to assign a unique identifier to the device within specific (local or global) domain where the identifiers are assigned to entities and are used. This unique identifier was generated by different mechanisms (**extraction** – which extracts unique identifier from a standard repository by performing look-up; **federation** – where identifier was extracted from different repositories from local and global organization and assigned uniquely; **random-algorithm generator** – popularly used for many thing identifiers to get uniquely assigned with fixing number of bits; **natural-biometric pattern**, iris pattern, vein pattern, and many other natural patterns).

Registration: It was a process of achieving a mechanism to store and retrieve information associated with an identifier for a particular entity. This process was initiated by regulation bodies to associate information related to identifier during any stages of identity life cycle. Examples are regular bodies assigning car license plates, telephone numbers and MAC address for devices that are interacting with internet related to a particular LAN network.

Resolution: It was a mechanism, based on the entity identifier, of getting the information how to interact with entity and how to access the services by a user/application.

Example includes a unique URL assigned to web page or web site managed with domain name system to resolve IP address to domain name.

Security, Privacy, and Data Protection: Security for identifiers was mainly concerned with authenticity of identifier so that only valid entities will access the device identity and untrusted and fake entity will not access the IoT system. Privacy and data protection are concerned with human-related information like their cars, personal devices, goods, and health. Encryption can be an important source for managing privacy and data protection.

Interoperability Issues: This mechanism comes into picture when multiple identifier schemes are followed for IoT solutions. There are three interoperability issues: First, the same entity is used for different identifier schemes. Second, activities are related to each other, but identifiers are different. Third, the same entity classes with different identifier schemes are used for application that runs across different domains.

6.7 Registry and Data Stores

IoT device registry was critical for performing any task using these devices in any application environments. Modeling this device registry using ontology was a better idea to automate the process of registry and its binding and provisioning management without any difficulty. Figure 6.2 (Hirmer et al. 2016) illustrates a better approach for automating the device registration using ontology and further binding it for further communication in application environments.

The architecture in Figure 6.2 consists of the following main parts:

(i) Device registry, which stores meta-data about the IoT devices;
(ii) Device ontology, which contains binding information;
(iii) Device adaptors, which extract the information from the IoT devices and deploy them directly on a thing or on an adaptor platform;
(iv) Resource Management Platform (RMP) (Hirmer et al. 2016), which provisions IoT devices by pull-and-push approaches.

This architecture was applied through a method that enables automated IoT device registration, IoT device binding, and IoT device provisioning of data in the following five consecutive steps.

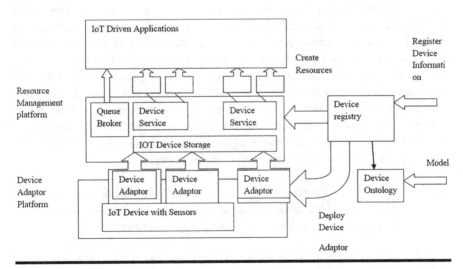

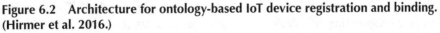

Figure 6.2 Architecture for ontology-based IoT device registration and binding. (Hirmer et al. 2016.)

Step 1: Task Definition
- *Input*: IoT thing identifier, IoT device identifier(s), *optional*: ontology snippet;
- *Output*: IoT thing identifier, IoT device identifier(s), *optional*: ontology snippet.

In this step, the IoT things and devices that have to be registered are defined. This step contains a unique identifier of the IoT thing, and depending on specific functionality, the IoT device was also registered with IoT device identifier. Ontology holds the complete information about IoT things and devices that are specified in task definition. If any IoT thing and device information was not available, then ontology snippet was used for adding their information to task definition, and for further process, step 2 was performed.

Step 2: Ontology Traversal
- *Input*: IoT thing identifier, IoT device identifier(s), *optional*: ontology snippet;
- *Output*: List of IoT device specifications, IoT device identifier, IoT device identifier(s).

Based on the information available from the task definition of step 1, the specific information about IoT things and devices is taken from ontology. Ontology gives technical details that are necessary for an automated IoT device registration and binding, and for device provisioning, and can also be used as meta-data source by IoT device-driven applications. This ontology contains IoT device-specific details in terms of accessing their accuracy, frequency, etc. about IoT device binding in terms of the respective adaptor in an IoT device adaptor repository, and information about IoT devices of a thing. SensorML, an XML-based language, was used for efficient storage and retrieval of information. SPARQL queries are used for automated editing and extension. As the ontologies are capable of integrating heterogeneous, dynamic environments, they are accepted for performing IoT device registration while traversing through it and searching for corresponding record entry of the IoT device binding, which will be explained in the next step.

Step 3: IoT Device Adapter Deployment/Automated IoT Device Binding
- *Input*: List of IoT device specifications, thing identifier, IoT identifier(s);
- *Output*: List of successfully deployed IoT device adapters.

The next step in ontology after binding IoT devices was to extract the information regarding provisioning of IoT device data. To extract the IoT device data from corresponding IoT devices, they require adaptors for connection with the IoT devices through serial interface connections, retrieve data as stream, and send to RMP (Hirmer et al. 2016) using HTTP protocol or MQTT message protocol.

The device adaptors retrieve the information about sensors from the repositories, and they parameterize the information using RMP's URL and provide IoT device information to RMP directly. The adaptor deployment can be realized by runtime environment example using Raspberry Pi with secure socket hash (SSH) connections. In most cases, these adaptors are self-implemented, such as FIWARE or Open MTC. Sometimes these adaptors are embedded into machine and need machine-to-machine standards.

Step 4: IoT Device Data Provisioning
- *Input*: List of successfully deployed adaptors;
- *Output*: REST resource URI(s), queue topic(s).

Once an IoT device adaptor was deployed and activated, it starts sending data to the RMP. Here, the data can only be accessed by the IoT device-driven applications after the fourth step was processed. At first, the interfaces are established for registered IoT devices; then, they send data to IoT device data storage and REST framework developed IoT device services. To enable pull-to-push approach for IoT device data provisioning, IoT device services will manage pull approach for retrieving IoT device data directly from IoT device data storage. The push approach was made possible by the creation of Queue Broker to hold the information and publish IoT device-driven application upon the use of IoT device data.

Step 5: IoT Device Deactivation
- *Input*: Thing identifier, IoT device identifier(s);
- *Output*: List of successfully deactivated IoT devices.

The final step was IoT device deactivation when there is no need for provisioning. To do this, first refer the IoT device from device registry, find active IoT devices which are using that information for connecting to device adaptors, and terminate them. Then, clear the data from the IoT device data storage, and delete any REST message information from queue. Thus, IoT device deactivation was done to save energy and cost.

6.7.1 Data Life Cycle Management in IoT for Device Data Stores

The data life cycle management in IoT (Abu-Elkheir et al. 2013) for device data stores is shown in Figure 6.3. This figure shows that IoT device data stores start from production to storage in edge devices and from collection to aggregation in front end of communications with other IoT devices. The application/services component deals with query processing for both history and current instances in real time. The back end components deal with pure storage of device data for archiving and updating stored data and performing any pre-processing as required to support for processing and analyzing the data. The complete data life cycle management

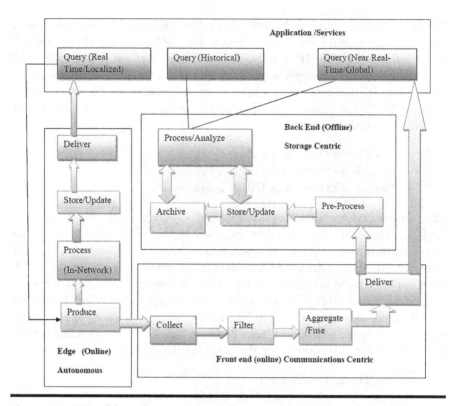

Figure 6.3   Data life cycle management in IoT. (Abu-Elkheir et al. 2013.)

components are divided in two categories: online (communication-sensitive operations) and offline (storage-sensitive operations).

Communication-Sensitive Operations: Produce, collect, aggregate, process (in-network), query, filter, update.

Storage Sensitive Operations: archiving, storage/update after processing, pre-processing of stored data.

Query: This component of data life cycle was mostly dealt with the interaction of real-time environment application services where the query was executed and the results were sent for further processing and analyzing for offline components for permanent storage.

Produce: It is the major component from where this life cycle was initiated for producing data from IoT devices at edge end (in-network) and front end (communications with other IoT devices).

Collect: This collects IoT device data during communication with other IoT devices for integrating and sending their information to further components for summarizing its results.

Filters: This component takes care of deleting the information generated during the collection of data from different IoT devices during integration and tries to send the required information to further components for processing.

Aggregate: This component does summarize all the information from different IoT devices that are integrated for giving the data for back end.

Pre-Processing: It manages many aspects related to missing data, unrelated data, and data cleaning as IoT device data comes in different formats from different sources.

Storage/Update Archiving: This component plays a prominent role in holding data permanently for long-term storage. It takes care of managing IoT device data in defining their type, structure, and other formats of data for easy storage at centralized data store.

Deliver: This component provides the final results to external environment to take necessary decision regarding the output of IoT device data store after getting processed by all components in life cycle.

Process/Analysis: This was a critical component that meant for online processing of IoT device data as it is gathered both in network and in back end. This component does processing of IoT device historical data and predicts future trends in terms of managing its information.

6.7.2 Data Management Framework for IoT Device Data Stores

Figure 6.4 gives the detailed layered architecture for data management framework (Abu-Elkheir et al. 2013) for IoT device data stores. The framework was divided in to six major layers, namely, things layer, communications layer, data layer, federation layer, query layer, and applications/analysis layer. Each layer has its own significance in terms of IoT device data store management.

Things Layer: It consists of actual entities that generate data from the real-time environments and forming groups such as IoT subsystems, mobile and stationary client. This layer consist of in-network query optimizer/executor for generating the query for further processing with related real-time data from the entities and getting the results for responding the system to the clients who are using these entities.

Communications Layer: This layer only uses the latest communication technologies or protocols for transferring the data to the next stacked layers.

Data Layer and Source Layer: Both layers have a critical task to manage the IoT device data for supporting it in many forms and storing the results in persistent data storage. The source layer reports the actual identity of the entities if any new IoT components are added and get notified to data layer to hold the data generated from this layer. The data layers use different data stores for holding metadata, object data, and structured and unstructured data and managing only local IoT devices that are involved in generating the integrated data. The publish/subscribe module and the

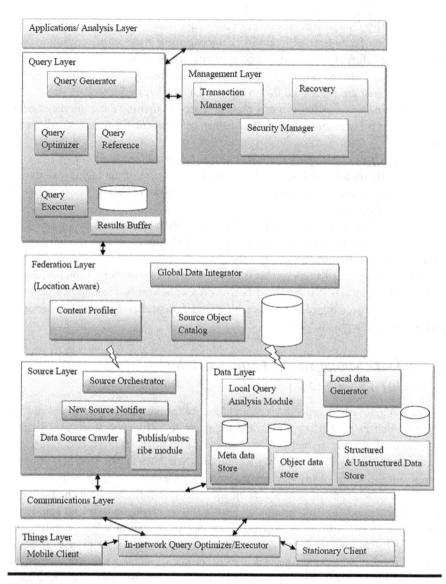

Figure 6.4 Data management framework for IoT device data store. (Abu-Elkheir et al. 2013.)

local query analyzer and local data generator of these layers do support in handling any issues related to IoT device data for local IoT system.

Federation Layer: This layer was the center of layered architecture, which tries to manage the integrated global data for IoT subsystem. It creates content profiler for different IoT devices that are involved in generating data and reporting for query layer for further processing. It uses data layer support for holding the local data store and local query optimizer for processing and reporting this layer for getting location aware about other IoT devices and integrating with them for further analysis with global data integrator.

Query Layer: This layer was popular for its major functionality in IoT data management for optimizing queries, executing and referencing them to generate information for the next layer in this framework.

Application/Analysis Layer: This layer was topmost in stack, which actually uses the stored IoT data for further analysis or usage by applications for managing the data and responding to external system users.

6.8 Device Provisioning

Device provisioning was a mechanism of making available IoT devices for managing their assigned task in the application environment. It needs the creation and registration of the following components of IoT device:

1. Creating certificate for IoT device that is involved in managing the operations, registering them, and placing theme in registry repositories;
2. Attaching a policy that specifies the rules and regulations to manage the IoT device;
3. Referring each IoT device with unique identity;
4. Assigning values to the set of attributes for the IoT device.

To provision an IoT device, every application framework provides a template that describes the resources required for them. All IoT devices need the aforementioned components, i.e., a certificate, policy, unique identifier, and set of attributes for device. Certificates are mostly used by IoT devices to interact within that application framework. Policies determine the operations to be performed within that real-time environment of the application framework.

Templates contain specific values assigned to the variables during device provisioning. A specific data structure like dictionary is used to hold the variable values like key value pair as used in template. The same template can be used by multiple IoT devices during provisioning. Different values can be assigned to the template variables in the dictionary and used in the application environment.

The application framework provides four ways for provisioning IoT devices:

1. *Single-Device Provisioning*: It uses a template for device provisioning, and it is good option when provisioning is done once at a time.
2. *Just-in-Time Provisioning*: It uses a template for registering and provisioning IoT devices when they are connected to the application framework.
3. *Bulk Provisioning*: It uses many single-device provisioning template values stored in a file of persistent data storage of that application framework.

In this technique, the desired characteristics of the IoT devices are known and grouped according to the requirements of the operations to be performed in real-time environment.

4. *API Calls*: Every application framework uses the specific APIs for provisioning the IoT devices programmatically.

6.9 Stream Processing and Processing

Big data in IoT provides two ways of data processing, i.e., batch processing and stream processing (Namiot et al. 2018). Batch processing of data was done by first storing data in huge data stores and then by scalable programming model that was used to process the data (a good example is Google MapReduce), whereas stream processing was a reactive and instant processing of data as it is available at the IoT device and performs analysis on the data and gives instant results to take dynamic decisions in the real-time environments. Batch processing works on fixed data, whereas stream processing operates on continuous data as it arrives while running the IoT device in the application environment. Many application frameworks manage stream processing and use Apache Storm, Apache Kafka, and Apache Flick as analytics examples.

Stream processing processes the stream of data and performs a series of operations on it as it was generated from the IoT devices from the application environment. The real-time processing of streamed data should include the following functionalities: (a) integrating with various data sources; (b) event detection methods such as collecting, filtering, and predicting; (c) online data discovery and monitoring; (d) components failure detection; and (e) performance, scalability, and real-time responsiveness.

Stream processing in IoT can include the following study directions:

1. Sensing data for data measurement;
2. Networking devices for data transmission;
3. Middleware to manage data aggregation;
4. Performing data analytics;
5. Understanding behavior of IoT devices for data interaction.

6.9.1 Stream Processing Architecture for IoT Applications

The stream processing architectures evolved because of the following reasons:

1. To achieve low latency for actively processing timely data;
2. To remove the gap between business models that are built on huge data volumes and computer architectures;

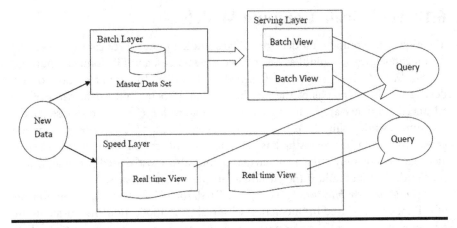

Figure 6.5 Lambda architecture. (Marz 2017.)

3. To process data as it arrives at creating a more predictable workload by stream processing.

The two popular stream processing architectures for IoT applications are Lambda architecture and Kappa architecture.

Lambda Architecture (Marz 2017): Figure 6.5 gives the clear diagram for Lambda architecture. This architecture is mostly built on top of MapReduce and storm for stream processing applications. In this architecture, the data records are simultaneously sent to both batch system and stream processing system in parallel for running the query, and the final results are combined for both systems and produced for the external environment. In this architecture, the logic needs to be executed twice to get the results. The complexity of this architecture was that it needs to feed data simultaneously into two pipelines and finally merges the results to get the final output.

Kappa Architecture (Uesugi 2017): Figure 6.6 gives the neat sketch of kappa architecture. It was clear from the diagram that it does involve only stream processing of data. It doesn't depend on any relational databases or NoSQL for data store. It uses the log records of the data stores and works with specific patterns for sending them for stream processing. It doesn't use any batch processing mechanism like in Lambda architecture. The specific patterns used for this architecture are as follows: (a) It uses Kafka cluster for employing log data stores that are generated for multiple subscribers for reprocessing; (b) it can frequently shift from one job to another job for reprocessing the log records and generate results for new output tables; (c) it can stop the jobs that are not responding and switch to new job for generating new output tables; and (d) it can stop all jobs that are not responding and delete their respective output data.

6.10 High-Scale Compute Models

The high-scale compute models for IoT are studied under three categories: (1) big data technologies, (2) middleware architecture services, and (3) cloud computing.

Big Data Technologies for IoT (Ahmed et al. 2017): The use of number of IoT devices was increasing as of the number of human beings on earth. Most of the advanced products are using this IoT technology for effective response to the consumers while using them in any real-time applications. Thus, the information generated during its processing has made IoT to shift for big data where its generated data is not only stored and managed but also mostly used for analytics to predict the product failure and sustain all its performance issues.

Middleware Architecture Services for IoT (Alarbi 2017): The major components of IoT that are involved in interaction with real-time application environments are sensors and actuators. The communication protocols and interfaces between these sensors and actuators with other networked devices use some middleware APIs for processing their connectivity and gathering information between these IoT devices.

Cloud Computing for IoT: The huge data generated from these IoT devices made local data store complex; hence, they need large data centers for processing this information and storing them in cloud. Cloud provides one-point solution for managing interoperability issues as it connects more number of IoT devices that are involved in communication and are compatible with storage and easy processing of data. It increases the remote processing power using a wide range of resources in cloud.

6.11 Corton Intelligence Suite Use Cases

Corton Intelligence Suite provides the scope of building business intelligence (BI) (Sindol 2016), which uses big data and advanced analytics to offer services with different application frameworks such as Microsoft Azure IoT and AWS IoT. It builds

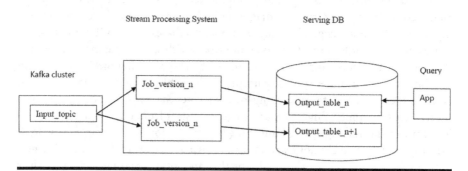

Figure 6.6   Kappa architecture. (Uesugi 2017.)

the gap between the data, i.e., generated from various IoT devices, Apps to the people who utilize these data for analysis and automate different application services. It major components are information management, big data stores, machine learning algorithms, intelligence components like bot frameworks, and finally visualization and dashboard for easy interaction with real-time environments.

Corton Intelligence Suite was popularly used in many business applications; some examples of the application scenarios are as follows.

Financial Services: It was one of the best application scenarios where the applications of Corton Intelligence are suitable because an intelligent system was needed to predict the fraud transactions made by the hackers without knowledge of actual customers. The historical data and trends of customers influence fraud people without their knowledge for gaining more profit within short span of time. Corton Intelligence applies complex machine learning algorithms and predictive models to analyze fraudulent transactions and protect trusted customers' valuable money. Many scenarios of financial services like credit/debit card fraud, online shopping fraud, and other means of stealing confidential data of customers are very popular where Corton Intelligence was applied for analyzing online behavior of hackers.

Retail: In retail business, predicting customer behavior in buying products, optimizing availability of products, forecasting the needs of consumers, and enabling right business actions towards product sales can be applicable scenarios where Corton Intelligence was applied to make the job of retail company simpler. Small IoT devices can be used in stores to sense the items seen by the customers and read the data of purchases made by them so as to analyze their buying habits, purchase history, and understand the better customer preferences in buying products.

Healthcare: The more profitable business utilizes Corton Intelligence Suite very effectively in analyzing patients' health records and predicting the breakthrough of diseases because wide climatic changes in urban, semi-urban, and rural areas caution government to run health camps and avoid major critical health issues. Optimizing the resources usage inside the hospitals and providing good hygienic environment are essential so that patient's health can be monitored and appropriate action can be suggested to their close relatives in avoiding any mishap with patients.

Manufacturing: This area needs huge information regarding the usage of equipment and the collection of different issues related to productivity of the product-supported components to have timely delivery of product to customers. Any disturbances during production stage can be easily predicted by Corton Intelligent Suite so that higher authorities will take necessary action in order to continue manufacturing of a product without any huge business loss.

Public Sectors: All public sector organizations such as transport, electricity, and water supplies of government departments can take support of Corton Intelligent

Suite for predicting and forecasting the needs of the people living in a locality. The usage of public resources can be easily analyzed and checked for scarcity and can fulfill timely needs of people without any delay and resolve their issues within short span of time.

References

Abu-Elkheir, M., Hayajneh, M. and Ali, N. (2013). Data management for the Internet of Things: Design primitives and solution. *Sensors, 13*(11), 15582–15612.

Ahmed, E., Yaqoob, I., Hashem, I.A.T., Khan, I., Ahmed, A.I.A., Imran, M. and Vasilakos, A.V. (2017). The role of big data analytics in Internet of Things. *Computer Networks, 129*, 459–471.

Alarbi, M., and Lutfiyya, H. (2017), Sensing as a service middleware architecture. *IEEE 6th International Conference on Future Internet of Things and Cloud (FiCloud)*, Barcelona, pp. 399-406.

Ali, W.B. (2016). Big data-driven smart policing: Big data-based patrol car dispatching. *Journal of Geotechnical and Transportation Engineering, 1*(2), 1–6.

Atzori, L., Iera, A. and Morabito, G. (2010).The Internet of Things: A survey. *Computer network* [Online], *54*(15), 2787–2805. doi:10.1016/j.comnet.2010.05.010 [Accessed 24th June 2019].

Belem Pacheco, L., Pelinson Alchieri, E. and Mendez Barreto, P. (2018). Device-based security to improve user privacy in the Internet of Things. *Sensors, 18*(8), 2664.

Chaudhuri, A. (2018). Internet of Things, for Things, and by Things.

DigiCert, Inc. (2017). www.digicert.com/internet-of-things/device-identity-management.htm [Accessed 30th April 2019].

Ge, M., Bangui, H. and Buhnova, B. (2018). Big data for Internet of Things: A survey. *Future Generation Computer Systems, 87*, 601–614.

Hashem, I.A.T., Yaqoob, I., Anuar, N.B., Mokhtar, S., Gani, A. and Khan, S.U. (2015). The rise of "big data" on cloud computing: Review and open research issues. *Information Systems, 47*, 98–115.

Hirmer, P., Wieland, M., Breitenbücher, U. and Mitschang, B., 2016. Automated sensor registration, binding and sensor data provisioning. In *CAiSE Forum at the 28th International Conference on Advanced Information Systems Engineering*, Ljubljana, pp. 81–88.

Hsieh, H.C. and Lai, C.H. (2011). Internet of Things architecture based on integrated PLC and 3G communication networks. In *IEEE 17th International Conference on Parallel and Distributed Systems*. IEEE, Tainan, pp. 853–856.

Marz, N. (2017). Lambda architecture. http://lambda-architecture.net [Accessed 24th May 2018].

Namiot, D., Sneps-Sneppe, M. and Pauliks, R. (2018). On data stream processing in IoT applications. In *Internet of Things, Smart Spaces, and Next Generation Networks and Systems*. Springer, Cham, pp. 41–45.

Natallia, S. (2018). www.sam-solutions.com/blog/internet-of-things-iot-protocols-and-connectivity-options-an-overview/ [Accessed 4th May 2019].

Pandya, H.B. and Champaneria, T.A. (2017). Enhancement of security in IoTSyS framework. In *Proceedings of International Conference on Communication and Networks*. Springer, Singapore, pp. 31–43.

Perera, C., Zaslavsky, A., Compton, M., Christen, P. and Georgakopoulos, D. (2013). Semantic-driven configuration of internet of things middleware. In *Ninth International Conference on Semantics, Knowledge and Grids*. IEEE, Beijing, pp. 66–73.

Reinsel, D. and Gantz, J. (2012). The digital universe in 2020: Big Data. *Bigger Digital Shadows, and Biggest Growth in the Far East*, *12*, 2014–2019.

Sindol, D. (2016). www.mssqltips.com/sqlservertip/4360/introduction-to-microsoft-cortana-intelligence-suite/ [Accessed 24th April 2018].

Thinxstream Technologies (2018). www.thinxtream.com/whitepapers/thinxtream-iot-and-big-data-wp-006.pdf [Accessed 5th May 2019].

Uesugi, S. (2017). Kappa architecture. http://milinda.pathirage.org/kappa-architecture.com [Accessed 24th May 2018].

Chapter 7

Algorithms for Big Data Delivery over Internet of Things

R. Indrakumari, T. Poongodi,
K. Thirunavukkarasu, and S. Sreeji

Galgotias University

Contents

7.1 Introduction

The increasing use of smart devices is continuously increasing the amount of data every minute. Data are collected, connected, and exchanged or transferred. Due to this, many new technologies, such as cloud and wireless sensor networks (WSNs), related to big data have emerged. The development in technology and the convergence of digital electronics, wireless communication, and micro-electromechanical systems (MEMSs) have paved the way for the emergence of Internet of Things (IoT). In the current scenario, research proves that, by 2030, more than one trillion devices will be connected. Therefore, there is an urgent need for big data technologies and applications. Big data technologies are interrelated to each other and therefore should be developed jointly. New trends are accompanied by numerous development and improvement expectations in all areas and come with concerns about security and violation of privacy. Many big data techniques are available to solve challenges. Frameworks are available to collect data from various sources using forms like eXtensible Markup Language (XML), JavaScript Object Notation (JSON), streaming, and textual data from sensors. Distributed collection of data makes the database unstructured, and hence data integration is needed. The major issue is to transform sensor data into knowledge. The most important procedure in statistical analysis lies in sampling sensor data. Some of the statistical analysis methods are the network-based spatial aggregation, the Euclidean-based spatial aggregation, the network-based parameter aggregation, and the Euclidean-based parameter aggregation. Researchers proposed parallel processing techniques to resolve the statistical queries, in which multiple servers apply statistical analysis in parallel, thus enriching the performance.

The rest of this chapter is organized as follows. Section 7.2 introduces WSNs. Section 7.3 discusses about the ecosystem. Section 7.4 describes the technologies and protocols. Section 7.5 illustrates the protocols and standards for routing. Section 7.6 explains the session layer protocol. Section 7.7 discusses communication techniques and methodologies. Section 7.8 concludes the chapter.

7.2 Wireless Sensor Network

A WSN consists of sensors, a microcontroller, and a transceiver, and the functionality of sensor nodes becomes mandatory in several domains. Generally, sensors are classified based on the readiness of field deployment in terms of scalability, energy efficiency, and cost. In common, they are categorized as physical, chemical, and biological sensors. A WSN comprises a data acquisition and distribution network. The complete network is controlled and managed by a central station. During the data acquisition process, data is acquired from a heterogeneous environment, and it is being transmitted to the main station using various wireless distribution technologies such as computers, wireless local area network (WLAN), cellular phones, Wi-Fi, and Bluetooth. The gathered data will be taken into consideration for further processing and analysis. The significant characteristics of WSNs include

- Energy harvesting
- Fault tolerance
- Mobility of nodes
- Scalability in terms of large-scale deployment
- Handling heterogeneous data and nodes
- Ease of use
- Robustness against harsh environmental conditions.

The protocol stack used in sensor nodes contains the following layers (Figure 7.1):

- *Physical Layer*: The main responsibility lies in carrier frequency generation, frequency selection, modulation, signal deflection, and data encryption.
- *Data Link Layer*: It focuses on data frame detection, multiplexing of data streams, medium access, reliable point-to-point (P2P) and multipoint connections, and error control.
- *Network Layer*: It specifies the details about assignment of addresses and packet forwarding.
- *Transport Layer*: Its responsibility lies in the reliable transmission of packets.
- *Application Layer*: It handles interaction with the end user and serves as a channel through which data can be requested.

The recent advancement in technology has a significant impact on the environmental changes, and it leads to serious concerns in terms of climate change and pollution. According to the report released by Intergovernmental Panel on Climate Change in 2014, it is confirmed that human activities influence the climate system since they have a huge impact on the environmental changes and such activities have been continuously increasing over the past decades [1]. Environmental monitoring system collects the relevant information related to the ecosystem from which new ideas and understanding can be obtained, and ultimate adaption and mitigation happen in this system which addresses the degradation level of the biosphere [2]. Another focus area is monitoring the ambience in indoor spaces, and it is meant not only for comfort but also for the health of the occupants [3]. At last, it significantly reduces greenhouse gas emissions also.

The parameters that are monitored in a WSN include humidity, temperature, rainfall, light intensity, atmospheric pressure, air quality affected by pollutants like CO, CO_2, SO, etc. The data acquisition helps in identifying the physical properties such as temperature, salinity, and soil moisture, and if these can be known in the agricultural field, significant resource savings can be achieved. Several monitoring applications depend on WSN because of its advantages such as lower maintenance, lower cost due to absence of cables, scalability, and variable network technologies [4]. WSNs have been successfully implemented in various fields such as current consumption monitoring in larger buildings [5]; natural disaster prevention [6]; environmental monitoring [7]; process control in industrial environments; gear condition surveillance; location tracking of assets, people, or hazardous gases; and dosimetry of radiology operators in electronic healthcare applications [8,9].

The extensively used protocols in various applications, like environment monitoring system, have less reliability and latency requirements, e.g., Wi-Fi based on IEEE 802.11 standard [10], Bluetooth – IEEE 802.15.1, and ZigBee – IEEE

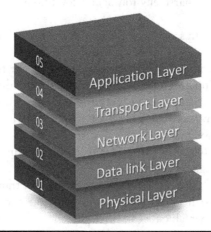

Figure 7.1　WSN OSI layer.

802.15.4 [11]. Among various IEEE standards, IEEE 802.15.4 operates with less power consumption and low cost at normal data rates; hence ZigBee is widely used in a number of wireless applications such as monitoring and control which need wireless connectivity. It is an energy-efficient technique, but it does not comply with firm reliability and latency and requires some additional hardware for packaging and transmitting data to the Internet. Wi-Fi based on IEEE 802.11 provides higher throughput and transmission range when compared to ZigBee but with high energy consumption.

The designing of low-power-consumption sensors such as the ESP8266 and RN131C/G from Espressif Systems and Roving Networks made this technology more impressive to be implemented in applications based on wireless sensors. The sensors based on these techniques avail the benefits of the IP-network compatibility and existing infrastructure and use protocols such as Hypertext Transfer Protocol (HTTP) and User Datagram Protocol (UDP). Bluetooth smart or Bluetooth Low Energy (BLE) was introduced with the objective of increasing the capability of Bluetooth as a power-constrained device like wireless sensors [12]. However, the utilization of Bluetooth Internet gateways is required to send and receive data in monitoring applications.

In the industrial sector, in the presence of heavy interference, the IEEE 802.15.4.e, ISA100 wireless (IEC62734), and the WirelessHART (IEC62591) are used in order to achieve high update rates, reliability of data transmission, high availability, and determinism [13]. These offer a secure and reliable low-power wireless process for noncritical monitoring applications. The Internet plays a significant role for transferring information from sensor networks to central stations for further processing. The deployment of sensors at larger distances provides the benefit of collecting environmental data from wider geographical areas. This is made possible by designing new transceivers with low power consumption and wider ranges by establishing the Internet connection. The developed sensors are a part of the network with Internet connection capabilities that allow users and things to get connected anytime, anywhere, with anyone and anything, using a network/path and service [14].

7.3 Ecosystem

Seven layers form the ecosystem. The bottom layer is the application layer, and the second layer consists of sensors. Sensors play a vital role in communication, and multiple sensors are needed to communicate and gather information before accessing the Internet. The interconnection layer is the third layer that allows the data generated by the sensors to be transmitted to data center. The other layers are the integration, analytics, software-defined networking, and service layers, respectively. The IoT protocol is the highly financed topic in academia and industry. The fast evolution of Internet, miniature hardware technology, and machine-to-machine communication has facilitated IoT technologies. Special protocols are designed for routing. Session layer protocols are designed to enable communication among sensors. Security and management protocols are also available in the session layer.

7.4 Protocols for IoT

The third layer of the IoT ecosystem, the interconnection layer, consists of three layers as shown in Figure 7.2.

These are the data link layer, network layer, and session layer. The sensors and the devices can be connected using data link layer. Routing of data from different sensors is supported by the network layer. Communications between subsystems are enabled by the session layer. Apart from these protocols, various security- and management-related protocols are defined for IoT.

7.4.1 Data Link Protocol

The data link layer includes the following physical and media access control (MAC) layer protocols.

7.4.1.1 IEEE 802.15.4

IEEE 802.15.4 [15] is a protocol standard for low-power personal area networks. IEEE 802.15.4 is a data link protocol used in the MAC layer. This protocol states how the communication among the nodes is happening. This standard specifies

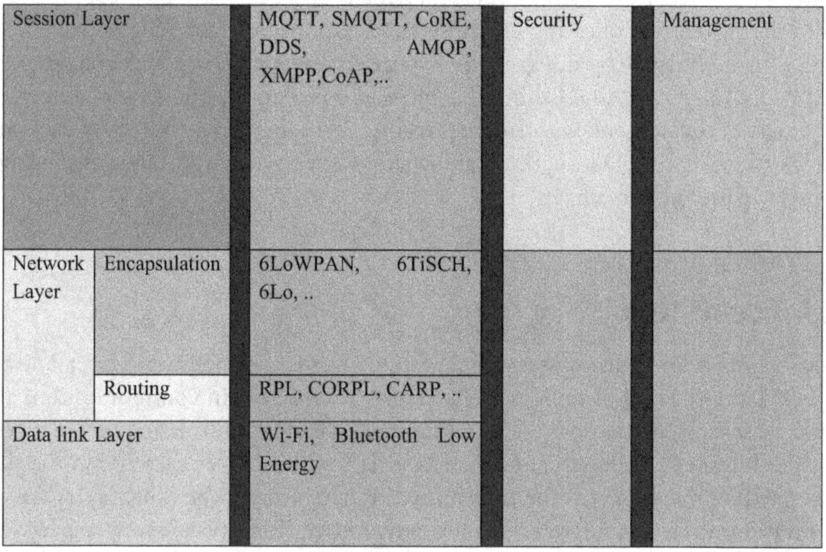

Session Layer		MQTT, SMQTT, CoRE, DDS, AMQP, XMPP,CoAP,..	Security	Management
Network Layer	Encapsulation	6LoWPAN, 6TiSCH, 6Lo, ..		
	Routing	RPL, CORPL, CARP, ..		
Data link Layer		Wi-Fi, Bluetooth Low Energy		

Figure 7.2 IoT protocols.

the frame format, headers, destination, and source addresses. The network topologies which support IEEE 802.15.4 are star, mesh, and cluster tree. The channel access modes for this standard are a beacon-enabled (BE) mode. The limitations of IEEE 802.15.4 are unbounded delay, limited communication reliability, and no protection against interferences/fading. For these limitations, IEEE 802.15.4 is not suitable for many scenarios where the applications need reliability and timeliness. The conventional IEEE 802.15.4 frame formats is not appropriate for low-power IoT devices. To overcome this, IEEE 802.15.4e was developed to support low-power-constrained IoT devices. The extended version in Figure 7.3 uses channel hopping and time synchronization to facilitate reliability and minimal communication cost.

IEEE 802.15.4e includes Low Energy (LE), Information Elements (IE), Multipurpose Frame, MAC Performance Metric and Fast Association (FastA) as functional enhancements when compared to IEEE 802.15.4 (Figure 7.4).

This figure depicts the operating frequency bands of IEEE 801.15.4 standard: 16 channels of 2.4 GHz, ten channels of 915 MHz, and one 868 MHz channel.

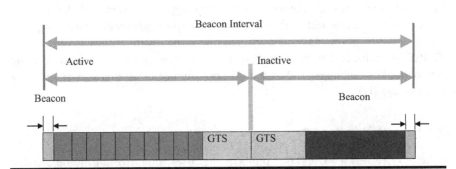

Figure 7.3   IEEE 802.15.4 superframe structure.

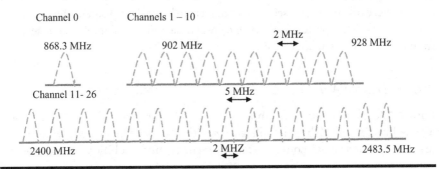

Figure 7.4   IEEE 802.15.4 operating frequency bands.

7.4.1.2 IEEE 802.11ah

It is the lightweight minimum overhead version of the IEEE 802.11 standard to satisfy IoT needs. IEEE 802.11, also called Wi-Fi, is a widely used wireless standard in conventional networking. The Wi-Fi standards are not appropriate for certain applications due to their high power consumption and frame overhead. To overcome this limitation, the task group initiated the standard 802.11ah that supports power friendly communication suitable for sensors and motes [16]. The MAC layer features of IEEE802.11ah are synchronization framing, efficient bidirectional packet exchange, increased sleep time, short MAC frame, and null data packet.

7.4.1.3 ZigBee Smart Energy

ZigBee is the commonly used IoT standard dedicated for medium-range communication in remote controls, healthcare systems, and smart homes. The supported topologies for this standard are star, cluster tree, and peer-to-peer. A coordinator is located at the center of the star topology and the cluster-tree topology but can be present anywhere in the peer-to-peer topology. This standard defines two stack profiles, ZigBee and ZigBee Pro, which support full mesh networking with low processing power and memory. ZigBee Pro provides better features than ZigBee, includes scalability using stochastic address assignment, security using symmetric-key exchange, and enhanced performance using many-to-one routing mechanisms [17].

7.4.1.4 WirelessHART

WirelessHART is a MAC layer protocol that uses time division multiple access (TDMA) in MAC and works on top of IEEE 802.15.4 PHY. For encryption of messages and to check for integrity, most advanced encryption algorithms are applied; thus, this standard is more reliable and secure. The architecture of WirelessHART is shown in Figure 7.5. It consists of a gateway to connect the wireless to wired devices, network manager, security manager, field devices, routers, access point, and adapters. This protocol offers end-to-end security and implements security from a source to destinations [18].

7.4.1.5 LoRaWAN

LoRaWAN is a long-range communication, wide area network wireless technology dedicated for IoT-based applications with features like power saving, minimal cost, bidirectional communication, security, and mobility. The low-power

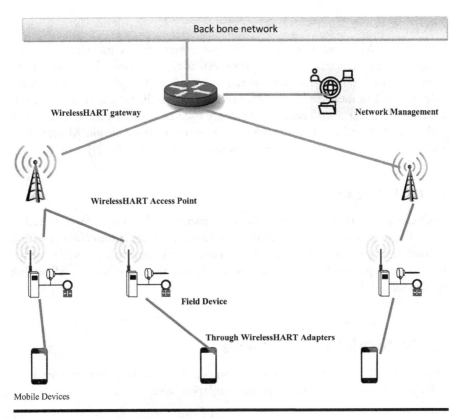

Figure 7.5   WirelessHART architecture.

feature makes it suitable for scalable wireless networks with millions of devices. It supports low cost, redundant operation, and low-power energy harvesting technologies to satisfy the near future requirements of IoT with ease-of-use features and mobility [19].

7.4.1.6 Weightless

Special interest group (SIG), a non-profit global organization has developed a new wireless technology called Weightless that uses ultra-narrow bands in the sub-1 GHz ISM (Industrial, Scientific and Medical) frequency band for the MAC layer. Here, two standards are in practice: Weightless-W and Weightless-N. Weightless-N is the first standard that works based on TDMA along with frequency hopping to reduce the interference. Weightless-W also accommodates the same features with television band frequencies [20] (Figure 7.5).

7.4.1.7 Z-Wave

Z-Wave is a MAC standard, consumes low power, and is intended for home automation applications. But it is now extended to various IoT applications including small commercial domains and smart homes. It works under a point-to-point communication method which can cover up to 30 meters. It uses Carrier-sense multiple access with collision avoidance (CSMA/CA) for media access along with small ACK (acknowledgment) messages for trusted transmission. Master–slave architecture is followed here where the master controls the slave [21].

7.4.1.8 EnOcean

EnOcean is a wireless technology that saves energy, and it is used for automation and IoT applications. The notion of this standard is to utilize resourceful harvesting of motion or any form of environmental energy and convert it to usable energy. It has a small packet size and is used in ventilation, air conditioning, and heating applications [22].

7.5 Network Layer Protocols

This section illustrates the protocols and standards for routing. The network layer is divided into the routing layer and encapsulation layer.

7.5.1 Network Layer Routing Protocols

7.5.1.1 Routing Protocol for Low-Power and Lossy Networks (RPL)

RPL, designed at Internet Engineering Task Force (IETF), is a distance-vector protocol for routing in applications. RPL is based on destination-oriented directed-acyclic graphs (DODAGs) that contain only a single route from every leaf node to the root. Each node transmits a DODAG information object (DIO) and advertises it as a root. A DIO is transmitted on the network, and the entire DODAG is built gradually. A destination advertisement object (DAO) is transmitted from the node to its parents when initializing a communication. The root node decides the route to the destination. When a new node intends to join the network, it sends a DODAG information solicitation request, and a DAO acknowledgment is sent by the root. The RPL node is a stateless or stateful protocol. In a stateless protocol, the root has the entire knowledge about the DODAG. The stateful node keep track off its parents and children and hence when communicating, there is no need to go through the root [23].

7.5.1.2 Cognitive RPL (CORPL)

CORPL is a standard that is the extension of RPL and depends upon DODAG technology with some modifications. This standard is intended for cognitive networks and uses DODAG topology. CORPL standard uses opportunistic forwarding to send a packet from a source to a destination. Every node of CORPL standard records the details of forwarding set and updates its modification to its neighbor with the help of DIO messages. Based on the updated information, every node energetically updates its neighbor [24].

7.5.1.3 Channel-Aware Routing Protocol (CARP) and E-CARP

CARP is a routing protocol based on distributed networks and developed for underwater communication. CARP is a lightweight packet forwarding protocol used for applications. To choose the forwarding route, it considers historical link quality measurements. Data forwarding and network initialization are the two situations that are considered in CARP. During data forwarding, hop-by-hop technology is used to route packets from sensor to sink. CARP does not support the reusability of previously collected data, and hence E-CARP is designed to allow the sink node to save previously received sensory data. E-CARP drastically minimizes the communication overhead [25].

7.5.2 Network Layer Encapsulation Protocols

7.5.2.1 IPv6 over Low-Power Wireless Personal Area Network (6LoWPAN)

IPv6 is the first IETF standard that encapsulates the long headers of IPv6 in IEEE802.15.4. Low-power wireless personal area network (6LoWPAN) accommodates many features like different networking topologies, different length addresses, low power consumption, scalable networks, long sleep times, and reliability. Header compression is used to minimize the transmission overhead and fragmentation to support multi-hop delivery. Four types of header are used in 6LoWPAN; they are 6loWPAN header (00), dispatch header (01), mesh header (10), and fragmentation header (11). Some of the application areas of 6LoWPAN are general automation, home automation, smart grid, and industrial monitoring (Figure 7.6).

7.5.2.2 6TiSCH

The goal of 6TiSCH is to combine the best features of Time Synchronized Channel Hopping (TSCH) and IPv6 through the IETF upper stack. 6TiSCH stores the frequencies and their corresponding time slots in a matrix format called the channel

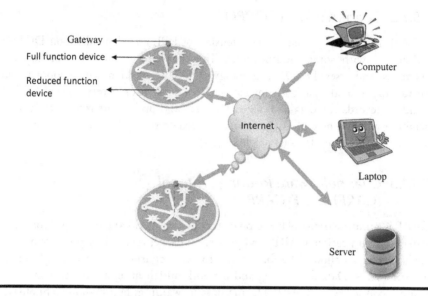

Figure 7.6   6LoWPAN architecture.

distribution usage matrix. The matrix is split into small chunks which hold times and frequencies and is known to all nodes in the network.

7.6 Session Layer Protocols

7.6.1 MQTT

In 2013, the Organization for the Advancement of Structured Information Standards (OASIS) has developed the standard Message Queue Telemetry Transport (MQTT). At one end, it connects the user and applications, and at the other end, it connects the network and communications. It is based on publish–subscribe architecture as shown in Figure 7.7.

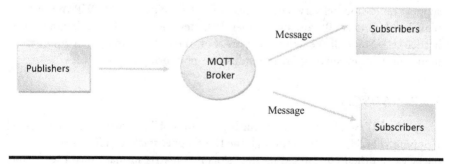

Figure 7.7   MQTT architecture.

This architecture consists of three major components: (1) publishers, (2) subscribers, and (3) the broker. In the IoT environment, the publishers are the lightweight sensors that establish a connection with the broker to transmit their data. Subscribers are applications which are connected to the broker that informs the arrival of new data. The purpose of the broker is to categorize sensory data and transmit it to subscribers who are interested in the particular topic.

7.6.2 SMQTT

Secure Message Queue Telemetry Transport (SMQTT) is an extension of MQTT and provides encryption based on lightweight attribute. It is a publisher-and-subscriber protocol intended to design device-to-device communication based on transmission control protocol (TCP) through a broker. The encryption method used here uses multicast features; that is, when a message is encrypted, it is delivered to multiple nodes. The encryption algorithm consists of four phases: setup phase, encryption phase, publish phase, and decryption phase. The subscribers and the publishers register with the broker and obtain a master secret key based on the developer's choice. The encrypted data is published and sent to subscribers by the broker.

7.6.3 AMQP

Advanced message queuing protocol (AMQP) is a standard designed for the financial industry based on TCP communication using publish–subscribe architecture. Here the broker is divided into exchange and queue components as shown in Figure 7.8. The exchange components receive the message from publisher and distribute the messages to queues. The sensory data are received by the subscribers which are connected to queues [26] (Figure 7.8).

7.6.4 DDS

Data distribution service (DDS) standard, developed by the Object Management Group (OMG), uses publish–subscribe architecture used for machine-to-machine (M2M) communication [27]. This protocol provides reliability service with outstanding quality of service levels with the help of the brokerless architecture suitable for M2M communication. The quality criteria are urgency, security, reliability, durability, and priority. Two sublayers are present here: data-local reconstruction which allows the integration of DDS in the application layer and data-centric publish–subscribe sublayer which is responsible for message delivery. The work of the publishers is to distribute sensory data. The data writer gets the permission from the publisher to send data to the subscriber which in turn delivers the data to big data applications. The data writer and the data reader act as brokers in the broker-based architecture.

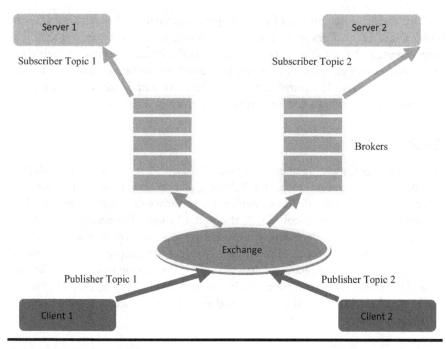

Figure 7.8 AMQP architecture.

7.7 Secure Communication in IoT and Big Data

There is a problem in managing big data because everyone in the world is claiming the smartest things that are available nowadays. With the large number of heterogeneous, fragmenting group of users is highly challenging in the rapidly growing industries. There are security challenges when communicating or transferring the sensitive data to the central repository for further analysis. The security challenges in IoT big data are perceived from the aspects of the physical challenge as well as the virtual challenge. First, the physical challenge is complicated when multilevel security options are preferred for the network devices. Firewall is significantly vital for the network devices since the data has to flow across many organizations and things becomes complex eventually. While retrieving information from various sources, the virtual challenge comes into existence.

The main target of security-based attacks is the communication between devices in the environment. The significant components considered in the communication process are devices and gateways. The central point is the gateway which controls the complete network and its related processes. Once the gateway is attacked, then the whole network is affected, and the communication process will get interrupted. The interference is viewed as a serious virtual threat that must be handled carefully at the time of communication between devices.

In the environment, a communication link is established to enable a smooth continuous traffic flow. However, the communication resources become unavailable due to interference that in turn leads to Denial of Service (DoS) in big data and IoT environment. It may also occur because of jamming in the physical communication channel between devices. The communication process is not completed in a single step; it involves many steps and devices such as sensors, actuators, and gateways throughout the whole communication process. Signal interception is perceived as a common and serious threat during the communication process. These attacks secretly relay or distort/alter the information that is being transmitted between two users. It is caused due to unauthenticated access, less protection in traffic flow, and insecure physical and virtual network resources.

Intrusion occurs at the physical level due to insecure firmware and software, user interfaces, and unprotected network resources. It paves the way for the attacker to get access and to authenticate himself in a big data environment. The attacker accesses data and the functionality of communication devices; consequently the available information is read by them. This process is referred to as exploitation; it occurs when an attacker attempts to access the communication resources when data is being transferred. A countermeasure for such malicious activity can be provided by limiting the access privileges to the physical resources and data by incorporating access control mechanisms. Hence, the physical threats can be avoided by employing access restriction on physical devices as well as gateways in the environment in order to preserve confidentiality and integrity of the communication process.

In the communication process, gateways play a significant role since they connect a variety of sensors and devices that communicate with each other. Once a gateway is hijacked, the devices involved in the communication process are also open to attackers. Henceforth, big data can be hacked, or it makes the communication resources unavailable, which imposes a serious threat in the big data environment. The frequent installation of new devices, replacement of damaged devices, and removal of unwanted and malfunctioning devices make the environment more dynamic. Security threats can also increase because fake gateways and devices can be deployed by the malicious users. Hence, end-to-end encryption (E2EE) assists in preventing unauthorized access so that an unauthorized person cannot have access to the information that is being transmitted.

In end-to-end communication, even the information that is being communicated will not be accessible in gateways. But the drawback of E2EE is in managing keys by the endpoint nodes. The intruder reads the data by acquiring the cryptographic key created by the end nodes. Hence, a solution is to be provided to authorize and authenticate the communication process.

Security is the major concern and is highly challenging in the big data environment since it involves billions of devices and different technologies that claim solutions for various categories of security threats. The security mechanisms ensure the integrity and correctness of data that is being transmitted via communication devices and gateways. The data should be transmitted to the destination node without any tampering and distortion in its journey. A trust can be made between the communication devices where any confidential data can be transmitted. The communication of big data can be secured by incorporating the security mechanisms mentioned in Figure 7.9.

Identity checking in a big data environment is necessary to protect the data from threats if any devices seek permission for accessing data or resources that are already involved in the communication process. The process of identity checking of different components such as sensors, gateways, devices, or servers is significant, but it is difficult due to the involvement of a large number of devices and restricted communication methodologies. In addition, the lifetimes of devices are too short, and the same identity cannot be offered for a long time in case of hacking. A lightweight token/private encryption key certificate can be used as a strong mechanism to authenticate the devices. URL and device IP can be associated together to provide strong identification of any type of devices. We can opt for hardware and software security tokens for authorization and identification. The generated one-time passwords can also be utilized for this purpose within a stipulated amount of time.

It is not the data alone that must be protected using encryption technique; the secret keys should also be kept completely confidential in order to ensure a high degree of authentication. The issue lies in maintaining the secret or encryption keys somewhere in the environment. The hardware intrinsic security can be incorporated by which a secret key need not be maintained permanently; rather it can be generated whenever it is needed for the authentication process. Once the process is

Anti-Tampering & Detection,

Authenticated Encryption,

Authorization,

Access Control,

Data Protection & Confidentiality

Figure 7.9 Secure communication.

over and the secret key is no longer needed, it must be removed from the storage devices, i.e., temporary storage device, registry. The key generation algorithm should be developed in such a way that the key should not be tracked by any step of the communication process and no key should be reused.

Privacy preservation is a major concern at the time of deploying big data techniques [28]. Cryptographic approaches may handle the issue of privacy preservation; however, these do not scale for larger datasets. K-anonymity, secure multiparty computation (SMC), data transformation and correlating into vector spaces, and differential privacy based on data sanitization method have focused on the scalability issue. Security models are required to be developed to support security proofs and analysis in order to provide solutions [29].

Gathering data from different organizations and storing them in a central repository needs confidentiality and privacy concerns. A strong distributive and collaborative approach is required to concentrate on these concerns. Different organizations must maintain data in their own datasets and cooperate with other data mining processes to learn the results without revealing the data from their own datasets. It includes the following:

(i) Techniques must be identified in such a way that two parties can build a decision tree without trying to learn each other's datasets, and the result can be learned from the final decision tree.

(ii) Specialized privacy preservation techniques for clustering, association rules, k-nearest neighbor classification need to be identified.

Novel approaches with new cryptographic primitives should be examined since the existing techniques are still inefficient.

In a distributed environment, users have to communicate with different service providers, and the protection of information becomes more difficult in such a scenario. Classification techniques, perceptual hashing techniques, and Zero-Knowledge Proof of Knowledge (ZKPK) protocols are combined together to address this issue. ZKPK protocol is used to authenticate the user, and this combined approach can be used for the secure usage on mobile phones. Novel identification and authentication techniques are to be investigated focusing on recent encryption techniques. Communication of big data should be secured by incorporating various security services [30]. Security can be provided at different layers of IP stack by using standardized security mechanisms. E2EE can be used to provide secure communication between a source and destination, or it can be offered on a per-hop basis between neighboring devices.

An Intrusion Detection System (IDS) is essential to identify malicious activities and imposters in the network, and firewalls are significant to prevent unauthorized access. Nowadays, various types of attacks are possible against a network, and they can breach the available security services. An attacker aims to disrupt a network by launching DoS attacks. It is significant to protect communication as well as the sensitive data stored in a device. Many devices are very tiny with resource-constrained wireless nodes, and practically it is not possible to protect or physically safeguard each device with the Trusted Platform modules or smart cards. This lack of security paves the way to expose data to theft and attacks by hackers and fraudsters. Secure communication presently requires several levels of configuration and algorithms, encourages users to prefer functionality over security, and discourages them staying away from protection-based implementation.

7.8 Conclusion

IoT is considered as a major source of big data, and it is ineffective without analytics. Big data analytics is needed to process a huge volume of high-frequency data that is generated. This chapter discusses about technologies such as WSNs required to process the generated big data. The IoT ecosystem explains the architecture and protocols associated with each layer. Data generated by devices flow freely, and hence there is a high chance of malicious attacks on data security. Secure communication techniques are also discussed in this chapter.

References

1. R. K. Pachauri and L. A. Meyer (Eds.), "Climate change 2014: Synthesis report," in *Contribution of Working Groups I, II and III to the Fifth Assessment Report of the Intergovernmental Panel on Climate Change*, Core Writing Team, IPCC, Geneva, Switzerland, 2014, p. 151.
2. M. Harris, "Mules on a mountain," *IEEE Spectrum*, vol. 53, no. 6, pp. 50–56, June 2016.
3. L. Zhang and F. Tian, "Performance study of multilayer perceptrons in a low-cost electronic nose," *IEEE Transactions on Instrumentation and Measurement*, vol. 63, no. 7, pp. 1670–1679, July 2014.
4. H.-H. Lin, H. Y. Tsai, T. C. Chan, Y. S. Huang, Y. S. Chu, Y. C. Chen, T. S. Liao, Y. M. Fang, B. J. Lee, and H. C. Lee, "An open-source wireless mesh networking module for environmental monitoring," in *Proceedings of the IEEE International Instrumentation and Measurement Technology Conference (IMTC)*, IEEE, Pisa, Italy, pp. 1002–1007, May 2015.
5. J. P. Amaro, R. Cortesão, J. Landeck, and F. J. T. E. Ferreira, "Harvested power wireless sensor network solution for disaggregated current estimation in large buildings," *IEEE Transactions on Instrumentation and Measurement*, vol. 64, no. 7, pp. 1847–1857, July 2015.
6. G. Werner-Allen, K. Lorincz, M. Ruiz, O. Marcillo, J. Johnson, J. Lees, and M. Welsh, "Deploying a wireless sensor network on an active volcano," *IEEE Internet Computing*, vol. 10, no. 2, pp. 18–25, March 2006.
7. M. T. Lazarescu, "Design of a WSN platform for long-term environmental monitoring for applications," *IEEE Journal on Emerging and Selected Topics in Circuits and Systems*, vol. 3, no. 1, pp. 45–54, March 2013.

8. D. Magalotti, P. Placidi, M. Paolucci, A. Scorzoni, and L. Servoli, "Experimental characterization of a wireless personal sensor node for the dosimetry during interventional radiology procedures," *IEEE Transactions on Instrumentation and Measurement*, vol. 65, no. 5, pp. 1070–1078, May 2016.

9. D. Magalotti, P. Placidi, M. Dionigi, A. Scorzoni, and L. Servoli, "Experimental characterization of a personal wireless sensor network for the medical X-ray dosimetry," *IEEE Transactions on Instrumentation and Measurement*, vol. 65, no. 9, pp. 2002–2011, September 2016.

10. G. Mois, T. Sanislav, and S. C. Folea, "A cyber-physical system for environmental monitoring," *IEEE Transactions on Instrumentation and Measurement*, vol. 65, no. 6, pp. 1463–1471, June 2016.

11. J. Gutierrez, J. F. Villa-Medina, A. Nieto-Garibay, and M. A. Porta-Gandara, "Automated irrigation system using a wireless sensor network and GPRS module," *IEEE Transactions on Instrumentation and Measurement*, vol. 63, no. 1, pp. 166–176, January 2014.

12. K.-H. Chang, "Bluetooth: A viable solution for? [Industry perspectives]," *IEEE Wireless Communication*, vol. 21, no. 6, pp. 6–7, December 2014.

13. D. Dujovne, T. Watteyne, X. Vilajosana, and P. Thubert, "6TiSCH: Deterministic IP-enabled industrial Internet (of Things)," *IEEE Communications Magazine*, vol. 52, no. 12, pp. 36–41, December 2014.

14. P. Guillemin and P. Friess, "Internet of Things strategic research roadmap," in *European Research on Cluster Internet Things*, Brussels, Belgium, Technical Report, September 2009.

15. IEEE802.15.4-2011, "IEEE standard for local and metropolitan area network–part 15.4: Low-rate wireless personal area networks (LR-WPAN)," in *IEEE Standards*, pp. 1–225, April 2012.

16. M. Park, "IEEE 802.11ah: Sub-1-ghz license-exempt operation for the internet of things," *IEEE Communications Magazine*, vol. 53, no. 9, 2015, pp. 145–151.

17. Zigbee, "Zigbee resource guide," 2016, www.nxtbook.com/nxtbooks/webcom/zigbee_rg2016/#/0).

18. M. Nobre, I. Silva, and L. A. Guedes, "Routing and scheduling algorithms for WirelessHART networks: A survey," *Sensors*, vol. 15, no. 5, 2015, pp. 9703–9740.

19. N. Sornin, M. Luis, T. Eirich, T. Kramp, and O. Hersent, "LoRaWAN specification," *LoRa Alliance*, January 2015, www.loraalliance. org/portals/0/specs/LoRaWAN%20Specification%201R0.pdf.

20. I. Poole, "Weightless wireless – m2m white space communications-tutorial," 2014, www.radioelectronics.com/info/wireless/weightless-m2m-white-space-wireless-communications/basics-overview.php.

21. Z-Wave, "Z-wave protocol overview," April 2006, https://wiki.ase.tut.fi/courseWiki/images/9/94/SDS10243_2_Z_Wave_Protocol_Overview.pdf.

22. EnOcean, "EnOcean – The world of energy harvesting wireless technology," 2015, www.enocean.com/en/technology/white-papers.

23. T. Winter, P. Thubert, A. Brandt, J. Hui, R. Kelsey, P. Levis, K. Pister, R. Struik, J. Vasseur, and R. Alexander, "RPL: IPv6 routing protocol for low-power and lossy networks," IETF RFC 6550.

24. A. Aijaz and A. H. Aghvami, "Cognitive machine-to-machine communications for Internet-of-Things: A protocol stack perspective," *IEEE Internet of Things Journal*, vol. 2, no. 2, 2015, pp. 103–112.

25. S. Basagni, C. Petrioli, R. Petroccia, and D. Spaccini, "Carp: A channel-aware routing protocol for underwater acoustic wireless networks," *Ad Hoc Networks*, vol. 34, 2015, pp. 92–104.

26. OASIS, "Oasis advanced message queuing protocol (AMQP) version 1.0," 2012, http://docs.oasisopen.org/amqp/core/v1.0/os/amqp-core-complete-v1.0-os.pdf.

27. Object Management Group, "Data distribution service (DDS)-v1.4," April 2015, www.omg.org/spec/DDS/1.4.

28. W. Jonker and M. Petković (Eds.), "Data security challenges and research operations," *SDM 2013*, LNCS 8425, Springer International Publishing Switzerland 2014, pp. 9–13, 2014. doi:10.1007/978-3-319-06811-4_2.

29. D. Sarkar and A. Nath, "Big data – A pilot study on scope and challenges," *International Journal of Advance Research in Computer Science and Management Studies*, vol. 2, no. 12, p. 919, 31 December 2014, ISSN: 2371-7782.

30. J. Feng, Y. Chen, and P. Liu, "Bridging the missing link of cloud data storage security in AWS," in the *7th IEEE Consumer Communications and Networking Conference – Security for CE Communications (CCNC '10)*, Las Vegas, NV, January 9–12, 2010.

31. Z. Ding, X. Gao, J. Xu, and H. Wu, "IoT-StatisticDB: A general statistical database cluster mechanism for big data analysis in the Internet of Things," in *2013 IEEE International Conference on Green Computing and Communications and IEEE Internet of Things and IEEE Cyber, Physical and Social Computing*, IEEE, Beijing, China, 2013.

Chapter 8

Big Data Storage Systems for IoT – Perspectives and Challenges

Rajalakshmi Krishnamurthi and Parmeet Kaur

Jaypee Institute of Information Technology

Contents

8.1 Introduction

The Internet of Things (IoT) is the concept of interconnecting different objects or things that surround us through sensors, actuators, smart phones, tags, radio frequency identification (RFID), etc. These objects interact with each other in order to perform a common goal as per human requirements to enhance human quality of living (QoL). The applications of IoT are smart city, smart grid, smart transport, smart healthcare systems, smart education, smart building, smart farming, etc. According to Gartner Report envisage, by 2020 there will be 50 billion of such interconnected IoT objects across the globe. It is expected that heterogeneous connected things of IoT generate voluminous data every moment [1–3]. In addition, a number of IoT applications using data analytics are developed that involve control and optimization at real time through cognitive decision-making mechanism based on voluminous data gathered from IoT sensors. In addition, these data possess complex properties such as veracity and velocity.

8.1.1 Data Processing in IoT

Data processing involves collection and manipulation of data and converting it into meaningful information. In general, it is a cycle with three fundamental stages such as input, processing, and output. In general, in the first step, the collected data is transformed into a machine-readable form. The second step uses different data manipulation techniques such as classification, sorting, and computation to transform the data into meaningful information. The last step presents processed data to

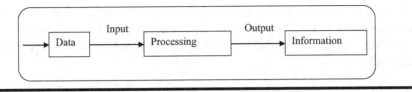

Figure 8.1   Data processing for IoT systems.

the end user as meaningful information. Figure 8.1 depicts the mechanism of data processing for IoT systems.

The nature of IoT or sensor data comprises a continuous stream of data, and the time interval between successive updates of the data is very small – usually minutes, seconds, or even milliseconds. The data produced provides information about the system. For example, it can be temperature, pressure, flow rate, heart rate, etc. Data processing in IoT introduces some new considerations such as the following: what kind of information the end user is interested in? What type of queries is answered using the IoT devices? For example, a user is interested in receiving an alarm whenever a manufacturing machine's temperature exceeds a threshold limit.

8.2   Big Data Analytics for IoT

It is now a known fact that we are surrounded by massive volumes of data [4]. A rapid rise in the number of devices connected to Internet is a major causal factor for this data deluge. Data from applications such as social networking, monitoring and surveillance, e-commerce, and many more running on devices, such as mobile phones and sensors, is constantly adding to the existing volumes. Further, this data is of multiple types, such as text, images, and videos, as well as of different forms, i.e., structured, unstructured, or semi-structured. This data that cannot be stored or processed efficiently with traditional methods and database management tools for traditional data is referred to as big data.

8.2.1   What Is Big Data?

The word "big" does not refer to size or volume alone. In practice, big data is characterized by three v's other than that for volume. These are as follows.

8.2.1.1   Velocity of Data

Tweets from Twitter; posts from Facebook or any other social data streams; data from our smartphones and online gaming; and data and logs from networking devices, such as the routers, switches, and firewalls, are generating massive amounts of real-time data which is valuable only if processed at high speeds. This type of data is known as high-velocity data. Consumers of that data, for operations and analytics, require all the data as soon as possible, and hence the drive towards high-velocity data.

8.2.1.2 Variety of Data

The data we are increasingly inundated with consists of text documents, images, audio files, videos, web pages, etc. All of this data may not fit into the traditional row–column structure of relational database management systems (RDBMSs) and is referred to as *unstructured data since it cannot be mapped to pre-designed fields. Data generated by social media, mobile phones, websites, scientific applications, etc. all fall in this category. There also exists data, such as XML documents, which is semi-structured.*

8.2.1.3 Veracity of Data

Veracity of data refers to the uncertainty of data. A collection of data may be the result of data ingestion from multiple sources. Knowledge of the source of the available data, for instance, is highly important. If the source of data is not trust-worthy, the efforts of extracting value from data are useless. Table 8.1 summarizes various selection factors between RDBMS and Not only SQL (NoSQL).

Thus, in general, big data involves a large amount of data. However, in many instances, it may imply data is streaming in the system at a high speed or is in a complex structure or being generated by multiple sources.

Table 8.1   Comparison of RDBMS and NoSQL

	Traditional Data	*Big Data*
Application characteristic	Typically for centralized applications	In distributed applications generally
Type of data	Structured	Unstructured, semi-structured, or structured
Velocity of data	Moderate	High
Volume of data	Moderate	High
Veracity of data	Low	High
Variety of data	Low	High

8.2.2 Need for Data Analytics in Big Data

Handling and storing big data is obviously a great challenge and needs special tools and methods. Further, if this data is processed effectively, it can be transformed into practically useful information. This has led to the quest for big data analytics.

IoT devices are contributing to the generation of big data every second. IoT devices in homes and offices are giving rise to data from smart appliances, smart meter, smart parking spaces, and multiple other avenues. If this data is harnessed, it can lead to better policy decisions and improved quality of life. For instance, data from smart meters can be leveraged for better energy-producing and energy-regulating decisions. Similarly, data from smart parking spaces can be used to save fuel consumption. In this data-driven world, turning data into valuable information by discovery of useful patterns and connections within data can be rewarding in terms of monetary gains. Therefore, big data analytics is being pursued in academia and industry with great zeal.

Moreover, big data has also moved the level of analytics from descriptive analytics of traditional data to predictive and prescriptive analytics. Data analytics was earlier limited to gaining insights into what had happened earlier. However, the volumes and heterogeneity of available data now is making it possible to make predictions based on this data. Further prescriptive actions are also being recommended using the information extracted from the data. For instance, data regarding electricity usage can be analyzed to the find details of usage (descriptive level), unravel patterns, and make it possible to predict the usage of electricity in coming days (predictive analytics). These insights may further be used for policy designs, setup of power plants in a region, etc. (prescriptive level).

8.2.3 Role of Big Data Analytics in IoT

Trillions of GBs of data are being generated through the IoT. It is undoubtedly difficult to manage this data, yet its importance cannot be undermined. Each device connected to the Internet is a potential source of information, and data from multiple such sources can be integrated to yield high-value information. Moreover, IoT devices provide an additional advantage in that they collect, analyze, and communicate data in real time. Hence, the data from IoT devices is capable of functionalities that may not be achievable otherwise. A few examples of useful data collection in real time are as follows:

- Forest conditions for detection of forest fires and remedial actions
- Activity monitoring of senior citizens for emergency situations
- Tracking of young children for protection against untoward incidents
- Temperature monitoring of factory equipment for maintenance
- Anomaly detection
- Switching power off in the absence of people in a room.

Since in IoT the unstructured data are collected via the Internet, big data for the IoT need lightning-fast analysis with large queries to gain rapid insights from data to make quick decisions. Hence, the need for big data in IoT is compelling. Hence, from this perspective, big data is the fuel that drives the running of the IoT.

Analytics of data streamed from IoT devices can aid rapid decision-making, for improvement of both quality of life as well as business intelligence. Big data analytics tasks are generally regarded under the following categories [5–7].

Classification: It is a supervised learning method where prior knowledge is utilized as training data to further classify data into classes. Here, the class assigned to a data object is one of the predefined classes. Classification finds multiple applications in IoT such as anomaly detection in manufacturing, emergency detection in healthcare, and sensor localization problem. Classification techniques are based on algorithms such as K-NN, Bayesian networks, support vector machines, and decision trees.

Clustering: This is a very commonly used method in big data analytics due to its unsupervised approach. It is used to group similar data objects into groups or clusters based on the data feature values, thus easing data analysis. K-means, fuzzy c-means, hierarchical clustering, etc. are popular clustering algorithms. These find application in various IoT areas such as anomaly detection, routing problem, and data aggregation.

Prediction: The third category of big data analytics is predictive analytics that uses historical data, i.e., training data, to predict values or trends for future. A number of statistical, data-mining, and machine-learning algorithms are used for developing predictive models. Linear regression, random forests, etc. are some examples used for prediction.

With respect to analytics of IoT big data, analytics tasks are categorized as follows:

- *Streaming Analytics*: This refers to analytics performed over data or event streams, i.e., analysis of volumes of in-motion datasets. This is an important category in IoT on which multiple applications are based such as detection of abnormal activities and commercial transactions and traffic tracking.
- *Spatial Analytics*: Some IoT applications rely on location of objects such as targeted marketing and finding parking slots. These applications need to analyze geographical data to identify patterns and relationships between objects.
- *Time Series Analytics*: Analytics of time-based data is involved in IoT applications such as weather monitoring and health monitoring. Patterns or trends in data are studied over time for extracting useful information.
- *Prescriptive Analysis*: This refers to determination of action that is required for a specific scenario based on analytics performed. For example, monitoring of equipment may indicate anomalous behavior and necessitate the need for prescriptive analysis to control the situation.

8.2.4 Architecture of Big Data Analytics in IoT

The architecture of big data analytics in IoT may be represented by a layered architecture. The lowest layer is the IoT device layer consisting of sensors and objects containing sensors. These are responsible for collecting the required data from the system. These devices are connected to each other by means of a wireless network. The network may be based on Bluetooth, Wi-Fi, ZigBee or a similar communication medium. Further, the IoT gateway is responsible for connecting the IoT devices' network to the Internet. Once the connection to the Internet is done, the data coming from the IoT is stored in cloud-based storage where it is processed and analyzed by multiple big data analytics applications. Results of analytics are available to users through application programming interfaces (APIs) or dashboards.

8.3 Data Storage and Access for IoT

A major challenge for IoT systems is storing and handling of large volumes of data. This challenge is compounded by continually incoming data from heterogeneous devices. In such a scenario, efficient data storage and access is highly crucial.

8.3.1 Distributed Storage Systems

An effective way of data storage is to rely on cloud-based distributed storage systems. Therefore, in general, IoT applications make use of platform-as-a-service model of cloud computing. This alleviates the need for upkeep of private storage infrastructure. PaaS provides flexible, on-demand storage that is highly scalable and can be used to store IoT data.

Depending on an organization or user's requirements, cloud storage can be used in a public, private, or hybrid model. Requirements of high security for data can be met using private clouds; else public cloud can be used to store the voluminous IoT data.

8.3.2 NoSQL Databases

Relational databases were the obvious choice for applications until a few years ago. However, recent times have seen the emergence of a new *paradigm* in the databases: the NoSQL. What has driven the use of NoSQL in IoT is the imperative need for databases to address the requirements of being distributed, scalable, and open source. Additionally, the data does not conform to strict schemas, and hence, NoSQL is steadily appearing as an efficient and suitable alternative for IoT applications [8–10].

NoSQL databases, in general, possess the ability to distribute the database across multiple locations which may be geographically spread. In addition, they are designed to tolerate partial failures in the system. These databases allow localization of data, and hence, the failure of one or more database servers does not impede the continuous availability of service if other nodes are up and functioning. NoSQL databases also allow read-and-write operations from any node, regardless of its location. In this manner, they provide location independence to users.

The distributed nature of NoSQL databases arises due to the features of sharding and replication available with most of the databases in this family. Sharding is the capability to spread data across servers. Many NoSQL databases provide auto-sharding, whereby an application is not required to be aware of the presence of multiple servers or distribution of data between them. The queries are also transparently routed to the correct shards by the configuration servers. In effect, sharding can be considered as an equivalent of horizontal fragmentation of data. Moreover, sharding allows data and query load balancing across nodes. Most NoSQL databases also provide automatic data replication in order to prevent loss of data in the event of node failures.

8.3.3 Data Integration and Virtualization

An IoT system receives data from diverse or heterogeneous sources. In order to convert this into valuable information, this data needs to be integrated meaningfully. The coming together of processes, technical or organizational, to integrate data from multiple sources is called data integration. As the number of IoT devices is growing rapidly, data integration is gaining significance for it to be used for benefit. For effective integration of data from IoT devices, firstly, a proper communication medium should be selected for transmitting data from IoT devices. This could be a cellular system or a wireless one, such as Wi-Fi, ZigBee, or Bluetooth. Subsequently, consideration needs to be put to network topology and gateway nodes. Another factor of importance is that instead of conventional extract, load, and transform (ELT) model, publish–subscribe model suits the IoT better. The data being ingested into the system by a device should be forwarded to the service that has subscribed for this data. Quality of data needs to be given priority during integration process. Any missing or incorrect values can lead to loss of information and hence loss in business. Apart from quality, data security should be implemented [11,12].

The IoT is also leading to the trend toward data virtualization. Sensor data without context collected in a repository can be leveraged by multiple applications by addition of context. For example, sensors that provide data from monitoring vehicles can be integrated with vehicle maintenance records to predict if a part is required to be replaced. Data virtualization provides abstraction of data assets and extraction of useful information.

8.4 Dynamic-Data Handling in Big Data Storage Systems

With the increase in the application of big data, the major requirement is to meet the dynamic nature of data and to achieve outstanding performance. In aspect, the conventional static databases fail to handle the demand of dynamic data in real time. Particularly, in case of IoT systems where data are obtained from sensors, networked devices, web logs, finance generates voluminous dynamic data. Hence, dynamic data mining is the best way to handle the dynamism and also to identify the hidden knowledge with this dynamic data. The process flow of dynamic-data handling is depicted in Figure 8.2. This process involves current data, historical data, and new data to perform extraction of knowledge based on rules applied on the dynamic data sources [13]. Authors in [14] proposed a dynamic framework based on data sensitivity within the Hadoop cluster. The aim of the framework was to protect the data from the untrusted users. Data sensitivity was estimated in real time on the Hadoop cluster. Authors in [15] proposed data transformation based on an iterative process that aimed to generate data schema based on real-time optimization. The experimental results of low latency querying in big data systems achieved a query latency of ~99%.

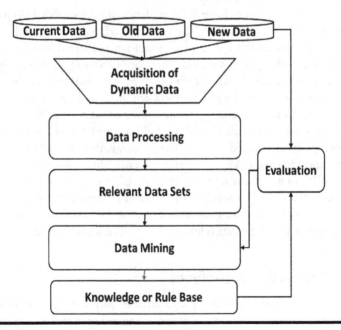

Figure 8.2   Dynamic-data-handling mechanism.

8.4.1 Dynamic Data Assimilation Mechanisms

Primarily the data assimilation (DA) technique aims to simulate real-time data obtained from various IoT-based monitoring systems [16]. DA technique is an efficient method that integrates numerical models for simulation with the observational data or experimental variables. The DA provides the probability distribution function (PDF) of various stochastic variables that are involved in running simulation. As huge amounts of data are involved in real-time systems, the convergence of IoT, big data, and data assimilation techniques provides best results in simulation and forecasting.

In recent years, the trend of connecting heterogeneous devices through Internet and IoT is exponentially growing as a means to share and exchange information. In fact, a voluminous amount of data termed as big data are generated through this interconnection of heterogeneous IoT sensors and devices. Hence, the analysis of such huge amount of big data requires efficient algorithms and analytical techniques. According to [17], the processing of big data analytics for IoT is of four categories namely heterogeneous data handling, high-dimensional big data handling, distributed big data processing, and parallel big data processing. The primary objective of the big data analytics for IoT is to obtain valuable insight into complex information data structures in addition to maintaining performance factors such as high throughput, uninterrupted data streaming, reliable data transfer, and low latency for larger data processing system.

Authors in [18] discussed the variational data assimilation (VarDA) mechanism for an IoT-based big data system. The goal of VarDA mechanism is to provide insight into dynamic complex data of air pollution IoT-based monitoring system. For the purpose of this study, numerical simulations and predictive analytics tools were involved to analyze dynamic data on transport pollution and its impact on individual commercial buildings, city infrastructure, and entire area of city. The input to the VarDA is from heterogeneous sensors based on methods like finite element analysis, open source data handling, fluid dynamics, and fluidity modeling.

Authors in [19] addressed the simulation for weather prediction based on big data assimilation (BDA). DA is the primary mechanism for numerical weather prediction (NWP), in which the data obtained are IoT-based physical sensor data. To meet the demand of big data involved in weather prediction, the big data prototype system was proposed. The next-generation BDA has the specification of 10 petaflops computing systems, and the data is fetched from Himawari-8 geostationary satellite.

8.4.2 Interpolation Techniques

Interpolation is defined as a technique to retrieve only a specific set of data from the voluminous amount of unwanted information in big data. Distributed systems like Hadoop by Apache Software Foundation provide distributed data storage and processing over a cluster of computers to handle massive dynamic real data [20,21].

These clusters provide abundant hardware commodity. The powerful mechanism namely normalization and interpolation are used to handle dynamic data through Hadoop Distributed File System (HDFS) structure. The objective of the normalization technique is to eliminate redundancy in big data. The objective of the interpolation search is to retrieve specific useful data.

The traditional sequential search also known as linear search is limited to find a target element within a given list of elements [22,23]. Moreover, each element in the given list is compared sequentially to match with the required target element. Hence, the worst-case scenario will be to search through all the elements of the entire list. On the other hand, in the binary search mechanism, the given list is partitioned into lower-level and higher-level elements. In this, the search is bounded within one of the levels. This limits the search objective, because if the target element is present in the other half of the elements, the search is limited. Interpolation search is an enhanced method of binary search.

The principle of working in interpolation search techniques involves two cases. In the first case, if the target element is found in the list, then the return value is the index of the element. In the second case, if the target element is not found, the original list of elements is divided into two equal parts. The target value is compared with the middle element. Then, the target element is further searched within the sublist of the divided parts. The process is repeated on both the levels of the sublists created during each probing of the target element. The complexity of the linear search is $O(n)$, binary search is $O(\log n)$, and the interpolation search is $O(\log(\log n))$ where "O" represents time complexity, and "n" represents the number of elements in the cluster.

8.5 Heterogeneous Datasets in IoT Big Data

In recent years, the advent of big data systems led to the enhancement of conventional data analysis techniques and machine learning algorithms. In a traditional enterprise scenario, the major data sources are the web with structured data, independent data archives, data mining techniques, and knowledge discovery procedures [21,24]. Generally, such organized data are stored in and retrieved from spreadsheets, HTML files, XML files, RDBMSs, etc. Moreover such data are carefully examined, pre-processed, anomaly free, and hidden patterns are discovered through the Knowledge Discovery from Data (KDD) mechanism. Further, organized internal resources include data from manufacturing industries, sales/customer data, or financial system data of an organization. Similarly, the external organized data sources are industry standardized data, scientific information data, government organization open data, etc. Figure 8.3 depicts the categories of heterogeneous data for big data.

On the other hand, unstructured data include largely text messages, pixel images, and framed videos. The objective in unstructured data through web search

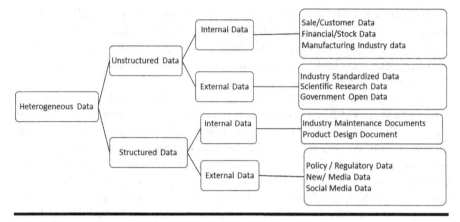

Figure 8.3 Heterogeneous data for big data.

tool is to find the relevant data or relevant text from a large amount of data of documents [25]. The traditional search technique includes metadata-based tools and search engines. Particularly, language-based tools and machine learning techniques are available depending on the dynamic requirements of users during web interaction.

However, between structured data and unstructured data, prevails the heterogeneous data that poses a greater challenge as handling a huge amount of such data is beyond the ability of existing data handling and analysis techniques. The major challenge for heterogeneous data is to (1) bridge the existing keyword-dictionary-based search engine and tools for retrieving data from structured big data and (2) bridge the database evaluation systems such as precision and recall metrics for the language-based big data systems. In summary, there exist large amounts of heterogeneous data that cannot be handled by existing data analysis mechanisms and require an enhanced solution for the data science research community.

8.5.1 Data Cleaning for Heterogeneous Data

The major challenge in integrating heterogeneous data from different types of databases is that these databases are not compatible with datasets other than those they can store. Datasets are in different formats such as CSV, XML, JSON, PDF, etc. With structured datasets, the problem is in identifying the rows and columns. Large datasets available as open web pages, which are accessed through http request, commonly involve dictionary files with details of domain terminology associated with large datasets. In turn, the size of open data is of a number of document web pages, out of which only few data items are suitable to be analyzed further [26]. The solution to these kinds of problems is to write a customized code to reconcile the heterogeneous data compatibility issues with programmers or developers with domain knowledge in data engineering.

However, the problems that arise in turn are the data cleaning ways to handle the missing information and unknown or irrelevant data entry within the datasets that cause trouble for integrating heterogeneous data. Regarding the date format used across different datasets, the various formats are DD-MM-YY, MM-DD-YY, text representation, and so on. In fact, the data cleaning problem is elevated in case of dictionary terms used in the special domain of expert. For example, in case of medical data, the disease name and the various features related to the diagnosis methods are specific to domain experts.

8.5.2 Data Integration

Data integration involves four main mechanisms: (1) dataset annotation, (2) code mapping, (3) data linking, and (4) resource description framework (RDF) [27,28].

8.5.2.1 Dataset Annotation

This involves adding comments or text fields to the data. Data annotation is in a human-readable simple format. The user with no domain knowledge will be assisted to understand the underlying domain-specific things.

8.5.2.2 Code Mapping

This method involves writing mapping codes to integrate different data in terms of their relationship such that all their relationships are encoded into a data warehouse framework. Thus, combined queries can be used to get responses from the integrated databases.

8.5.2.3 Data Linking

This involves creating a special format such that different data items and their relations are expressed in terms of URL, unique identifiers, and data annotations. Thus, these unique identifiers can be used to resolve the data integration problem.

8.5.2.4 Resource Description Framework

An example of the practical application of RDFs is the Wikipedia data [29]. In Wikipedia, each data item is assigned two data integration parameters namely (1) a unique identifier and (2) a set of relations between different data items of Wikipedia. In fact, the data items are linked to other database-domain vocabularies. However, the challenges in diversely linked databases include the complexity of managing these links, cycle in linked data, and handling of different formats within the database information.

8.5.3 Dimensionality Reduction

Dimensionality reduction involves the selection of suitable feature sets [30–32]. This feature-selection process can be performed using several algorithms namely genetic algorithms, simulated annealing, hill climbing, swarm intelligence algorithms, and evolutionary algorithms. The merits of feature selection include a speed-up of feature-classification process, enhanced technique for feature classification, and improvement in accuracy of feature classification. The feature-selection process involves two subprocesses namely feature ranking and subfeature selection. Feature ranking involves the ranking of all the features based on some threshold values. Feature selection involves the optimal selection of important features. There are three subapproaches within feature selection, namely filter, embedded, and wrapper approaches. In the filter approach, first the features are selected, and then a classification algorithm is applied upon them. In the embedded approach, the feature-selection process is carried along with a classification algorithm. In the wrapper approach, a classification algorithm is applied upon the dataset to identify the optimal feature sets.

The reasons for dimensionality reduction are as follows:

i. It is inefficient in terms of time and cost to have all features of the datasets.
ii. Machine learning algorithms perform poorly in terms of large set features in datasets.
iii. Dimensionality reduction provides more meaningful data and also captures easily the hidden pattern within the datasets.

8.5.4 Big Data Analytics for Heterogeneous Data

According to International Data Corporation (IDC) envisage, by 2022, the big data industry and allied data analytics industry are estimated to improve by 13.2% in terms of five-year predicted compound annual growth rate (CAGR). In fact, IDC approximates the worldwide revenue of big data industry as $274.3 billion. Big data involves three types of analytics, namely descriptive, predictive, and prescriptive as depicted in Table 8.2.

8.5.4.1 Descriptive Analytics

Descriptive analytics involves the analysis of historical data along with real-time data to gather information for future business. The primary aim of descriptive analytics is to analyze the faults and successful processes in the history of a business. This "history" can refer to seconds, minutes, hours, or several years ago. The standard methods in mathematical statistics, such as aggregation, summation, mean, and standard deviation, are used in descriptive analytics. A popular example for descriptive analytics is a social networking site, which provides information such

Table 8.2 Types of Big Data Analytics

Parameters	Descriptive Analytics	Predictive Analytics	Prescriptive Analytics
Value	Analysis of historical data	Predicting the future	Proactive methods to make events happen
Complexity/ difficulty	Low	Medium	High
Outcome	Hindsight	Insight	Foresight of the process
Analytics level	Reporting	Forecasting	Optimization

as the average number of likes, average number of posts, average number of replies, and number of site views. The outputs in descriptive analytics are in terms of effective data visualization, drill-downs, and comprehensive reports. The big data tools for descriptive analytics are Tableau, Qlik View, Power BI, and Rapid Miner.

8.5.4.2 Predictive Analytics

Predictive analytics provides an understanding of an organization's big data for its future progress. The future prediction is achieved through an assessment of the likelihood factor based on probabilities and statistical forecasting methods. The statistical methods are applied on the historical data obtained from HR payroll software, enterprise resource planning software, customer relationship modules, etc. The input data for predictive analytics can be internal data of an organization or external data from social media. The primary objective of predictive analytics is to perform the optimization function to achieve good outcomes and also to carry out stochastic optimization for a better understanding of good outcomes and to handle uncertainties within the datasets. The most popular area of predictive analytics is the sentiment analysis of users in social networking. The text inputs fetched from social websites are provided for the learning model. Then the sentimental score is estimated to determine various types of sentiments such as positive, neutral, and negative feelings of the users.

8.5.4.3 Prescriptive Analytics

Prescriptive analytics involves decision-making, taking actions, and then studying the impacts of those decisions and actions. It addresses the events that will occur in future, when they will occur, and why they will occur. Basically, the analysis involves making several decisions to provide foresight into the future. Machine learning algorithms, rule-based programming models, and mathematical programming models are used in combinations in prescriptive analytics. However, a high

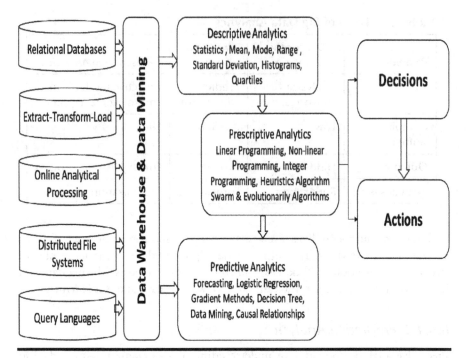

Figure 8.4 Decision and action mechanisms based on descriptive, predictive, and prescriptive analytics.

level of complexity is involved in this approach. The input for data analysis includes real-time data, historical data, big data, and transactional datasets. The outcomes of this analysis include optimized solutions, foresight into future processes, and methods to achieve the required outcomes. Figure 8.2 depicts instances of how decision and action mechanisms are performed based on descriptive, predictive, and prescriptive analytics. Figure 8.4 depicts the decision and action mechanisms based on descriptive, predictive, and prescriptive analytics.

8.6 Semantic Analytics for Big Data

Semantic data have been traditionally related to the concept of semantic web. Both semantic data and semantic web concepts are technically interrelated [29,33]. In a way, the semantic web aims to incorporate machine-based semantic processing for WWW with information objects such as data sources, hyperlinks, and services. The objectives of the semantic web are to provide semantic features for WWW information. The major difference between database-based semantic data and WWW-based semantic web is that the former requires schemas and metadata. The metadata provides query structuring, logical meaning to the query, and precision in accessing data. The semantic data aims to provide machine-processed data in the WWW. Hence, for big data, the semantics plays a crucial role for an insightful understanding of data on the web. Basically there are two types of methods for semantic data processing, namely RDF and Web Ontology Language (OWL).

8.6.1 Resource Description Framework (RDF)

RDF provides a simple data model and supports distributed resource statements on the web. The RDF allows a formal representation of semantics and also extensible support for URI based domain specific vocabulary. The description of RDF is defined through URL triples with embedded standard meanings. The RDF is primarily based on graph-based data specifications, network semantics, and URL identifiers [34,35].

8.6.2 Web Ontology Language (OWL)

The OWL is a logic-based language that adapts to the various requirements of the web. The OWL consists of various logic operators and meaning definition methods in a distributed manner [36,37]. OWL provides a rich resource of domain-based vocabulary as metadata with inbuilt classes, relations, bounds, equality, and properties of entities. The OWL is proven to be cost effective in term of scalability and computation complexity. OWL's semantics is rich in logical reasoning methods for different data.

8.7 Conclusion

This chapter focuses on big data for IoT and the various solution approaches from three perspectives, namely data storage and access, data processing, and data analysis mechanisms. This chapter discusses data storage and access mechanisms such as big data distributed storage systems, NoSQL databases, data integration, and data virtualization for the IoT ecosystem. Next, this chapter addresses different types of big data such as heterogeneous data, dynamic data, and weak semantic data gathered from IoT systems. Further, this chapter presents the data processing, data quality, and knowledge discovery tools on the IoT data. Finally, this chapter addresses the different big data analysis mechanisms such as predictive, descriptive, and prescriptive analytics.

References

1. J. Gubbi, R. Buyya, S. Marusic, and M. Palaniswami, "Internet of Things (IoT): A Vision, Architectural Elements, and Future Directions," *Future Generation Computer Systems*, vol. 29, no. 7, pp. 1645–1660, 2013.

2. L. Atzori, A. Iera, and G. Morabito, "The Internet of Things: A Survey," *Computer Networks*, vol. 54, no. 15, pp. 2787–2805, 2010.
3. S. Bandyopadhyay, M. Sengupta, S. Maiti, and S. Dutta, "A Survey of Middleware for Internet of Things," in A. Özcan, J. Zizka, D. Nagamalai D. (eds) *Recent Trends in Wireless and Mobile Networks*, pp. 288–296. Springer, Berlin, 2011.
4. M. K. Saggi and S. Jain, "A Survey towards an Integration of Big Data Analytics to Big Insights for Value-Creation," *Information Processing & Management*, vol. 54, no. 5, pp. 758–790, 2018.
5. S. Thrun and L. Pratt, eds., *Learning to Learn.* Springer Science & Business Media, New York, 2012.
6. H. Zhang, "The Optimality of Naive Bayes," *AA*, vol. 1, no. 2, p. 3, 2004.
7. A. Y. Ng and M. I. Jordan, "On Discriminative vs. Generative Classifiers: A Comparison of Logistic Regression and Naive Bayes," in T. G. Dietterich, S. Becker, and Z. Ghahramani (eds) *Advances in Neural Information Processing Systems*, pp. 841–848. MIT Press, Cambridge, 2002.
8. V. Abramova, J. Bernardino, and P. Furtado, "Which NoSQL Database? A Performance Overview," *Open Journal of Databases*, vol. 1, no. 2, pp. 17–24, 2014.
9. D. Intersimone, "The End of SQL and Relational Database? (Part 2 of 3)," *Computerworld*, 10 February, 2010.
10. A. T. Kabakus and R. Kara, "A Performance Evaluation of In-Memory Databases," *Journal of King Saud University – Computer and Information Sciences*, vol. 29, no. 4, pp. 520–525, 2017. doi:10.1016/j.jksuci.2016.06.007
11. J. Qiu, Q. Wu, G. Ding, Y. Xu, and S. Feng. "A Survey of Machine Learning for Big Data Processing." *EURASIP Journal on Advances in Signal Processing*, vol. 2016, no. 1, p. 67, 2016.
12. Y. Liu, Y. Wang, and Y. Jin, "Research on the Improvement of MongoDB Auto-Sharding in Cloud Environment," in *2012 7th International Conference on Computer Science & Education (ICCSE)*. IEEE, Melbourne, 2012.
13. S. Shai Shalev-Shwartz and S. Ben-David, *Understanding Machine Learning: From Theory to Algorithms.* Cambridge University Press, New York, 2014.
14. H. A. Idar, K. Aissaoui, H. Belhadaoui, and R. F. Hilali, "Dynamic Data Sensitivity Access Control in Hadoop Platform," In *2018 IEEE 5th International Congress on Information Science and Technology (CiSt)*, pp. 105–109. IEEE, Marrakech, 2018.
15. L. Ordonez-Ante, T. Vanhove, G. Van Seghbroeck, T. Wauters, B. Volckaert, and F. De Turck, "Dynamic Data Transformation for Low Latency Querying in Big Data Systems," in *2017 IEEE International Conference on Big Data (Big Data)*, pp. 2480–2489. IEEE, Boston, MA, 2017.
16. K. Hiroi, D. Murakami, K. Kurata, and T. Tashiro, "Investigation into Feasibility of Data Assimilation Approach for Flood Level Estimation Using Temporal-Spatial State Space Model," in *2019 IEEE International Conference on Big Data and Smart Computing (BigComp)*, pp. 1–5. IEEE, Kyoto, 2019.
17. H. Nagao, "What Is Required for Data Assimilation that Is Applicable to Big Data in the Solid Earth Science? Importance of Simulation-/Data-Driven Data Assimilation," in *17th International Conference on Information Fusion (FUSION)*, pp. 1–6. IEEE, Salamanca, 2014.
18. R. Arcucci, C. Pain, and Y.-K. Guo, "Effective Variational Data Assimilation in Air-Pollution Prediction," *Big Data Mining and Analytics*, vol. 1, no. 4, pp. 297–307, 2018.

19. T. Miyoshi, G.-Y. Lien, S. Satoh, T. Ushio, K. Bessho, H. Tomita, S. Nishizawa, R. Yoshida, S. A. Adachi, J. Liao, and B. Gerofi, "'Big Data Assimilation' Toward Post-Petascale Severe Weather Prediction: An Overview and Progress," *Proceedings of the IEEE*, vol. 104, no. 11, pp. 2155–2179, 2016.

20. L. Wang, "Heterogeneous Data and Big Data Analytics," *Automatic Control and Information Sciences*, vol. 3, no. 1, pp. 8–15, 2017.

21. L. Zhang, Y. Xie, L. Xidao, and X. Zhang, "Multi-Source Heterogeneous Data Fusion," in *2018 International Conference on Artificial Intelligence and Big Data (ICAIBD)*, pp. 47–51. IEEE, Chengdu, 2018.

22. N. Dey, H. Das, B. Naik, and H. S. Behera, eds., *Big Data Analytics for Intelligent Healthcare Management*. Academic Press, London, 2019.

23. P. A. Tak, S. V. Gumaste, S. A. Kahate, "The Challenging View of Big Data Mining," *International Journal of Advanced Research in Computer Science and Software Engineering*, vol. 5, no. 5, pp. 1178–1181, 2015.

24. J. Zhang, X. Yang, and D. Appelbaum, "Toward Effective Big Data Analysis in Continuous Auditing," *Accounting Horizons*, vol. 29, no. 2, pp. 469–476, 2015.

25. L. Wang, "Heterogeneous Data and Big Data Analytics," *Automatic Control and Information Sciences*, vol. 3, no. 1, pp. 8–15, 2017.

26. M. Cammarano, X. Dong, B. Chan, J. Klingner, J. Talbot, A. Halevey, and P. Hanrahan, "Visualization of Heterogeneous Data," *IEEE Transactions on Visualization and Computer Graphics*, vol. 13, no. 6, pp. 1200–1207, 2007.

27. K.-U. Sattler, S. Conrad, I. Geist, and G. Saake, "Example-Driven Integration of Heterogeneous Data Sources," in *Fifth IFCIS International Conference on Cooperative Information Systems*, 2000.

28. D. Keim, H. Qu, and K.-L. Ma, "Big-Data Visualization." *IEEE Computer Graphics and Applications*, vol. 33, no. 4, pp. 20–21, 2013.

29. G. E. Modoni, M. Sacco, and W. Terkaj, "A Survey of RDF Store Solutions," in *2014 International Conference on Engineering, Technology and Innovation (ICE)*, pp. 1–7. IEEE, Bergamo, 2014.

30. C. Onal, O. Berat Sezer, M. Ozbayoglu, and E. Dogdu, "MIS-IoT: Modular Intelligent Server Based Internet of Things Framework with Big Data and Machine Learning," in *2018 IEEE International Conference on Big Data (Big Data)*, Seattle, WA, pp. 2270–2279, 2018.

31. M. A. Razzaque, M. Milojevic-Jevric, A. Palade, and S. Clarke, "Middleware for Internet of Things: A Survey," *IEEE Internet of Things Journal*, vol. 3, no. 1, pp. 70–95, 2016.

32. Z. Liu and J. Heer, "The Effects of Interactive Latency on Exploratory Visual Analysis," *IEEE Transactions on Visualization and Computer Graphics*, vol. 20, no. 12, pp. 2122–2131, 2014.

33. M. Banane and A. Belangour, "A Survey on RDF Data Store Based on NoSQL Systems for the Semantic Web Applications," in M. Ezziyyani (ed) *Advanced Intelligent Systems for Sustainable Development (AI2SD'2018). AI2SD 2018. Advances in Intelligent Systems and Computing*, vol. 915. Springer, Cham, 2019.

34. K. Botond, W. Terkaj, and M. Sacco, "Semantic Virtual Factory Supporting Interoperable Modelling and Evaluation of Production Systems," *CIRP Annals – Manufacturing Technology*, vol. 62, no. 1, p. 443446, 2013.

35. M. Stocker, E. Baranizadeh, A. Hamed, M. Rönkkö, A. Virtanen, A. Laaksonen, H. Portin, M. Komppula, and M. Kolehmainen, "Acquisition and Representation of Knowledge for Atmospheric New Particle Formation," in J. Hřebíček, G. Schimak,

M. Kubásek, and A. E. Rizzoli (eds) *Environmental Software Systems. Fostering Information Sharing. ISESS 2013. IFIP Advances in Information and Communication Technology*, vol. 413. Springer, Berlin, 2013.

36. Y. Zhang, M. D. Pham, O. Corcho, and J. P. Calbimonte, "SRBench: A Streaming RDF/SPARQL Benchmark," in P. Cudré-Mauroux et al. (eds) *The Semantic Web – ISWC 2012. ISWC 2012. Lecture Notes in Computer Science*, vol. 7649, pp. 641–657. Springer, Berlin, 2012.

37. A. Milicic, A. Perdikakis, S. El Kadiri, D. Kiritsis, S. Terzi, P. Fiordi, and S. Sadocco, "Specialization of a Fundamental Ontology for Manufacturing Product Lifecycle Applications: A Case Study for Lifecycle Cost Assessment," in P. Herrero, H. Panetto, R. Meersman, and T. Dillon (eds) *On the Move to Meaningful Internet Systems: OTM 2012 Workshops. OTM 2012. Lecture Notes in Computer Science*, vol. 7567, pp. 69–72. Springer, Berlin, 2012.

Chapter 9

Key Technologies Enabling Big Data Analytics for IoT

S. Karthikeyan, Balamurugan
Balusamy, and Firoz Khan
Galgotias University

Contents

9.1 Introduction

Internet of Things (IoT) is the connection between sensors, Internet, cloud server, user, and the environment. The objective of IoT is to minimize the work of humans using sensors and the Internet. It is a global infrastructure where all the sensors work automatically and can be configured by the user whenever and wherever it is needed. Here devices communicate with each other and makes our life easy, where huge manpower will be needed to replace the Internet of Things. Sensors for temperature, proximity, infrared frequency, pressure, light, ultrasonic frequency, smoke, gas, acceleration, and alcohol are used to observe the environment and send notifications to the user in case of any critical situations (Ashton 2009).

Big data analytics is the process of analyzing a huge volume of data to produce a desired output. In business (Mikalef et al. 2018), people need an increase in sales after the launch of every product (Russom 2011). Here analytics will help industries find the need of their customers. This can be achieved by analyzing previous data provided by customers themselves such as feedback, reviews, ratings, and other parameters (Gubbi et al. 2013). IoT is the process of recording data continuously using sensors or actuators. Then the user accesses the data from the cloud (Ashton 2009). As data is generated without any intervention, the normal cloud data turns into big data, which leads to the use of big data analytics in the IoT to produce meaningful data (Lavalle et al. 2011). Big data analytics is not just about the tools to analyze and modify data (Rialti et al. 2019); there are different technologies for analytics in the IoT (Russom 2011). The key technologies include predictive analytics and IoT databases such as relational and non-relational databases (Gubbi et al. 2013). The databases can be chosen based upon the need of the user and the design of the IoT environment. NoSQL database is a structureless database as it can be redesigned at any point of time owing to the absence of static schema in the database (Dias et al. 2018). As IoT works with different types of devices and actuators, it is difficult to work with a table-oriented database. Hence, NoSQL is preferred to store IoT data Once data is stored in the distributed cloud, big data will come into picture. Analytics tools can be used to forecast the results effectively using the IoT data (Dias et al. 2018).

9.2 IoT for Big Data Analytics

Big data analytics and the IoT are two different applications, having unique methodologies to perform their defined operations. IoT data are generated continuously from sensors, and this leads to big data generation; the data may be either or structured or unstructured. Big data analytics can be used to predict or take decisions (Kundhavai and Sridevi 2016).

9.2.1 Big Data

In the IoT, sensors sense the elements in all surroundings, which results in the generation of a huge amount of data. Data that is generated is called streaming data and is characteristic of being continuous (Kundhavai and Sridevi 2016).

Examples of Sources of Big Data
- Social media
- Stock market
- Education industry
- Healthcare
- Movies and entertainment
- Weather prediction
- Transportation industry
- Smart homes
- Banking sector

9.2.2 Big Data Processing

9.2.2.1 Stream Analytics

It is the one of the familiar big data technologies and is used to detect abnormalities in data by using queries; the detection time will vary as per the data used (Hu et al. 2014). If the level of temperature goes high, then this analytics will notify the user about the high temperature. It is also called as stream process, real-time analytics, or complex event processing (Ranjan 2014). Here the techniques analyze big datasets of large size, i.e., petabytes and zetabytes of data, for extracting value from the data. It is the process of handling a large volume of data; handling involves storage, analysis, and visualization. If there is no processing technique, then the data cannot be used to produce meaningful results (Ranjan 2014).

9.2.2.1.1 Batch Data Processing

It deals with past or historical data of an organization. It initially stores data and then performs analytics.

Examples: Payroll and billing systems.

9.2.2.1.2 Real-Time Data Stream Processing

It handles data that exist live in the IoT device. It starts with analytics, and data may be stored or may not be stored depending upon the devices. Complex event processing helps in making decisions by observing possible patterns from many sources (Kejariwal et al. 2015).

9.2.3 *Big Data Analytics*

Big data analytics enables us to detect similar or hidden patterns, any related correlation between entities (Govindan et al. 2018), which will enhance the efficiency and performance of data. It gives real value to the data. It performs information collection, organization, and data analysis to find hidden patterns in a large volume of data (James et al. 2017).

9.2.3.1 *Big Data Analytics Challenges*

There are challenges in the steps involved in implementing big data analytics. In order to overcome the issues in handling a large volume of data, the following concepts should be considered:

- Storage
- Analytics
- Visualization
- Data curation
- Data search
- Data capture
- Data heterogeneity.

The above challenges are explained in Figure 9.1.

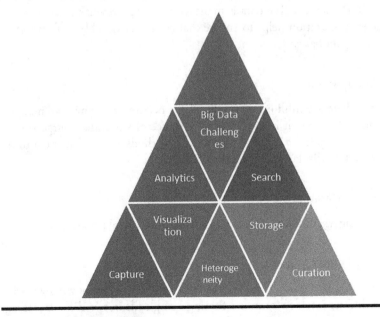

Figure 9.1   Big data challenges.

9.2.3.1.1 Storage

Storage is a place where the recorded IoT data will be stored, so the security and privacy issues need to be taken into consideration. It must be able to store all types of data formats (Cooper et al. 2009).

9.2.3.1.2 Analytics

Big data is nothing without analytics in which large volumes of data are extracted and processed to produce meaningful information. It computes a large volume of data, has frameworks such as MapReduce and Hadoop that helps in taking decision from large volume of data (Dean et al. 2008), and leads to increased business revenue and better marketing and decisions (Cooper et al. 2009).

9.2.3.1.3 Visualization

As there are huge amounts of data, it is not possible to make decisions or predict something with documents containing a lot of text, images, and so on. Visualization helps to represent large volumes of such data in the form of graphs, maps, charts and, through pictorial representation, makes the derivation of results faster.

9.2.3.1.4 Data Curation

It is the process of collecting large volumes of data from different sources and organizing them in the servers. The data is managed from the time it's created, modified, and deleted. Curation helps to ensure that data is retrievable in future if it's needed on an urgent basis.

9.2.3.1.5 Data Search

It is estimated there are millions of search results occurring in any search engine in the Internet, Data search is about the importance of searching a large volume of data, web crawling, indexing, and many basic methods are implemented in the World Wide Web to display search results faster.

9.2.3.1.6 Data Missing

It is one of the biggest challenges in big data from a statistical perspective.

9.2.3.1.7 Duplicate Data

It is one of the critical issues in big data, as the users may be unknowingly storing same files in different storage locations. Storing a single file in two different storage locations generates twice the volume of data.

9.3 Technologies of IoT Big Data Analytics

Big data analytics is used along with the IoT in many applications to predict outcomes, find the possibilities of events to have happened in the past, and to show some alternatives for the result. In part, we will be discuss on the major technologies, such as cloud computing, fog computing, edge computing, relational databases, non-relational databases, and tools used for performing big data analytics.

9.3.1 Cloud Computing

It is on-demand computing, which provides resources such as a server with storage space and virtual operating systems. Applications and tools which are needed on rental basis will be given to the user by the cloud service provider by using the Internet. The major requirement in cloud computing is that the systems must be connected to the Internet all the time to ensure less downtime and high uptime (Doukas et al. 2012). It came into existence when it was harder to manage the files in the traditional file system (Cai et al. 2016).

The IoT data gets stored in the cloud server, then the stored data can be retrieved by the IoT user at any point of time (Stergiou et al. 2018). The recorded IoT data will be stored in the cloud and can be accessed by the user at any time irrespective of geographical location (Cai et al. 2016).

9.3.2 Fog Computing

It is also called as fogging or fog network. It transmits data by bridging the communication between the user's devices such as mobiles and the cloud server (Aazam et al. 2014). The devices are also called as edge devices and perform computation and store data. In simple terms, it is a process of extending the cloud computing to the end user or enterprises (Bonomi et al. 2012). It is closer to the IoT users as the cloud server can be in any geographical location, but the fog will be near the user, making the information reach faster, which is explained in Figure 9.2.

Advantages
- Reduced latency
- Faster response time
- Increased efficiency
- Performance even with unavailable bandwidth
- Improved consistency
- Better security
- Increased business agility
- Less operation cost

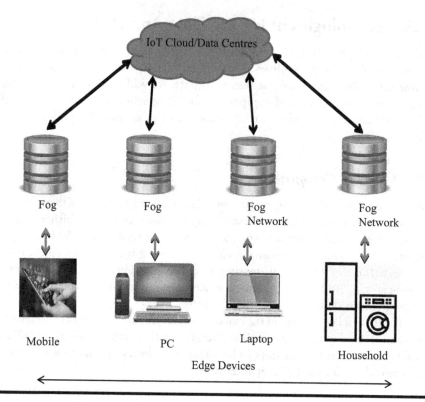

Figure 9.2 Architecture of edge, cloud, and fog computing.

Examples of Applications
- Mining
- Electrical grid
- Trains
- Wind farms
- Oil wells
- Pipelines

9.3.3 Edge Computing

As IoT devices are increasing exponentially every day, it's hard to compute, store, process, and retrieve the data from the centralized cloud due to load in the network (Satyanarayanan 2017). Here edge computing is used to reduce the latency between the devices and the cloud. Even the data centers have many resources. Still the transfer rate and response time are challenges in the network topology of the IoT environment (Shi et al. 2016).

It is the small data centers that store the data locally and send the recorded IoT data to the central IoT cloud.

Advantages
- Reduction in traffic
- Less response time
- Easy access of data
- Increased performance
- Local storage

9.3.4 Data Virtualization

It is the process of managing the data by storing and retrieving it without physical access to it and by saving memory space, as virtual memory is being used instead of physical memory. It is the process of consolidating the data from multiple sources to develop single point of access as the user doesn't know the locations of servers (Pangal et al. 2008).

An organization uses different types of servers. By using virtualization, it is possible to make the data available in single location (Weng et al. 2004).

It plays a role in the following:

- Business integration
- Data integration
- Enterprise search.

Advantages
- Decrease in data errors
- Better workload management
- Reduction in data storage
- Improved access speed
- Reduced support time

9.3.5 Data Quality Assurance

It is the process of assessing data to check whether it behaves as intended. It consists of the following steps (Gudivada et al. 2017):

1. Defining the objective
2. Assessing previous state
3. Verifying the gap between the objective and achieved state
4. Improving the current plans as per the needs
5. Implementing the mechanism to the problem
6. Checking if the data works as intended.

9.3.6 Data Preprocessing

It is the process in which raw data will be converted into a meaningful form so that decisions can be taken based on them.

The following steps are carried out in this process:

- Data cleansing
- Data transformation
- Data reduction.

9.3.7 Data Cleansing

Data may contain a lot of unrelated information, and some values may also be missing. To solve this issue, data cleansing can be used (Maletic et al. 2000).

9.3.8 Data Transformation

Here the cleansed data will be converted into a form which will be easy to manipulate. The conversion of data from one form to another form is called as data transformation.

9.3.9 Data Reduction

The process of reducing the duplicates in the database can be called as data reduction. Here all the redundant values will be removed from the system.

9.3.10 Data Fabric

Distributed cache is the process of making copies of data in the memory, which can then be made available in the cluster for a user. A data grid will partition the data in the memory, and then the clusters will contain only subsets of these data (Chung et al. 2011).

The following features are needed for the functioning of data grids:

- Query distribution
- Transaction distribution
- Computation of the available data.

9.4 In-Memory Data Fabric

It is dependent on main memory storage rather than disk-based storage system. It is the place where memory computing components will be used without any constraints. It will be able to do load balancing and schedule the computations.

A node can contain keys and values:

Node 1 = Key1 and Value1
Node 2 = Key2 and Value2
Node 3 = Key3 and Value3

Each node will have keys and values, and read operation and write operation have been performed in this memory data fabric.

9.5 Distributed Storage

It is the process of storing data on multiple servers; it can even act as a single server virtually.

It contains three different things:

■ Object
■ File
■ Block.

9.6 Data Integration

It is the process of merging data from many sources into a single unit. It is used to achieve effective decision-making in the form of business intelligence (Dong et al. 2013).

The elements involved include the following:

■ Data sources
■ Master server
■ Clients.

It contains the following processes:

■ Ingestion
■ Data cleansing
■ ETL (extract, transform, load) mapping
■ Transformation.

9.7 IoT Data Management Requirements

Data management is the process of managing the data lifecycle, i.e., generating, processing, storing, and retrieving data with the defined architecture, principles, and standards. Here IoT is the layer between the objects and the sensors that generate the data and the applications that use the data to analyze it. Here a large volume of heterogeneous data will be recorded by the sensors and distributed geographically in all places of the globe. In the scenario of IoT, data management has additional features for storage, processing, logging, and auditing for offline analysis (Abu-Elkheir et al. 2013).

9.7.1 Requirements in IoT Data Storage

Elements in data storage include the following:

- Generation
- Collection
- Aggregation
- Preprocessing
- Storage archiving
- Processing.

9.7.2 Data Heterogeneity

Data will be heterogeneous in form, i.e., unstructured, semi-structured, or structured, and in content. In the IoT environment, data can be temperature measurements, pressure readings, geographical location data, textual data, identification addresses, and so on.

9.7.3 Semantic Interoperability

It is the process of switching on services, agents, and applications to exchange data in a unique way. In the IoT, data will be stored in different applications. So cloud databases must be managed by the user. Interoperability is the unifying of formats, language modeling, and query languages, through knowledge representation and ontologies.

9.7.4 Scalability

A database is said to be scalable when it is able to execute many requests with less downtime and then enable the data to be stored on different new hardware. As data is recorded continuously, the hardware must support the high throughput with the help of services such as cloud computing and scalable databases.

9.7.5 Real-Time Processing

Most of the IoT applications generate real-time data in an environment. In healthcare, past data can be used to predict similar cases of diseases or any kind of disorder that can happen to the individual. Here past data will be outdated once the need for real-time data comes into the picture. IoT applications should generate real-time data for all needs of the user.

9.7.6 Security

Mobiles, sensors, and other devices which play a role in the recording of data use human details, which leads to intruders' invasion into the IoT cloud. Hence, data must be secured from the intruder or the attacker. IoT applications should give privilege to the authenticated individuals of the system. It can be done by using some encryption methodology.

9.7.7 Data Aggregation

It is the process of merging the data from many sources and removing the duplicates to provide valid and genuine information. As the IoT generates large volumes of data, they must be consolidated to extract primary and useful data it can be seen figure 9.3 (Abu-Elkheir et al. 2013).

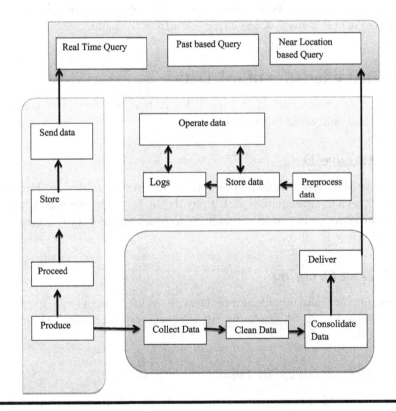

Figure 9.3   IoT data management.

9.7.8 Generation

It is the process in which different types of data are generated. As a result, they will be stored in the IoT server so that they can be retrieved whenever necessary.

9.7.9 Collection

The sensors in the IoT may store data for a specific time. Data might be gathered at certain points for efficient transmission.

9.7.10 Communication Layer

This layer is used to transport raw data; that is, the data collected by the sensors are transmitted through the communication layer to reach the database (Abu-Elkheir et al. 2013).

9.7.11 Data Repositories

They are used to store the recorded sensor data, which can then be processed whenever the user needs to access or retrieve it from the repositories.

9.8 Characteristics of IoT Data

The IoT data possess certain characteristics such as ordering, data generation, retrieval, and expiry seen in figure 9.4.

9.8.1 Massive Data

The generated data is directly proportional to the number of devices. Hence, the IoT will have a huge amount of data. Every day, new IoT devices with new applications are being built, and this is resulting in generation of large volumes of data (Abu-Elkheir et al. 2013).

9.8.2 Data Ordering

Sensors contain timestamp in most of the cases, which helps in arranging the data in a desired sequence. This ordering helps to process the data with less downtime (Figure 9.4).

9.8.3 Data Retrieval in Time

A user always wishes to retrieve data from a system with a secure connection and fast uptime.

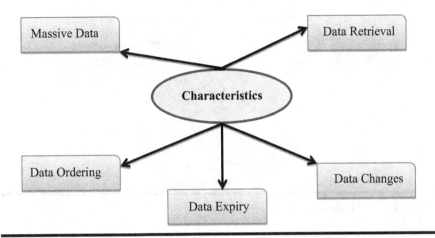

Figure 9.4   IoT data characteristics.

9.8.4 Data Changes

The advantage of IoT data is it is static in nature, and consistency is a benefit in IoT, as the data is rarely replaced or updated.

9.8.5 Data Expiry

As IoT data is stored in a centralized database, older data that will not be needed can be deleted, and data can be aggregated to reduce the space of the database or the cloud.

9.9 Database Management System in IoT

IoT is all about sensors, data, cloud, and the Internet. The following topics describe the methods and way of storing the data in the cloud, database, or any file system (Abu-Elkheir et al. 2013). The process of storing, retrieving, and handling data by using standard systems can be called as database management (Abu-Elkheir et al. 2013).

9.9.1 Database in IoT

A database is a collection of data that are accumulated in a centralized location and can be retrieved from server (Abu-Elkheir et al. 2013). These data can be either structured, unstructured, or semi-structured. Most of the time, data can be in the form of text.

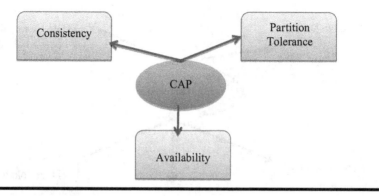

Figure 9.5   CAP theorem.

These database characteristics include those mentioned in the CAP (consistency, availability, partitioning) theorem (Figure 9.5):

■ Consistency
■ Availability
■ Partitioning.

9.9.1.1 Consistency

If any transaction has been done by the user, it has to be completed without any failure of the system. This can be called as consistency, which is nothing but achieving a transaction without any delay or failure. It should do what operation it is intended to do for the transaction.

9.9.1.2 Availability

The data or the transaction should be available to users continuously. To accomplish this, data are replicated and stored in multiple machines or nodes, so that they can be retrieved in case of any failure that occurs in the other servers.

9.9.1.3 Partition Tolerance

It possesses the ability to retrieve the data in times of any failure or if the data is inaccessible. It is achieved by redirecting the request to other active nodes. Traditional databases based on SQL (structured query language) focus on ACID (atomicity, consistency, isolation, durability) properties.

9.9.2 ACID Properties

9.9.2.1 Atomicity

Here a transaction can be either complete or incomplete. A transaction can be successfully executed or it may not be initiated. Atomicity will not start the process and end the transaction with any failure.

9.9.2.2 Isolation

Here transactions are executed without any interference and independently. Here it is isolated from the failure of transaction and delay in transaction.

9.9.2.3 Durability

It is the property of being reliable and robust during a transaction. The transactions will be stored as logs and retrieves the data from the database in any critical situations.

9.10 Object-Oriented Database (OODB)

It represents data in the form of objects and classes, uses the principle of object-oriented programming, and is implemented by combining features of a relational model with object-oriented principles shown in Figure 9.6 and Table 9.1.

9.11 Centralized Database

This database is stored and managed in a single location. It can be a central computer or server like a mainframe computer. In education, a single database is used to store and retrieve the data. The data will be accessed from multiple locations, but the server will be stored in a single location as shown in Figure 9.7.

Examples: Colleges, industries, organizations, and so on.

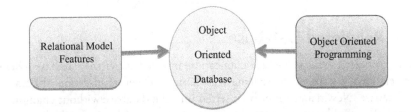

Figure 9.6   OODB model.

Table 9.1   OODB Model Features

S. No.	Relational Database Features	Object-Oriented Programming
1.	Integrity	Inheritance
2.	Concurrency	Polymorphism
3.	Query processing	Encapsulation

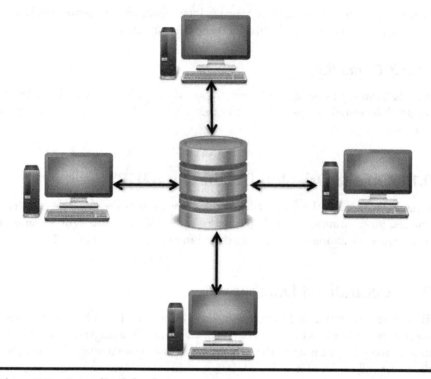

Figure 9.7   Centralized database.

9.12 Relational Database

It is a structured database, where data can be inserted as per the database schema. In a relational database, the schema will be defined before insertion of data into the database. New data cannot be inserted into the database without changing its schema. These tables are connected to each other and can be accessed by using join operations. It is based on SQL, which provides the interface between the user and the database server.

Table 9.2   Relational Database

Student Details				
Admission Number	Name	Age	Mobile Number	Blood Group
1200	Akilan	29	7538495793	B+
1201	Manu	32	9243534534	O+
1202	Somesh	28	8645645645	B+
1203	Sreenarayanan	29	8564564564	O+
1204	Pasupathi	30	3453464445	B+

The student-details table (Table 9.2) shows a list of records (rows) and attributes (columns); it contains five records and five attribute names such as admission number, name, age, mobile number, and blood group.

9.13 Non-Relational Database

It stores data in the form of key-value pairs that are called as JSON documents. Here any data can be inserted at any point of time irrespective of the database schema, as the schema is dynamic in nature. These databases are not restricted to any standard format. With certain attributes, it is more prominent in applications where new data needs to be managed in the database. It is called as NoSQL as there is no structure definition in the database.

Table 9.3 shows a list of key value pairs with documents.

Table 9.3   MongoDB Documents

Key	Document
1001	{ Admission_Number: 1200 { Student_Details { Name: Akilan Age: 29 Mobile: 7538495793 Blood: B+ } } }
1002	{ Admission_Number: 1201 {Student_Details { Name: Manu Age: 32 Mobile: 9243534534 Location: India } } }

In a traditional database, we cannot add any new fields into the database without changing its schema, whereas in a non-relational database, any data can be added at any time irrespective of its schema.

9.13.1 MongoDB

MongoDB is a cross-platform document database used to store JSON-like documents. It is a document-oriented NoSQL database (Dias et al. 2018) used to store large data. It contains two types of relations: referenced and embedded (Chodorow 2013).

It mainly operates on the collection and documents.

Collection: It contains MongoDB documents.

Documents: It has key-value pairs.

Following are some important features of MongoDB:

1. Replication
2. Supporting ad hoc queries
3. Load balancing
4. Indexing
5. Duplication of data
6. Using JavaScript instead of procedures.

There are two keys 1001 and 1002 where key 1001 contains data about name, age, mobile number, and blood group and key 1002 contains name, age, mobile number, and location, as there is no location data in key 1001.

9.13.2 Cassandra

It is a distributed NoSQL Apache database which is highly scalable with high performance. It comes into picture when a large volume of data is stored in many servers. This offers high availability of data as there will not be a failure in the retrieval of data.

9.13.2.1 Features of Cassandra

9.13.2.1.1 Schema-Free Database

Data can be inserted in any format as there is no need to change the database schema on adding any new data in the database.

9.13.2.1.2 Replication

It is the process of making duplicates from the primary to the secondary servers so that the retrieval of data is easy.

9.13.2.1.3 Application Programming Interface

It works on a simple application programming interface (API) that is user friendly for any individual who uses the database as a beginner.

9.13.2.1.4 High Scalability

Any number of devices can be added at any time irrespective of any constraints.

9.13.2.1.5 Rigid Architecture

It is robust and strong as the servers will not fail at any point of time; even if one server fails, another one will be used to retrieve the data.

9.13.2.1.6 Fast Linear-Scale Performance

It offers faster response time as the throughput performance is high in the servers. It is fault tolerant.

9.13.2.1.7 Flexible Data Storage

It is flexible as it can store all the three types of data – structured, semi-structured, and unstructured.

9.13.2.1.8 Transaction Support

It supports ACID properties: atomicity, consistency, isolation, and durability.

9.13.2.1.9 Efficient Cassandra Write

The Read operation can be performed even if hardware resources are minimal in number1. Still the performance of the database is notable (Table 9.4).

Table 9.4   Comparison between Relational and Non-Relational databases

S. No.	Relational Database	Non-Relational Database
1.	It stores data in the form of tables	It stores data in form of key-value pairs in the form of tables
2.	It is used for a moderate volume of data	It is used for a large volume of data
3.	It is used for centralized applications such as enterprise resource planning (ERP)	It is used for decentralized applications such as web pages, IoT

(Continued)

Table 9.4 (*Continued*)   Comparison between Relational and Non-Relational databases

S. No.	Relational Database	Non-Relational Database
4.	Data velocity is lesser than that of non-relational database	Data velocity is higher than that of relational database
5.	Static schema	Dynamic schema
6.	It is called as SQL database	It is called as NoSQL database
7.	Joins will be used to combine two different tables	There are no joins in this database
8.	It cannot be further divided	It can be divided into documents, graphs, etc.
9.	It is preferred for storing structured data	It can store structured, unstructured, and even semi-structured data
10.	Examples • MySQL • SQLite • PostgreSQL • SQL server • Oracle database	Examples • MongoDB • Cassandra • Neo4j • Redis • DocumentDB • HBase
11.	Database schema needs to be changed in case of adding new fields in a table	Database schema need not be changed as it is dynamic in nature
12.	Vertical scalability	Horizontal scalability

9.14 Conclusion

Big data technologies are not associated just with tools alone, as the big data generated in the IoT are stored in the cloud. In this chapter, storing the data in server and cloud, fog, and edge computing as well as their architecture have been discussed. Big data processing methods such as stream processing and batch processing have also been discussed. This chapter also presents data management issues in IoT, such as issues in storing the data, and the types of databases, i.e., relational and non-relational databases, in which the data can be stored in the IoT server.

References

Aazam, Mohammad, and Eui-Nam Huh. "Fog computing and smart gateway based communication for cloud of things." In *2014 International Conference on Future Internet of Things and Cloud*, pp. 464–470. IEEE, Barcelona, 2014.

Abu-Elkheir, Mervat, Mohammad Hayajneh, and Najah Ali. "Data management for the Internet of Things: Design primitives and solution." *Sensors* 13, no. 11 (2013): 15582–15612.

Ashton, Kevin. "That 'Internet of Things' thing." *RFID Journal* 22, no. 7 (2009): 97–114.

Bari, Md Faizul, Raouf Boutaba, Rafael Esteves, Lisandro Zambenedetti Granville, Maxim Podlesny, Md Golam Rabbani, Qi Zhang, and Mohamed Faten Zhani. "Data center network virtualization: A survey." *IEEE Communications Surveys & Tutorials* 15, no. 2 (2012): 909–928.

Bonomi, Flavio, Rodolfo Milito, Jiang Zhu, and Sateesh Addepalli. "Fog computing and its role in the Internet of Things." In *Proceedings of the First Edition of the MCC Workshop on Mobile Cloud Computing*, pp. 13–16. ACM, Helsinki, 2012.

Cai, Hongming, Boyi Xu, Lihong Jiang, and Athanasios V. Vasilakos. "IoT-based big data storage systems in cloud computing: Perspectives and challenges." *IEEE Internet of Things Journal* 4, no. 1 (2016): 75–87.

Chodorow, Kristina. MongoDB: *The Definitive Guide: Powerful and Scalable Data Storage*. O'Reilly Media, Inc., Sebastopol, CA, 2013.

Chung, Eric S., James C. Hoe, and Ken Mai. "CoRAM: An in-fabric memory architecture for FPGA-based computing." In *Proceedings of the 19th ACM/SIGDA International Symposium on Field Programmable Gate Arrays*, pp. 97–106. ACM, Monterey, CA, 2011.

Cooper, Joshua, and Anne James. "Challenges for database management in the Internet of Things." *IETE Technical Review* 26, no. 5 (2009): 320–329.

Dean, Jeffrey, and Sanjay Ghemawat. "MapReduce: Simplified data processing on large clusters." *Communications of the ACM* 51, no. 1 (2008): 107–113.

Dias, Lucas B., Maristela Holanda, Ruben Cruz Huacarpuma, and Rafael T. de Sousa Jr. "NoSQL database performance tuning for IoT data-Cassandra case study." In *IoTBDS*, pp. 277–284, Funchal, 2018.

Dong, Xin Luna, and Divesh Srivastava. "Big data integration." In *2013 IEEE 29th International Conference on Data Engineering (ICDE)*, pp. 1245–1248. IEEE, Brisbane, QLD, Australia, 2013.

Doukas, Charalampos, and Ilias Maglogiannis. "Bringing IoT and cloud computing towards pervasive healthcare." In *2012 Sixth International Conference on Innovative Mobile and Internet Services in Ubiquitous Computing*, pp. 922–926. IEEE, Palermo, 2012.

Govindan, Kannan, T. C. Edwin Cheng, Nishikant Mishra, and Nagesh Shukla. "Big data analytics and application for logistics and supply chain management." *Transportation Research Part E: Logistics and Transportation Review* 114 (2018): 343–349.

Gubbi, Jayavardhana, Rajkumar Buyya, Slaven Marusic, and Marimuthu Palaniswami. "Internet of Things (IoT): A vision, architectural elements, and future directions." *Future Generation Computer Systems* 29, no. 7 (2013): 1645–1660.

Gudivada, Venkat, Amy Apon, and Junhua Ding. "Data quality considerations for big data and machine learning: Going beyond data cleaning and transformations." *International Journal on Advances in Software* 10, no. 1 (2017): 1–20.

Hu, Han, Yonggang Wen, Tat-Seng Chua, and Xuelong Li. "Toward scalable systems for big data analytics: A technology tutorial." *IEEE Access* 2 (2014): 652–687.

James, Blessing E., and Prince Oghenekaro Asagba. "Hybrid database system for big data storage and management." *International Journal of Computer Science, Engineering and Applications (IJCSEA)* 7, no. 3/4 (2017): 15–27.

Kejariwal, Arun, Sanjeev Kulkarni, and Karthik Ramasamy. "Real time analytics: Algorithms and systems." *Proceedings of the VLDB Endowment* 8, no. 12 (2015): 2040–2041.

Kundhavai, K. R., and S. Sridevi. "IoT and big data – The current and future technologies: A review." *International Journal of Computer Science and Mobile Computing* 5, no. 1 (2016): 10–14.

LaValle, Steve, Eric Lesser, Rebecca Shockley, Michael S. Hopkins, and Nina Kruschwitz. "Big data, analytics and the path from insights to value." *MIT Sloan Management Review* 52, no. 2 (2011): 21–32.

Maletic, Jonathan I., and Andrian Marcus. "Data cleansing: Beyond integrity analysis." In D. K. Barbara and F. R. Donald (eds) *IQ*, pp. 200–209. MIT, New York, 2000.

Mikalef, Patrick, Ilias O. Pappas, John Krogstie, and Michail Giannakos. "Big data analytics capabilities: A systematic literature review and research agenda." *Information Systems and e-Business Management* 16, no. 3 (2018): 547–578.

Pangal, Gururaj, Michael B. Schmitz, Vinodh Ravindran, and Edward D. Mcclanahan. "Apparatus and method for data virtualization in a storage processing device." U.S. Patent 7,353,305, issued April 1, 2008.

Ranjan, Rajiv. "Streaming big data processing in datacenter clouds." *IEEE Cloud Computing* 1, no. 1 (2014): 78–83.

Rialti, Riccardo, Giacomo Marzi, Cristiano Ciappei, and Donatella Busso. "Big data and dynamic capabilities: A bibliometric analysis and systematic literature review." *Management Decision* 57, no. 8 (2019): 2052–2068.

Russom, Philip. "Big data analytics." *TDWI* (Best Practices Report, Fourth Quarter) 19, no. 4 (2011): 1–34.

Satyanarayanan, Mahadev. "The emergence of edge computing." *Computer* 50, no. 1 (2017): 30–39.

Shi, Weisong, and Schahram Dustdar. "The promise of edge computing." *Computer* 49, no. 5 (2016): 78–81.

Stergiou, Christos, Kostas E. Psannis, Byung-Gyu Kim, and Brij Gupta. "Secure integration of IoT and cloud computing." *Future Generation Computer Systems* 78 (2018): 964–975.

Weng, Li, Gagan Agrawal, Umit Catalyurek, T. Kur, Sivaramakrishnan Narayanan, and Joel Saltz. "An approach for automatic data virtualization." In *Proceedings of the 13th IEEE International Symposium on High Performance Distributed Computing*, pp. 24–33. IEEE, Honolulu, HI, 2004.

Chapter 10

Internet of Things (IoT) and Big Data: Data Management, Analytics, Visualization and Decision Making

K. Padmavathi, C. Deepa, and P. Prabhakaran

PSG College of Arts and Science

Contents

10.1　Introduction

Nowadays, numerous new digital technologies are changing the world through digital adoption. These technologies have caused digital disruption in the lifestyle of people. Internet of Things (IoT) has widened the innovation landscape in technology, elevating the digital experience to a new level across the globe. These innovations are ubiquitous, whether it is lifestyle products, business operations, or governance. Digital technologies are working together to make IoT a reality.

The rapid growth in the number of devices related to IoT coupled with the exponential increase in data utilization illustrate how advancements in big data are associated with that of IoT. The control of big data in a continuously increasing network gives a push to non-trivial concerns regarding data collection ability, analytics, data processing, and security. Despite numerous studies on big data, analytics, and IoT, the concurrence of these technologies creates several possibilities for the advancement of big data analytics and IoT systems. Technologies such as IoT, artificial intelligence, machine learning, big data, and sensor technology can be incorporated to increase the efficiency of data management and knowledge discovery of applications.

IoT can enable big data and their related technologies, which are used to improve the performance of IoT devices. IoT, big data, and related technologies can be used to improve functions and operations in various applications as well as in diverse sectors. Both have extended their capabilities to a wide range of areas. Big data analytical process uses IoT-generated data from different physical devices, which is used to help or improve decision making. The role of big data in IoT is to process a large amount of data based on real-time processing or batch processing and to store the results using storage technologies [7]. IoT-big data process can be implemented using the following steps (Figure 10.1):

1. IoT device generates considerable amounts of data from various physical IoT devices. This IoT-generated big data depends on factors such as volume, velocity, and variety.
2. The large amount of big data is stored in big data management system.

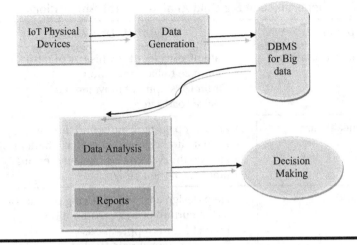

Figure 10.1   IoT-big data processing.

3. The stored IoT-big data is analyzed using big data analytic tools.
4. The reports are generated and used in decision-making processes.

10.1.1 The Importance of Data Analytics in IoT Applications

IoT with big data moves at the edge for ongoing decision making, such as recognizing crop designs in agricultural plants, detecting suspicious activities at ATMs, and anticipating driver behavior for an associated car. In IoT environment, big data technologies offer data storage, and big data analytical tools implement data analysis to make better decisions. IoT applications are important sources of big data and big data analytics. Table 10.1 shows the importance of big data analytics in IoT applications.

IoT with big data helps realize the future of a smart technological world. The convergence of IoT and big data can provide new opportunities in all applications [6].

10.2 Big Data Framework for IoT

Big data framework in IoT acts as the foundation for data analytics and visualization. The framework is divided into different layers with each layer performing a specific function, which is used for big data analytics. The big data framework can be used for the following tasks:

- Information extraction
- Massive datasets processing
- Environment optimization

Table 10.1 Importance of Big Data Analytics in IoT Applications

IoT Applications	Uses of Big Data Analytics
Smart transportation	• Minimize accidents by history of mishaps • Minimize traffic congestion • Optimize shipment movements • Ensure road safety
Smart healthcare	• Predict epidemics, cures and disease • Help insurance companies make better policies • Pick up the warning signs of any serious illnesses in their early stages
Smart grid	• Help design an optimal pricing plan according to the current power consumption • Predict future supply needs • Ensure an appropriate level of electricity supply
Smart inventory system	• Detect fraudulent cases • Strategically place an advertisement • Understand customer needs • Identify potential risks

- ■ Storage of large amounts of unstructured data
- ■ Unstructured data to structured data format
- ■ Data analysis

IoT-big data management performs a number of managerial activities, such as data collection, integration, storage, processing, analysis, and visualization, which are implemented using various models, architectures, and frameworks [2]. Various types of frameworks are used in IoT-big data management, data analysis, and visualization. In IoT-big data research, different big data frameworks, such as general framework, Cognitive-Oriented IoT Big-data (COIB) framework and machine-to-machine (M2M) framework, are implemented for performing various data management activities for data analytics and knowledge discovery. The big data management framework is used to securely manage the large amounts of data generated by IoT-enabled devices. In this section, we describe two specific frameworks used in IoT-big data activities [1].

10.2.1 The General Big Data Framework

The general big data framework architecture contains numerous mechanisms to handle ingestion, protection, process, and analysis of data that are massive and complex for file systems or database systems. The big data framework has multiple layers. Figure 10.2 shows the logical components that fit into the general big data framework for IoT.

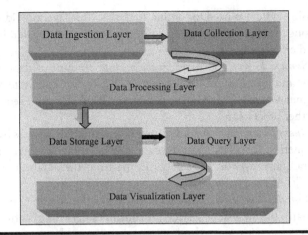

Figure 10.2 General big data framework.

i. *Data Ingestion Layer*: This layer extracts data from different data sources. The extracted data are categorized and prioritized. It takes data from various sources and puts it somewhere to access and process. Effective data ingestion process uses some parameters for categorizing, prioritizing, and validating data, such as
   - *Velocity*: Velocity of data is the speed at which data flows from different sources such as machines, networks, human interaction, and social media. The data flow can be massive or continuous.
   - *Size*: Data size refers the volume of data. Data is generated from different sources that may increase with time.
   - *Frequency*: Data can be processed by real-time processing or batch processing. In real-time processing, data is received through online sources at the same time. In batch processing, data is stored in batches, fixed at some time interval, and then moved further.
   - *Format*: Data can be in different formats such as structured, semi-structured, and unstructured.
ii. *Data Collector Layer*: This layer transports data from the ingestion layer to the rest of the data pipeline and transforms all data into a standard format. This layer performs the following functions:
   - *Data Transformation*: Transforms data into a standard format.
   - *Data Integration*: Integrates different types of data.
   - *Data Organization*: Organizes data using data pipeline.
   - *Data Refining*: Enhances, cleans, and improves raw data into useful data.
iii. *Data Processing Layer*: This layer provides a route for the data to various destinations. It focuses on specialized data pipeline systems for data processing. A batch processing system is used for offline analytics, and a real-time

processing system is used for online analytics. This layer provides some main functions for data processing, including parallel data transfer, import datasets, and efficient data analysis.

iv. *Data Storage Layer*: This layer stores a large amount of data and provides data for analysis. For example, Hadoop Distributed File System (HDFS) or Relational Database Management System (RDBMS) are used to store data for further processing.

v. *Data Query Layer*: This layer implements data analytic process by using interactive queries. This layer reads the data from a data storage layer. In rare cases, the data query layer accesses data directly from the data source. It provides the results of data analysis.

vi. *Data Visualization Layer*: This layer visualizes the outcome of the processes to humans, businesses, or services. It consumes data insights from the results of analytics applications. This layer saves, shares, and communicates insights for users. Moreover, it helps users generate questions by revealing the depth, range, and content of their data stores.

10.2.2 The Cognitive Adopted Framework (COIB) for IoT Big Data

IoT-big data management and knowledge discovery aims at COIB framework for real-time data management, along with implementation architecture [5]. COIB framework performs data collection, extraction, and analysis using real-time processing, which is used to enhance the decision-making process of applications. COIB framework performs data management activities through self-regulated monitoring. A COIB framework produces effective results in data management activities and knowledge discovery processes for large-scale industrial applications. Requirements for COIB framework implementation in industrial applications include:

■ High-speed internet connectivity
■ Efficiency of machines, that is, functional and operational

10.2.2.1 Functions of COIB Framework

COIB framework has four necessary functions for big data management activities, as shown in Figure 10.3.

i. *Data Aggregation*: COIB framework fuses large-scale data streams based on standard data semantics. In this framework, data aggregator checks data availability in periodical time interval from IoT data source. If data is available in IoT data source, data aggregator collects data and performs data integration. The aim of data integration is to achieve data with high consistency and completeness. Data quality is an important aspect to achieve desired results.

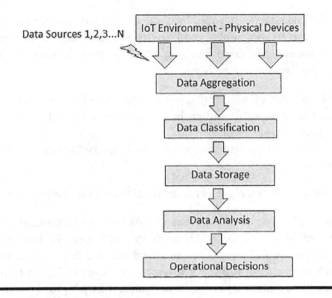

Figure 10.3   COIB framework.

ii. *Data Classification*: In COIB, the data classifier performs data classification which is used for formulating the fused data into multiple data groups based on properties. At the end of data classification process, each data group possesses homogeneous data.

iii. *Data Storage*: COIB framework uses HBase database management system for storing data. HBase Database Management Systems (DBMS) store IoT-big data from various data source using storage nodes controlled by a control node. Based on process or application, the entire IoT space is segmented into numerous segments. Each segment uses and implements individual HBase system for data storage.

iv. *Data Analysis*: Data analysis is required to turn IoT-big data into knowledge and actions, which are used to take decisions in real time. The COIB computational intelligence tool acts as a catalyst in data management activities, such as data analysis, knowledge discovery which produces the plans, and decisions for automation applications. COIB framework produces high-quality abstracts used to analyze IoT-big data and take operational decisions. The main aim of COIB framework is IoT-big data management and knowledge discovery.

10.3 IoT Big Data Management

Data can be defined as a systematic record of information for a particular activity or values. Different values of that information are represented together in a set. Data is a collection of facts and figures used for a specific purpose such as a survey or analysis [3]. When data is arranged in an organized form, it can be called information. Big data refers to complex and large datasets that need to be processed and analyzed to uncover valuable information that can benefit businesses and organizations. The term big data refers to:

■ A massive amount of data that grows exponentially with time.
■ Voluminous data that cannot be processed or analyzed using conventional data processing techniques.
■ Uses data mining, data storage, data analysis, data sharing, and data visualization concepts.

Based on their structure, big data can be classified into the following types:

i. *Structured*: Structured data refers to data that can be processed, stored, and retrieved in a fixed format. It refers to highly organized information that can be readily and seamlessly stored and accessed from a database by simple search engine algorithms. For instance, employee table in a company database will be structured as employee details, their job positions, their salaries, etc. in an organized manner.
ii. *Unstructured*: Unstructured data refers to data that lacks any specific form or structure. This makes it very difficult and time-consuming to process and analyze unstructured data. Email is an example of unstructured data.
iii. *Semi-structured*: Semi-structured data refers to data containing both the formats mentioned above, that is, structured and unstructured data. To be precise, it refers to data that, although has not been classified under a particular repository (database), contains vital information or tags that segregate individual elements within the data.

Data management refers to management of information and data for secure and structured access and storage. Data management embodies the creation of knowledge management policies, analysis, and architecture; database management system (DMS) integration; information or data security; and information supply, identification, segregation, and storage [4]. Data management encompasses various techniques that facilitate and ensure that data control and flow from creation to processing, utilization, and deletion is smooth. Data management is enforced through organized infrastructure of technological resources and governing framework that outline the executive processes used throughout the lifecycle of the data. This is a large area and is just an overarching term for an entire segment of IoT.

10.3.1 IoT Data Lifecycle

The lifecycle of data in an IoT system is illustrated in Figure 10.4. It starts from data production to aggregation, transfer, optional filtering, and preprocessing, and, finally, to storage and archiving. Querying and analysis are endpoints that initiate

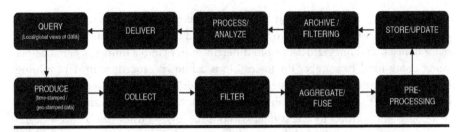

Figure 10.4   IoT data lifecycle and data management.

(request) and consume data production; however, data production can be set to be "pushed" to IoT-consuming services.

Querying: Data-intensive systems rely on querying as the core process to access and retrieve data. In the context of IoT, a query can be issued either to request real-time data to be collected for temporal monitoring or to retrieve a certain view of the data stored within the system. The first case is typical when a (mostly localized) real-time request for data is needed. The second case represents more globalized views of data and in-depth analysis of trends and patterns.

Production: Data production involves sensing and transfer of data by the "Things" within the IoT framework and reporting this data to interested parties periodically (as in a subscribe/notify model), pushing it up the network to aggregation points and subsequently to database servers, or sending it as a response triggered by queries that request the data from sensors and smart objects. Data is usually time-stamped and possibly geo-stamped, can be in the form of simple key-value pairs, or may contain rich audio/image/video content, with varying degrees of complexity.

Collection: The sensors and smart objects within the IoT may store data for a certain time interval or report it to governing components. Data may be collected at concentration points or gateways within the network where it is further filtered and processed, and possibly fused into compact forms for efficient transmission. Wireless communication technologies such as Zigbee, Wi-Fi, and cellular are used by objects to send data to collection points.

Aggregation/Fusion: Transmitting raw data out of the network in real-time is often prohibitively expensive given the increasing data streaming rates and the limited bandwidth. Aggregation and fusion techniques deploy summarization and merging operations in real-time to compress the volume of data to be stored and transmitted.

Delivery: As data is filtered, aggregated, and possibly processed either at the concentration points or at the autonomous virtual units within the IoT, the results of these processes may need to be sent further up the system, either as final responses or for storage and in-depth analysis. Wired or wireless broadband communications may then be used to transfer data to permanent data stores.

Preprocessing: IoT data possibly come from different sources with varying formats and structures. Data may need to be preprocessed to handle missing data, remove redundancies, and integrate data from different sources into a unified schema before being committed to storage. Preprocessing is a known procedure in data mining called data cleaning. Schema integration does not imply brute-force fitting of all the data into a fixed relational (tables) schema, but rather a more abstract definition of a consistent method to access data without having to customize access for each source's data format(s). Probabilities at different levels in the schema may be added at this phase to IoT data items to handle uncertainty that may be present in data, or to deal with the lack of trust that may exist in data sources.

Storage/Update and Archiving: This phase handles the efficient storage and organization of data, as well as the continuous update of data with new information as and when it becomes available. Archiving refers to the offline long-term storage of data that is not immediately needed for the system's ongoing operations. At the core of centralized storage is the deployment of storage structures that adapt to the various data types and the frequency of data capture. RDBMSs are a popular choice involving the organization of data into a table schema with predefined interrelationships and metadata for efficient retrieval at later stages.

NoSQL key-value stores are gaining popularity as storage technologies for their support of big data storage without relying on relational schema or strong consistency requirements typical of relational database systems. Storage can also be decentralized for autonomous IoT systems, where data is retained at the objects that generate it and is not sent up the system. However, due to limited capabilities of such objects, storage capacity remains limited in comparison to the centralized storage model.

Processing/Analysis: This phase involves the ongoing retrieval and analysis operations performed and stored and archived data to gain insights into historical data and predict future trends, or to detect data defects that may trigger further investigation or action. Task-specific preprocessing may be needed to filter and clean data before any meaningful operations can occur. When an IoT subsystem is autonomous and does not require permanent storage of its data, but rather retains the processing and storage in the network, in-network processing may be performed in response to real-time or localized queries.

Looking back at Figure 10.4, the flow of data may take one of three paths: a path for autonomous systems within the IoT that proceeds from query to production to in-network processing, and then delivery, a path that starts from production and proceeds to collection and filtering/aggregation/fusion and ends with data delivery to initiating (possibly global or near real-time) queries, and finally a path that further extends production to aggregation and includes preprocessing, permanent data storage and archival, and in-depth processing and analysis. In the next section, the need for data management solutions that surpass the current capabilities of traditional data management is highlighted in light of the previously outlined lifecycle [8,9].

10.3.2 IoT Data Management Versus Traditional Database Management Systems

Based on the IoT data lifecycle discussed earlier, IoT data management system is divided into an online, real-time frontend that interacts directly with the interconnected IoT objects and sensors, and associate offline backend that handles the mass storage and in-depth analysis of IoT information. The data management frontend is communication-intensive, involving the propagation of query requests and results to and from sensors and sensible objects. The backend is storage-intensive, involving the mass storage of created data for later processes, as well as analysis and additional in-depth queries.

Although the storage elements reside on the backend, they interact with the frontend on a frequent basis through continuous updates, and are referred to as online. The autonomous edges in the lifecycle can be considered more communication-intensive than storage-intensive as they provide real-time data to certain queries.

This envisioned data management architecture is considerably different from the existing DBMS, which are mainly storage-centric. In traditional database systems, the bulk of data is collected from predefined and finite sources, and then stored in scalar form according to strict normalization rules in relations. Queries are used to retrieve specific "summary" views of the system or update specific items within the database. New information/data is inserted into the database when required via insertion queries. Query operations are usually local, with execution costs bound to processing and intermediate storage.

Transaction management methods guarantee the ACID properties to enforce overall data integrity. Even if the database is distributed over multiple sites, query processing and distributed transaction management are enforced. The execution of distributed queries is based on the transparency principle, which dictates that the database is viewed logically as one centralized unit, and the ACID properties are guaranteed via the two-phase commit protocol.

In IoT systems, the picture is dramatically different, with a massive and growing number of data sources: sensors, RFIDs, embedded systems, and mobile devices. Contrary to occasional updates and queries submitted to traditional DBMSs, data streams constantly from a multitude of "Things" to IoT data stores, and queries are more frequent with more versatile needs.

Hierarchical data reporting and aggregation may be needed for scalability guarantees as well as to enable more prompt processing functionality. The strict relational database schema and the relational normalization practice may be relaxed in favor of more unstructured and flexible forms that adapt to diverse data types and sophisticated queries. Although distributed DBMSs optimize queries based on communication considerations, optimizers base their decisions on fixed and well-defined schemas. This may not be the case in IoT where new data sources and streaming, localized data create a highly dynamic environment for query optimizers. Striving to guarantee the transparency requirements imposed in distributed DBMSs on IoT data management systems is challenging, if not impossible. Furthermore, transparency may not even be required in IoT because innovative applications and services may require location and context awareness. Although maintaining ACID properties in bounded IoT spaces (subsystems) while executing transactions can be managed, challenges exist for more globalized space. However, mobile data sources and how their generated data can be incorporated into the already established data space is a novel challenge that is yet to be addressed by IoT data management systems [5,9].

10.3.3 Common Problems in IoT Data Management

Working with IoT, information processing requires a shorter time span than with information collected from humans, with the following issues:

Scalability and Agility: The sheer size of IoT data traffic and its immediacy makes this data management issue most pressing.

Security: Security is a significant challenge for organizations planning and implementing IoT solutions. According to estimates, through 2022, half of all security budgets for IoT will go to fault remediation. Preventing unauthorized access has become forefront.

10.3.4 Applications of Database Management

Various applications are used in IoT database management [9]. Applications such as HBase, Cassandra, CouchDB, DynamoDB, and MongoDB databases used by IoT devices, that store large amounts of data and access them in a random manner, is discussed below.

i. *HBase*: HBase is a distributed column-oriented database built on top of the Hadoop File System (HDFS). It is open-source and horizontally scalable. HBase is a data model that provides quick random access to huge amounts of structured data. It leverages the fault tolerance provided by the HDFS. It is a part of the Hadoop ecosystem. It provides random real-time read/write access to data in the HDFS. Data is stored in HDFS either directly or through HBase. Data consumer reads/accesses the data in HDFS by randomly using HBase. HBase is laid on top of the HDFS and provides read and write access. HBase Databases are used in devices with COIB frameworks because they help in scalability and consistency in the data that is needed. Table 10.2 lists the differences between HBase and RDBMS.

   Features of HBase
   - *Scalability*: It supports scalability in both linear and modular form.
   - *Sharding*: It supports automatic sharding of tables, and is also configurable.
   - *Distributed Storage*: It supports distributed storage like HDFS.

Table 10.2   Differences between HBase and RDBMS

HBase	RDBMS
Is schema-less and doesn't have the concept of fixed columns schema	Is governed by its schema, which describes the entire table structure
Built for wide tables, and is horizontally scalable	Thin and built for small tables, and is hard to scale
No transactions	Transactional
Has de-normalized data	Has normalized data
Good for both semi-structured and structured data	Good for structured data

- *Consistency*: It supports consistent read and write operations.
- *Failover Support*: It supports automatic failover.
- *API Support*: It supports Java APIs so clients can access it easily.
- *MapReduce Support*: It supports MapReduce for parallel processing of large data volumes.
- *Back Up Support*: It supports back up of Hadoop MapReduce jobs in HBase tables.
- *Real-Time Processing*: It supports both block cache and Bloom filters. So, real-time query processing is easy.

ii. *Apache Cassandra*: The Apache Cassandra is a powerful open-source distributed database system that works extremely well to handle huge volumes of records spread across multiple commodity servers. It can be easily scaled to meet sudden increase in demand by deploying multinode Cassandra clusters, meets high availability requirements, and there is no single point of failure. It is one of the most efficient NoSQL databases available today. Table 10.3 lists the differences between Cassandra and RDBMS.

Features of Cassandra
- Elastic scalability
- Always on architecture
- Fast linear-scale performance
- Flexible data storage
- Easy data distribution
- Transaction support
- Fast writes

iii. *CouchDB*: CouchDB is an open-source NoSQL database based on common standards to facilitate web accessibility and compatibility with a variety of devices. NoSQL databases are useful for very large sets of distributed data,

Table 10.3   Differences between Cassandra and RDBMS

Cassandra	RDBMS
Used to deal with unstructured data	Used to deal with structured data
Has a flexible schema	Has a fixed schema
A table is a list of nested key-value pairs	A table is an array of arrays
Keyspace is the outermost container comprising data corresponding to an application	Database is the outermost container comprising data corresponding to an application
Tables or column are the entities of a keyspace	Tables are the entities of a database
Row is a unit of replication	Row is an individual record
Column is a unit of storage	Column represents the attributes of a relation
Relationships are represented using collections	There is a concept of foreign keys, joins, etc.

especially for large amounts of unstructured data in various formats, a characteristic of big data. Data in CouchDB is stored in a format called JavaScript object notification (JSON), and is organized as key-value pairs. The key is a unique data identifier and the value is the data itself, acting as a pointer to the data's location. All standard database functions are performed by JavaScript. Table 10.4 lists the differences between CouchDB and RDBMS.

Features of CouchDB
- Easy cross-server replication through instances.
- Support for conflict resolution and master set-up.
- Quick indexing and search and retrieval.
- Documents are accessed through browsers, and indices can be queried through HTTP.
- Index, combine, and transform operations are performed with JavaScript.
- Advanced MapReduce.

Table 10.4   Differences between CouchDB and RDBMS

CouchDB	RDBMS
Data is stored in documents	Data is stored in tables
Replication is easy	Replication is difficult

iv. *DynamoDB*: DynamoDB uses the NoSQL model, that is, it is a non-relational database system. DynamoDB is a hosted NoSQL database offered by Amazon Web Services (AWS). It offers *reliable performance* even as it scales, a *managed experience*, so you won't be SSH-ing into servers to upgrade the crypto libraries and *a small, simple API*, allowing for simple key-value access along with more advanced query patterns. Table 10.5 lists the differences between DynamoDB and RDBMS.

Features of Dynamo
- DynamoDB spreads data and requests traffic to multiple servers to provide better throughput and storage.
- Data is stored on a solid state drive and is replicated over multiple availability zones to provide high availability and fault tolerance.
- Allows you to decide the expiry time of items by allowing you to set a time-to-live parameter. The item will be deleted after this time expires, which makes storage management more efficient.
- We only have to pay for throughput, making it cost-effective.

v. *MongoDB*: MongoDB is an open-source document database that provides high performance, high availability, and automatic scaling. MongoDB is used in all modern applications that require big data, fast features development, and flexible deployment. Table 10.6 describes the difference between MongoDB and RDBMS.

Table 10.5 Differences between DynamoDB and RDBMS

DynamoDB	RDBMS(SQL)
Uses HTTP/HTTPS requests and API operations	The SQL database system uses determined connection and SQL commands
Uses the primary key, and a schema is not required to be defined in advance. Uses various data sources	Fundamental structure is a table, and its schema must be defined in advance before any operation
Only the primary key is available for querying. For more flexibility in querying data, one must use secondary indexes	All table information is accessible, and we can query exactly all data. SQL is rich in query processing
Information is stored as items in a table, and the item structure can vary as it is schema-less	Information is stored in rows of tables

Table 10.6 Difference between MongoDB and RDBMS

MongoDB (NoSQL)	RDBMS (SQL)
Non-relational and document-oriented database	Relational database
Coding starts without worrying about tables. Objects can be modified later at a low development cost	Need to design tables, data structure, and relations before coding
Provides JavaScript client for querying	Does not provide JavaScript client for querying
Collection-based and key-value pair	Table-based
Does not support foreign key, joins, and triggers	Supports foreign key, joins, and triggers
Provides only one level of locking	Provides very fine granularity of locking
Contains dynamic schema	Contains a predefined schema

Features of MongoDB
- Supports ad hoc queries.
- Supports map reduce and aggregation tools.
- Uses JavaScript instead of Procedures.
- It is a schema-less database written in C++.
- Provides high performance.
- Stores files of any size easily without complicating your stack.

10.4 IoT Data Analytical Technologies

Data analytics (DA) is defined as a process used to observe big and small datasets with varying data properties to extract meaningful conclusions and actionable insights. These conclusions are usually in the form of trends, patterns, and statistics that help business organizations in proactively using the data to implement effective decision-making processes.

10.4.1 Approaches and Methods for Data Analytics in IoT

The numbered items are approaches and the underlying methods are highlighted beneath each.

    i. *Applied Statistics*: In this approach, data is collected and analyzed through sampling to generalize metrics about a population. It uses the following different methods for data analysis:

Sigma Analysis: This is a very simple but powerful way to use statistics for detecting outliers in real time. When the average value of some measurement is characterized, it's often helpful to understand the variance as well. Knowing the variances helps to look at observations and measurements in real time to determine how many standard deviations (sigmas) these observations are away from the mean.

Statistical Hypothesis Testing: This is a method for testing whether an observation of a designed random variable is statistically significant, or unlikely to have occurred by chance. This is a powerful way to determine if a measured value is likely to be meaningful for making a business decision.

Analysis of Variance: This method determines whether differences exist between means for different groups. It is similar to statistical hypothesis testing application, but is useful to compare across multiple groups for statistical significance.

Lag Variogram: This method determines the periodicity of a process, which is useful in characterizing processes of unknown period or duration.

ii. *Probability Theory*: This approach involves the analysis of random processes related to a population to characterize likely or expected observations. It uses the following methods for data analysis:

Markov Chain Modeling: This method characterizes transition states in a process where the future state depends only on the current state, and is powerful when expected transitions involve a finite number of states.

Decision Tree Modeling: This structure is very popular for visualizing downstream probabilities. It uses a branching graph structure to model all possible consequences of a process with associated probabilities for each branch. It is useful for characterizing downstream probabilities at the leaves of the tree.

iii. *Unsupervised Machine Learning*: This approach includes algorithms that find hidden patterns or structures in large datasets using clustering, classification, and other statistically "heavy" methods.

Clustering: This method discovers patterns in data where elements in each cluster are most similar to one another than any of the elements in other clusters.

Data Mining: This is an automated process for identifying anomalies in data or hidden rules in data based purely on statistics. Typically, there is little reliance on theory or subject matter expertise in data mining approaches. Data mining can be useful to develop hypotheses, but may be dangerous as a holistic solution.

Random Forest Modeling: This method is a variant of decision tree optimization wherein all possible trees are constructed to create specific classes in data. The optimal tree, which is the best predictor of classes, is the model output.

iv. *Supervised Machine Learning*: This approach leverages algorithms that optimize the decision-making and reasoning skills of human beings by programmatically capturing hidden preferences and rules.

Classification: This method identifies which class an element belongs to given a training set of classes based on attributes of that element and comparison to other elements in each class.

Predictive Coding: This method actively trains an algorithm regarding which attributes are most important about an event or data element based on a human interaction determining which elements from random subsets are the most meaningful.

Reinforced Learning: This is a hybrid machine learning method where a training set is identified by an unsupervised algorithm. The training set is supervised by a predictive coding process where a human reinforces or discourages learning and refinement.

v. *Natural Language Processing (NLP)*: The NLP approach adds structure, computation, and quantities to traditional language to create analytic opportunity.

Term Frequency/Document Frequency Matrix: This method characterizes how anomalous a document is based on the ratios of words used in that document to the ratios of words used in all documents throughout a corpus.

Sentiment Analysis: This includes methods that determine the sentiment of written text based on the words used and the structure of the speech.

Topic Tagging: This method includes algorithms that determine the topic of a document based on the associations of words used and comparisons to "word bags" of interest.

vi. *Network Analysis*: This approach analyzes the structure of a network graph to determine the relationships between nodes and edges.

Network Descriptive Statistics: This method calculates descriptive measures to characterize network position and examine the change and evolution of the position over time.

vii. *Geospatial Statistics*: This approach provides analysis of data that has geographical or spatial relevance.

Kernel Density: This method graphically measures the point density of multiple observations in multiple dimensions. Kernel density can be extended to linear density and other creative variants; however, it is ultimately useful for "hot spot" characterization in two and three dimensions.

Local Outlier Factor: This method determines how likely an observation is given the proximity to its nearest neighbors, and is a powerful method to look for outlier observations in dense data that is very regularly measured. Although nearest neighbors can be considered spatially, they can also be extended to temporal proximity, scalar proximity, etc.

10.4.2 IoT Data Analytics Tools

IoT solutions find their use-cases across various industries – logistics, warehouse monitoring, manufacturing, quality management, facility management, vehicles in transit, etc. The volume of IoT sensor data is growing each day along with the need to analyze and gather insights from them [10,11]. As an organization, one needs a robust IoT analytics solution to analyze both historical and real-time data. There are many existing tools to analyze our data. Some of them are discussed below:

i. *Microsoft Azure Stream Analytics*: Microsoft's azure stream analytics can be easily integrated with azure IoT hub and azure IoT suite to perform real-time analytics on IoT sensor data. Azure stream analytics helps companies deploy AI-powered real-time analytics and unlock the full value from the data. It is also easy to create dashboards with power business intelligence (BI) and visualize the data and to view actionable insights.

It is a cloud computing service created by Microsoft for building, testing, deploying, and managing applications and services through Microsoft-managed data centers. It provides Software as a Service (SaaS), Platform as a Service, and Infrastructure as a Service and supports many different programming languages, tools, and frameworks, including both Microsoft-specific and third-party software and systems.

ii. *AWS IoT Analytics*: AWS IoT Analytics automates the most difficult tasks associated with the analysis of IoT data and is a fully managed service, which makes it easy to run complicated DA algorithms. It is one of the easiest IoT analytics platforms to run analytics on the edge and get accurate insights. With AWS IoT Analytics, only relevant data from the sensor are stored, the data is enriched with device-specific metadata such as device type and locations. AWS IoT Analytics is fully managed and can support up to petabytes of IoT data. Thus, IoT applications are easily managed, without worrying about the hardware and infrastructure. Using AWS IoT Analytics, users can easily run queries on IoT data, run time analytics, optimize data storage, and analyze using machine learning.

AWS IoT Analytics automates the steps required to analyze data from IoT devices. It filters, transforms, and enriches IoT data before storing it in a time-series data store for analysis. There are services to collect only the data that is needed from the devices, apply mathematical transforms to process the data, and enrich the data with device-specific metadata such as device type and location before storing it. Then, extracted data is analyzed by running queries using the built-in SQL query engine, or more complex analytics and machine learning inference. AWS IoT Analytics enables advanced data exploration through integration with Jupyter Notebooks. Additionally, it enables data visualization through integration with Amazon QuickSight.

Traditional analytics and BI tools are designed to process structured data. IoT data often comes from devices that record noisy processes (such as temperature, motion, or sound). Therefore, the data from these devices can have significant gaps, corrupt messages, and false readings that must be cleaned up before analysis. Further, IoT data is often only meaningful in the context of other data from external sources. AWS IoT Analytics enables us to address these issues and collect large amounts of device data, process messages, and store them. It also enables extracting data using queries and running sophisticated analytics on it. AWS IoT Analytics includes prebuilt models for common IoT use-cases so that it can answer questions, such as which devices are about to fail or which customers are at risk of abandoning their wearable devices.

iii. *SAP Analytics Cloud*: SAP Analytics Cloud has options to integrate IoT data to its analytics solution and analyze and visualize the data better. SAP Analytics cloud is enhanced with the power of predictive analytics and machine learning technology. SAP also has Streaming Lite module, which is a to-the-edge component designed to remotely deploy streaming projects. Streaming Lite is relevant for projects deployed on remote gateway devices – it is not required as part of a standard smart data streaming installations.

SAP Analytics Cloud (or SAP Cloud for Analytics) is a SaaS BI platform designed by SAP. Analytics Cloud is developed specifically with the intent of providing all analytics capabilities to all users in a single product. In addition to business planning, the other key components are BI (for reporting, dashboarding, data discovery, and visualization), predictive analytics, and governance, risk, and compliance.

Built natively on SAP HANA Cloud Platform (HCP), SAP Analytics Cloud allows data analysts and business decision makers to visualize, plan, and predict all from one secure, cloud-based environment. SAP claims this differs from other BI platforms, which often require data to be integrated from various sources and users to jump between different applications when performing tasks, such as creating reports. With all the data sources and analytics functions in one product, Analytics Cloud users can work more efficiently, according to SAP. The key functions are accessed from the same user interface that is designed for ease-of-use for business users.

iv. *IBM Watson IoT Platform*: Analytics is a part of IBM Watson's IoT platform. With this solution, users can easily analyze and visualize the IoT data and perform complicated analytics on the data from various IoT devices. IBM uses cognitive computing to extract valuable insights from structured and unstructured data and help users understand the data better. IBM Watson provides NLP, machine learning, and image and text analytics to enrich IoT apps. Watson IoT Platform Service is an IoT device message broker for device registration, IoT data management, and IoT device management. It also provides secure communication to and from devices by using MQTT and TLS.

Watson IoT Platform Service is built on the following key areas:

- *Connection Management*: Connect and control IoT devices.
- *Data Management*: Use device twins to normalize, transform, and review device data for use with the Watson IoT Platform components and other services.
- *Risk Management*: Configure secure connectivity and architecture with access control for users and applications.

v. *Cisco Data Analytics*: With Cisco Data analytics it's easy to run analytics applications in the entire network from the cloud to the fog. Cisco provides infrastructure and tools for businesses to perform analytics on the collected IoT data. Cisco IOx APIs helps companies to make the data available to internal applications to improve operational efficiency. Cisco IoT analytics infrastructure offers infrastructure for real-time analytics, cloud to fog, enterprise analytics integration, and analytics for security.

vi. *Oracle Stream Analytics and Oracle Edge Analytics*: Oracle's IoT Analytics solution is a combination of both Oracle Stream Analytics and Oracle Edge Analytics. Oracle's solutions help us develop analytics application that can read and analyze data from various sensors and devices and provide valuable insights. Both Stream Analytics and Edge Analytics can process and analyze huge volumes of streaming data collected from sensors and devices.

Oracle Stream Analytics is a new tool provided as a part of Oracle Event Processing technology platform. The Oracle Stream Analytics caters to the business needs of the users. This tool enables users to proactively identify and act on emerging streaming real-time threats and opportunities in their enterprise, as well as improve the operational efficiencies of their business. Oracle Stream Analytics helps in enhancing functional and operational efficiencies of businesses with actionable insight from real-time data by only processing and storing relevant data. Users can build applications and monitor them against the real-time streaming data within no time and with no complexity or knowledge of the underlying technologies using Oracle Stream Analytics.

10.5 Big Data Visualization Tools for IoT

Data visualization is a visual depiction of information. The visualization of data is an important part of an IoT application that is used to extract meaningful information from big data. Big data visualization brings new challenges in data processing because of the speed, size, and diversity of data. The variety of data brings challenges to visualization because of semi-structured and unstructured data. Big data visualization tools are used to analyze and evaluate data in real time. Data visualization creates and provides visual representations of large datasets [11]. The best visualization tools have the following properties:

- Easy to use
- Handle huge sets of data in a single visualization
- Output array must be in different charts, graph, and map types
- Cost

In this section, we discuss some important visualization tools in IoT-big data visualization.

i. *Tableau*: Tableau is one of the popular BI tools for data visualization. By using Tableau, users can create and distribute an interactive and shareable dashboard, which represents the data in the form of graphs and charts. Tableau provides a variety of visualization capabilities with different features in data visualization, which is used to enable data discovery in a smart manner. Tableau can access files from different data sources to process data. Tableau provides facility to connect to a variety of data sources with many systematic types, such as data systems organized in file formats (CSV, JSON, XML, MS Excel, etc.), relational and non-relational data systems (PostgreSQL, MySQL, SQL Server, MongoDB, etc.), cloud systems (AWS, Oracle Cloud, Google BigQuery, Microsoft Azure). It has different output options including multiple chart formats, mapping capability, etc.

Special Features of Tableau: All kinds of industries and data environments can get solutions using Tableau. Tableau has some unique features that are used to enable and handle data in an efficient manner. Its special features includes:

– *Data Blending*: Tableau allows you to blend different relational, semi-structured, and raw data sources in real time, without expensive up-front integration costs. The users don't need to know the details of how data is stored.

– *Real-Time Collaboration*: Tableau can filter, sort, and discuss data in real time which makes a valuable investment for commercial and non-commercial organizations.

– *Report Sharing*: Tableau shares the reports using a number of ways, for example, by publishing report to a Tableau server; via email Tableau Reader capability; by publishing Tableau workbook openly and giving access to anyone who has a link.

– *Visual Discovery*: Tableau explores and analyzes the data by using visual tools like colors, trend lines, charts, and graphs.

– *Centralized Data*: Tableau server provides a centralized location to manage all of the organization's published data sources. You can delete, change permissions, add tags, and manage schedules in one convenient location.

These features enable great flexibility and remove many restrictions. Tableau offers three distinct options: Tableau desktop, Tableau online, and Tableau server. The Tableau desktop is intended for individual user and enterprise use. Personal use implies that it is for an individual developer and supports six data sources. Enterprise use means that it is for business requirements and allows up to 44 data sources. Tableau Online is a cloud-based platform with a web interface. Tableau online may be used for free with its public option, but when the reports are hosted on a public server, all reports are shared publicly. Tableau Server is a full-fledged business tool for companies that operate their own servers and want to have complete control over data flows and full security of on-premise hosting.

Tableau is easy to apprehend as a working tool and its learning curve is pretty gentle. It strives to provide all of its powers to any kind of users. It also provides the ability to control the outcome through additional filtering with custom parameters. All data is communicated in a clear, attractive, and interactive manner. Tableau offers an insightful look at the data and allows compressing complex decision-making process efficiently. It is a powerful developer tools which is used to import data, build attractive visualization, and share and publish form.

Benefits of Tableau
- Attractive user interface.
- Supports mobile platforms.
- Powerful community collaboration.
- Reliable customer support.
- Hundreds of data import options.
- Mapping capability.
- Free public version available.
- Lots of video tutorials to walk you through how to use Tableau.
- Leadership in community building efforts (various training videos, blogs, forums, social network engagement).

Drawbacks of Tableau
- Non-free versions are expensive.
- Public version doesn't allow you to keep data analyses private.

ii. *Power BI*: Power BI is an important data visualization and BI tool that collects data from different data sources and converts it into interactive dashboards and BI reports. Power BI provides several software, connector, and services to the user by using different platforms. For example, Power BI desktop is used to create reports, Power BI service based on SaaS is used to publish the reports, and mobile Power BI app is used to view the report. Power BI provides a simple web-based interface with plenty useful features varying from customizable visualization to certainly limited controls of data sources. These services can be used by users to consume data and build BI reports.

Power BI implements data visualization using the following components (Figure 10.5):
- *Desktop*: creates reports and data visualizations by using dataset.
- *Gateway*: Power BI gateway keeps data by connecting to data sources without the need to move the data. It also allows to query large datasets.
- *Mobile Apps*: Power BI mobile app is used to connect data from anywhere. Power BI apps are supported by Windows, iOS, and Android platform.
- *Service*: Power BI service is a cloud service used to publish reports and data visualizations.

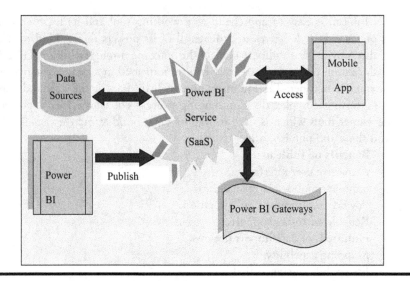

Figure 10.5 Components of Power BI.

Power BI supports a large range of data sources. It allows accessing and connecting to different flat files, SQL database, and webbing platforms such as Facebook, Google Analytics, and Salesforce objects. It also has ODBC connection that connects other ODBC data sources. The data sources used in Power BI are Flat Files, SQL Database, OData Feed, Blank Query, Azure Cloud platform, Online Services, and Blank Query.

Special Features of Power BI

– Power BI has a free basic version.
– It supports several ways to incorporate or import data like streaming data, cloud services, and excel spreadsheets.
– It has interactive dashboards with real-time processing.
– It integrates simple API with applications.
– It has several ways to share reports and dashboards.
– It support multiplatform like web, Desktop, and Mobile.

iii. *QlikView*: QlikView is a leading and powerful tool for visualizing data. It can read data from different data sources like files and relational databases. During data analysis, it always maintains the relationship between the data and this relationship can be seen visually using colors. It searches data from data sources by direct and indirect search.

Special Features of QlikView

– *Data Association*: QlikView has an ability to manipulate data associations automatically. It can recognize the relationships between various data items in a set without any preconfiguration by the user. So, users need not preconfigure the relationship between different data entities. The automation process increases the speed of the process in dashboard development.

- *Speed*: Qlikview handles data input for several users in the RAM of the server. This allows faster queries and quicker data exploration and amelioration of user experience with aggregations.
- *Aggregation*: There is no need to store precalculated aggregate values. It the data is held in memory, calculations are done automatically on the fly.
- *Data Compression*: Data can be compressed to 10% of its original size.
- *Visual Relationships*: The relationship between data is shown by colors, not in arrow or lines.
- *Direct and Indirect searches*: It extracts and gives results based on some related data because of the data association. User can also search for a value directly.

Benefits of Qlikview
- Attractive user interface
- Fast rendering of both graphs and tables
- Ability to mail reports in the convenient format of PDF
- Tools for building filters, charts, and tables
- Allows community collaboration

Drawbacks of Qlikview
- No ability to union bookmark results together
- No ability for non-technical staff to self-service
- Complications using QlikView as a enterprise tool

iv. *Klipfolio*: Klipfolio is a genuinely insightful tool for data visualization that enables data and process data in real-time solutions. Klipfolio supports and enables connectivity to a variety of data sources, both online and offline. The online sources integrate a range of cloud-hosted storages, including Google Sheets, Relational DBs, and other services that provide data in all kinds of forms. Klipfolio supports a different variety of offline services like MS Excel, CSV, XML, JSON, etc. All these data sources are used for integrating various metrics.

Klipfolio applies to facilitating the discovery of dashboards using diverse technological platforms, ranging from smartphones and tablets, to desktop computers and smart TVs. Klipfolio represents a powerful data dashboard building platform that enables access to the real-world lively data sources. It is best used for live monitoring and control over continuous data flows when their dynamics are of great importance and may require urgent decisions.

Klipfolio includes plain tables, bar charts, pie charts, line and area charts, a combination of those charts, as well as scatter plots. Klipfolio dashboards feature an extensive collaboration framework for sharing information with other users based on permissions, enabling notification, and distribution via email. User can implement all computations using different functions and formulas in worksheets. They can also create sheets with any type of visualization.

Special Features of Klipfolio
- Integration of multiple data sources
- Unlimited connection
- Management of access rights and restrictions for important information
- Mobile accessibility (iOS, Android, BlackBerry, Windows)
- Flexible REST connector for setting up custom data sources
- Secure connection to SQL databases
- Support for Excel, CSV, JSON, XML file formats
- Easy to use threshold indicators

Benefits of Klipfolio
- Flexibility of calculations and IT connectivity
- Attractive and smooth interface
- Continuous development
- Supports API and different data formats
- Real-time data analysis

Drawbacks of Klipfolio
- No options for ad hoc analysis and reporting
- No services for predictive analysis

v. *Geckoboard*: Geckoboard supports integration to a variety of services which makes it easy to connect with the demanded data sources. Data visualization is accomplished by dragging the desired data onto the area of the report, dropping it there, and then dragging/dropping data that needs to be visualized. It has a rich library which is used to prepare integrations with Facebook, twitter, Salesforce APIs. User can instantly visualize social media engagements or business data. It also provides an ability to develop a custom integration with your own data sources in two ways: Pull or Push. Pull implies that the particular widget makes a request for the data every N seconds from where it extracts the data. Push implies that user can feed the widget with data manually by sending an HTTP request to the special widget URL. Geckoboard gives the standard widget templates, such as line charts or histogram. User can also change the stylesheet for widgets, change the color schema, add two or more dashboards, or add multiple users.

Benefits of Geckoboard
- Integration with various services such as Google Analytics, Zendesk, Bitium, etc.
- An attractive, user-friendly interface

- Data transformation support
- Collaboration facilities
- Customization of visualizations
- Fused responsiveness
- Customer support and documentation are very helpful

Drawbacks of Geckoboard

- Lack of functionality
- Limited widgets library

vi. *Google Data Studio*: Google Data Studio gives visualization results based on web, which uses Google data sources for visualization. It provides easy access to data through data connectors. With Data Studio, users can allow others to view and edit the dashboard you are working on in the same way as Google Docs. It is quick to connect to data and figure out how the interface works.

User can create reports and dashboards as it is straightforward by using the following three steps:

1. pick the type of a visual,
2. drag and drop it into the report area positioning it in the desired location and
3. set up the metrics for visualization.

User can send invitations to access a report or a folder of reports via either email, or a shareable link, and choose to either grant permission to only view or allow editing.

Benefits of Google Data Studio

- Connectors to Google Data Sources
- Transformation tools for working with raw data
- Decent library of built-in visual types
- Great teamwork capabilities
- Great collaboration capabilities

Drawbacks of Google Data Studio

- Interactivity is not supported
- No functionality for blending data

10.6 Big Data as Source for IoT Decision Making

Not only big data and IoT depend on each other, as they also help each other, they hugely impact each other. As IoT grows, there will be more demand on businesses regarding big data capabilities. For example, as IoT-generated data is increasing at a rapid rate, conventional data storage technology is already being pushed to its limits. As a result, more advanced and innovative storage solutions are required to handle these growing workloads, resulting in updating the infrastructure of an organization's big data storage. Similarly, IoT-big data combined applications accelerate the scope of research in both the fields. Therefore, IoT and big data technologies carry interdependency and need to take decisions in various environments.

10.6.1 How Are IoT and Big Data Together Beneficial for Companies?

IoT will enable big data, big data needs analytics, and, in turn, analytics will improve processes for more devices. IoT and big data can be used to improve various functions and operations in diverse sectors [12,13]. Both have extended their capabilities to a wide range of areas. IoT big DA can be useful for a variety of IoT data to:

- Reveal trends
- Find unseen patterns
- Find hidden correlations
- Reveal new information

Hence, companies can benefit from analyzing large amounts of IoT big data and managing them to identify how they affect businesses. Consequently, it assists businesses and other organizations to achieve an improved understanding of data, and thus, making efficient and well-informed decisions. Every segment of businesses and industries can achieve some benefits by IoT-big data implementation.

10.6.2 Benefits of IoT and Big Data for Companies in Different Sectors

IoT and big data play a major role in the growth of companies in various sectors in today's world.

 i. Helps to increase the return on investment (ROI) for businesses

   IoT and big DA are transforming how businesses are adding value by extracting maximum information from data to get better business insights. With increased demand for data storage, companies prefer big data cloud storage which ultimately lowers the implementation cost for them.

 ii. Reshapes the future e-health system

   The combined features of IoT and big data can reshape the next generation of e-healthcare systems. Big data will lead hypothesis-driven research to data-driven research transformation. On the other hand, IoT will help control and analyze the different levels of connections between various sensor signals and existing big data. This will enable new ways of remote diagnosis with a better understanding of the disease, which will help in the development of innovative solutions in healthcare.

iii. Advantages in manufacturing companies

If manufacturing companies install IoT sensors within their equipment, they can collect significant operational data on machines. This will help them to obtain an in-depth view at how the business is performing and enable them to find out which equipment need repairing before significant problems arise. This prevents them from more considerable expenses by skipping the downtime or replacement of the equipment. Hence, investment in IoT and big data saves businesses money.

iv. IoT and big data will raise self-service analytics

With more inventions in the IoT field, most IT functions can be handled with data automation and integration. Additionally, big data tools will increasingly become self-sufficient and straightforward to perform basic functions. Hence, analytics as a service will become more of a self-service.

v. Benefits in the transportation industry

In the transportation sector, IoT sensors have been installed in vehicles as a way to track them as they go around the world. This not only help companies to keep a clos eye on their vehicles but also provides data regarding fuel efficiency, how drivers utilize their time, and delivery routes. This information can be indispensable for optimizing fleets and improving organizational productivity.

Working on real-time data is a high priority today and a necessity. As IoT and big data both enable on-demand and real-time action, the importance of deployment of these technologies is high. In this view, edge computing is also becoming very popular. As IoT and big data are closely linked, there are many examples of organizational benefits to put them to good use.

10.7 Conclusion

IoT devices are gathering huge amounts of data. Big data helps us to organize, generate, and store/retrieve the needed information/data using various applications and tools. Various frameworks and architecture are followed in different devices which help us to retrieve information. Here, we have discussed the COIB framework along with the general framework of IoT in big DA. This chapter also discusses the data lifecycle and data management. Various approaches used for this framework in dealing with data management are also presented. Similar to big data, analysis plays a vital role in collected data to make better decisions for any domains. Different approaches and tools that can aid in better analysis are also discussed. We also discussed how analyzed data undergo visualization process for better results. For this, various visualization techniques are also discussed aiding the users to have a better idea regarding which techniques to be used for a particular analysis.

Thus, overall, this chapter helps the user in dealing with various stages of big data in retrieval of better data for IoT devices. IoT along with big data have done better analysis in many areas, such as health, smart city, etc., which creates new opportunities for supporting decision making. In the future, the right mix of people, analytics, and things will be required to enhance organizational success and decision-making processes.

References

1. Abbasi, M.A., Memon, Z.A., Syed, T.Q., Memon, J., Alshboul, R., "Addressing the Future Data Management Challenges in IoT: A Proposed Framework", *International Journal of Advanced Computer Science and Applications*, Vol. 8, No. 5, pp. 197–207, 2017.
2. Siow, E., Tiropanis, T., Hall, W., "Analytics for the Internet of Things: A Survey", *ACM Computing Surveys*, Vol. 1, No. 1, Article 1, 2018.
3. Kundhavai, K.R., Sridevi, S., "IoT and Big Data – The Current and Future Technologies: A Review", *International Journal of Computer Science and Mobile Computing*, Vol. 5, No. 1, pp. 10–14, 2016.
4. Marjani, M., Nasaruddin, F., Gani, E., Karim, A., Hashem, I.A.R., Siddiqa, A., Ayaqoob, I., "Big IoT Data Analytics: Architecture, Opportunities, and Open Research Challenges", IEEE Access, Vol. 5, pp. 5247–5261, 2016.
5. Mishra, N., Lin, C.-C., Chang, H.-T., "A Cognitive Adopted Framework for IoT Big-Data Management and Knowledge Discovery Prospective", *International Journal of Distributed Sensor Networks*, Vol. 11, No. 10, p. 718390, 2015.
6. Ge, M., Bangui, H., Buhnova, B., "Big Data for Internet of Things: A Survey", *Future Generation Computer Systems*, Vol. 87, pp. 601–614, 2018.
7. Ramadan, R.A., "Big Data Tools – An Overview", *International Journal of Computer & Software Engineering*, Vol. 2, p. 125, 2017.
8. Rout, R., Mohanayak, R.K., "Big Data with Reference to IoT: Architecture, Opportunities and Challenges", *IOSR Journal of Engineering (IOSRJEN)*, Vol. 1, pp. 45–53, 2018.
9. Siddiqa, A., "A Survey of Big Data Management: Taxonomy and State-of-the-Art", *Journal of Network and Computer Applications*, Vol. 71, pp. 151–166, 2016.
10. Yerpude, S., Singhal, T.K., "Internet of Things and Its Impact on Business Analytics", *Indian Journal of Science and Technology*, Vol. 10, No. 5, pp. 1–6, 2017.
11. Soldatos, J., *Building Blocks for IoT Analytics*, River Publishers Series in Signal, Image and Speech Processing, River Publisher, Denmark, 2017.
12. Stankovic, A.J., "Research Directions for Internet of Things", *IEEE Internet of Things Journal*, Vol. 1, No. 1, pp. 3–9, 2014.
13. Tiainen, P., "New Opportunities in Electrical Engineering as a Result of the Emergence of the Internet of Things", Technical Report, AaltoDoc, Aalto University, 2016.

Chapter 11

Big Data Programming Models for IoT Data

T. Lucia Agnes Beena

St. Josephs College

Contents

11.1 Introduction

Nowadays, there is an abundant flow of data due to emerging technologies like cloud computing, edge computing, and Internet of Things (IoT). Many industries including healthcare, government, media and entertainment, manufacturing, and IoT generate large volumes of data every day. These industries need analytical models to improve their operational efficiency. The data produced in these industries are called big data because they are not only large they are rapid and in varied formats. Organizations such as McDonald's, Amazon, and Walmart are investing in big data applications for examining large datasets to expose hidden patterns, unknown correlations, market trends, customer preferences, and other useful business information. In big data programming, data-driven parallel programs are written by users to execute on large-scale and distributed environments. Numerous programming models are available for big data with different focus and advantages. Software developers use programming models to build the applications. Irrespective of the programming language and supporting Application Programming Interfaces (APIs), the programming models connect the underlying hardware architecture with the software. IoT applications, such as smart homes, wearables, and smart cities, generate large volumes of data for processing. Analyzing such large data volumes is an important challenge. This chapter discusses the various programming models that are suitable for IoT data processing.

11.2 Programming Paradigm

Programming languages are classified into the following paradigms based on their features [1]:

- Imperative
- Declarative

In imperative programming, the programmer educates the machine how to change its state. It includes procedural and object-oriented programming. In declarative programming, the programmer merely states the properties of the desired outcome and does not give the procedure for computing the outcome. It includes functional, logical, and mathematical programming. In this chapter, MapReduce, data flow of non-declarative types, functional, Standard Query Language (SQL)-based and statistical programming of declarative types, bulk synchronous parallel (BSP) of skeleton-based type and actor, and event-driven message-based programming are discussed.

11.2.1 MapReduce

Traditional programming models are not suitable to process huge volumes of data by standard database servers. Google solved this issue using MapReduce. MapReduce is a processing technique and a programming model for distributed computing to process huge amounts of data in parallel. MapReduce processes big data in two phases: Map and Reduce. Both phases have key-value pairs as input and output.

Map phase implements mapper function [2], in which user-provided code is executed on each key-value pair (k1, v1) read from the input files. The output of the mapper function would be zero or more key-value pairs (k2, v2), which are called intermediate pairs. Here the data is grouped based on the key, and the value is the information related to the analysis in the reducer.

Reduce phase takes the mapper output (grouped key-value data) (k2, v2) and runs reduce function on each key-value group. Reduce function iterates over the list of values associated with a key and produces outputs such as aggregations and statistics. Once the reduce function is executed, it sends zero or more key-value pairs (k3, v3) to the final output file. By default, MapReduce input and output files are in text file formats. The MapReduce paradigm [3] is shown in Figure 11.1.

A Word Count Example of MapReduce

Consider that the example.txt file contains the following text.
Pen, Paper, Eraser, Pencil, Pencil, Pen, Pen, Eraser, Paper

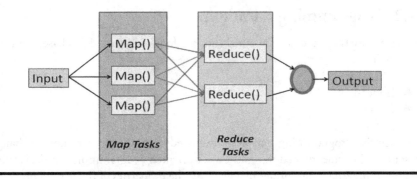

Figure 11.1 MapReduce paradigm.

To perform a word count on the example.txt using MapReduce, find the unique words and the number of occurrences of those unique words. The process of performing word count is depicted in Figure 11.2. To distribute the work among the map nodes, the given input is divided into three splits. Each mapper tokenizes the words and assigns a hardcoded value (1) to each of the tokens or words. Then, a list of key-value pair is created where the key is the individual words and value is 1. So, in the first line (Pen, Paper, Eraser), there are three key-value pairs – Pen, 1; Paper, 1; Eraser, 1. The mapping process remains the same on all nodes. After the mapper phase, during the partition process, sorting and shuffling are done, so that all the tuples with the same key are sent to the corresponding reducer. After the partition phase, each reducer will have a unique key and a list of values corresponding to that key. Now, each reducer counts the values present in that list of values. As shown in the figure, reducer obtains a list of values for the corresponding key and counts the number of ones in the very list and gives the final output as – Pen, 3. Finally, all the output key/value pairs are collected and written in the output file.

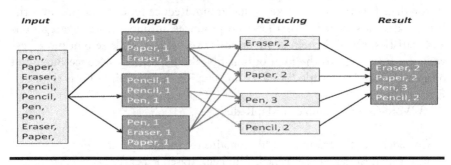

Figure 11.2 MapReduce word count process.

11.2.1.1 Hadoop

Hadoop is an implementation of MapReduce, an application programming model developed by Google [4]. Hadoop is an open-source software framework written in Java and comprises two parts: storage and data processing. The storage part is called the Hadoop Distributed File System (HDFS), and the processing part is called MapReduce.

11.2.1.1.1 Advantages of MapReduce

The advantages of MapReduce [3] programming include:

- Scalability
- Cost-effectiveness
- Flexibility
- Fast
- Security and authentication
- Parallel processing
- Availability and resilient nature

Scalability: Hadoop platform is highly scalable because it can store and process large datasets distributed across several servers, which operate in parallel mode. Additions of new servers add processing power. Hadoop MapReduce programming facilitates corporates to run applications from a large number of nodes possibly involving the usage of thousands of terabytes of data.

Cost-effective Solution: In a traditional model, raw data is transformed to the required format and valuable data alone are retained. If businesses have to change their plan, the original data may not be available. Hadoop's scale-out architecture with MapReduce programming allows data storage and processing in a very affordable manner. Data can also be used at a later time. This results in significant cost savings as the data is in terabytes.

Flexibility: Hadoop MapReduce programming facilitates business organizations to have access to various new sources of data and operate on different types of data, structured or unstructured. This enables organizations to generate value from all the data that can be accessed by them. From different data sources like social media, email, or clickstream, MapReduce can recommend systems, processing of logs, marketing analysis, warehousing of data, and fraud detection.

11.2.2 Functional Programming

In functional programming, the program is actually an expression that corresponds to the mathematical function. Functional languages support the construction of such expressions by allowing powerful functional constructs [5]. Because functional programs do not use variables, they cannot use assignments as there is nothing to assign to. Functional programs can use functions and recursive functions. Functional programming is based on Lambda calculus. Lambda calculus is a framework developed by Alonzo Church to study computations with functions.

Features of functional programming include [6]:

- Pure functions
- Recursion
- Referential transparency
- Higher-order functions
- Variables are immutable

Pure Function: These functions always produce the same output for the same arguments. They are immutable, that is, they modify the argument or global variables. This feature enables programmers to write parallel/concurrent applications.

Recursion: Functional programming does not support loops. Iteration in functional languages is implemented through recursion. Recursive functions repeatedly call themselves until it reaches the base case.

Referential Transparency: In functional programs, the value of the variables does not change throughout the program. To store some value, a new variable has to be defined. This avoids the chances of modifying the existing variables. The state of any variable is constant at any instant.

Higher-Order Functions: Some functions are treated as first-class variables that can be passed to functions as parameter, as well as returned from functions or stored in data structures. The higher-order functions can take other functions as arguments as well as return functions.

Variables are Immutable: In functional programming, modification of a variable after its initialization is not permitted. The existing variables cannot be modified, and therefore new variables can be defined. This helps maintain state throughout the runtime of a program. Once a variable is created and value is set, it is confirmed that the value of that variable will never change.

The functional programming frameworks Spark and Flink are discussed below.

11.2.2.1 SPARK

Spark was in the result of a 2009 project from the AMPLab at the University of California, Berkeley. Later, in 2013, Spark became an incubated project of the Apache Software Foundation [7]. Apache Spark is a general-purpose cluster computing system which offers efficient execution by performing in-memory data transformation. As a general-purpose data processing engine, Spark is suitable for use in a wide variety of applications. Spark supports interactive queries across large datasets, processing of streaming data from sensors or financial systems, machine learning tasks, and graph-parallel computation. Spark's extensive set of developer libraries and APIs render support for languages such as Java, Python, R, and Scala. Spark integrates well with data storage modules such as HDFS (Hadoop's data storage module), HBase, Cassandra, MapR-DB, MongoDB, and Amazon's S3.

11.2.2.1.1 Features of Spark

The key features are [7]:

■ Simplicity
■ Speed
■ Support

Simplicity: Spark offers a rich set of APIs. They are well documented and designed specifically for interacting quickly and easily with big data. This makes the work of the data scientists and application developers easy in using Spark for their requirements.

Speed: Spark is designed for faster execution when operating both in-memory and on-disk. Spark running in-memory can be 100 times faster than Hadoop MapReduce, as well as ten times faster when processing disk-based data compared to Hadoop MapReduce.

Support: Spark's extensive set of developer libraries and APIs render support for languages such as Java, Python, R, and Scala. Spark integrates well with data storage modules such as HDFS (Hadoop's data storage module), HBase, Cassandra, MapR-DB, MongoDB, and Amazon's S3. Commercial providers such as Databricks, IBM, and all the main Hadoop vendors deliver widespread support for Spark-based solutions.

11.2.2.2 Resilient Distributed Datasets (RDD)

The core structure of Spark is the RDD. RDD is a read-only collection of objects partitioned across a set of machines that can be restored if a partition is lost [8]. Users can explicitly cache an RDD in memory across machines and reprocess it in multiple parallel operations. Fault-tolerance is achieved by RDDs through the concept of lineage. In lineage, if a partition of an RDD is lost, the RDD rebuilds that partition based on the information about how it was derived from other RDDs.

Spark is implemented in Scala, a modern multiparadigm programming language which is a combination of object-oriented programming and functional programming. Using the modified version of Scala Interpreter, Spark allows the user to define RDDs, functions, variables, and classes, as well as to use them in parallel operations on a cluster. In interactive machine learning workloads, Spark can outstrip Hadoop by ten times and has the capability to scan 39 GB dataset with subsecond latency in interactive data processing [9].

Spark programmers construct RDDs from a file in an HDFS by parallelizing a Scala Collection, transforming an existing RDD, or changing the persistence of an existing RDD. Apache Spark RDD supports the following two types of operations [10,11]:

- Transformations
- Actions

11.2.2.2.1 Transformations

A transformation is a function that creates new RDD from existing RDDs; however, to work with the actual dataset, action is executed. Some of the transformations are [10]:

map(): Map is a transformation that passes each dataset element through a function and returns a new RDD representing the results

flatmMap(): Similar to map, but each input item can be mapped to zero or more output items and return a sequence rather than a single item.

filter(): Returns a new dataset formed by selecting those elements of the source that satisfy the Boolean function.

mapPartitions(): Similar to map, but runs separately on each partition of the RDD.

union(): Combines the current dataset with another dataset and returns a new united dataset.

intersection(): Returns the common elements from two datasets.

distinct(): Returns the distinct elements from two datasets.

join(): Combines pairwise RDDs on the basis of the key (Pairwise RDDs are RDD in which each element is in the form of tuples. Where the first element is key and the second element is the value).

groupByKey(): Returns a new dataset of (K, V) pairs, where the data is shuffled according to the key-value K.

reduceByKey(): Returns a new dataset (K, V), where the pairs on the same machine with the same key (K) are combined before the data is shuffled.

sortByKey(): Returns a new dataset of (K, V) pairs, where the data is sorted according to the key K.

11.2.2.2.1.1 Action

RDDs are created between transformations, but action is triggered when the actual dataset is accessed. Once the action is triggered new RDD is not formed. Thus, actions are Spark RDD operations that give non-RDD values. The values of action are stored on drivers or on external storage systems. An action is one of the ways of sending data from the executer to the driver. Executors are agents that are accountable for executing a task, while the driver is a JVM process that organizes workers and execution of the task. Some of the actions of Spark include [11]:

Count(): Returns the number of elements in the dataset.

Collect(): Sends all elements of the dataset to the driver program.

Save(): Evaluates the dataset and writes it to a distributed file system such as HDFS.

take(n): Returns n number of elements from RDD.

top(n): Extract top elements from mapFile with default ordering.

countByValue(): Returns number of times each key-value occurred in the given RDD.

reduce(): Combines dataset elements using an associative function to produce a result at the driver program.

fold(): Similar to reduce except that it takes an "Zero value" which will be used in the initial call on each partition

aggregate(): When applied on a dataset of (K, V) pairs, it returns a dataset of (K, U) pairs where the values for each key are aggregated using the given combine functions and a neutral "zero" value.

foreach(): If a particular operation is to be performed on each element of the dataset, foreach() function is applied.

11.2.2.3 FLINK

Apache Flink [12] is a recent open-source framework for distributed stream and batch data processing. It processes large amounts of data with very low data latency and high fault-tolerance on distributed systems. Flink offers a high fault-tolerance mechanism to consistently recover the state of data streaming applications. The features of Flink [13] are:

- Process batch and streaming data
- Ubiquitous applications deployment
- Scalability
- Influence in-memory performance

Process Batch and Streaming Data: Data-stream processing and batch data processing were traditionally considered as two different types of applications. A considerable number of today's large-scale data processing applications handle data that are produced continuously in real time. Some of the examples are web logs, application logs, sensors, or transaction log records of databases. Data-stream processing requires the order in which the events are ingested for the completeness of the results. Flink programs achieve this using windowing mechanism. Flink defines events based on event time, ingestion time, and processing time, so that programmers can code the events appropriately [14]. Batch data processing is a special type of streaming programme with a finite set of data that requires the order and time of occurrence of the events. To support batch processing, Flink has specialized data structures and algorithms for performing operators, such as join or grouping and some dedicated scheduling strategies. Flink also has specific APIs for processing batch datasets.

Ubiquitous Applications Deployment: Being a distributed system, Flink combines with all common cluster resource managers, such as Hadoop YARN, Apache Mesos, and Kubernetes. It can also run as a standalone cluster. Based on the application configuration file, Flink identifies the required resources automatically from the resource manager for deploying the application. In the event of a failure, the failed container is replaced by a new resource on request. All these operations are performed using REST calls, which pave the way for easy integration in any environment.

Scalability: Flink has the capability to run stateful streaming applications at any scale. Thousands of tasks are distributed and concurrently executed in a cluster by parallelizing the applications. Thus, an application has the power to control virtually unlimited amounts of CPUs, disk, memory, and network IO operations. Flink's asynchronous and incremental checkpointing algorithms maintain a large application state that guarantees minimal processing latency.

Influence In-Memory Performance: Flink applications enhance local state access. All computations are performed by accessing in-memory using access-efficient, on-disk data structures. Flink uses cache-efficient and robust algorithms that gracefully handle memory pressure.

11.2.3 SQL-Based Programming Models

A large amount of data is generated every second in web. Commercial organizations process generated huge amounts of data to get insights and produce products based on those insights. SQL is a tool used by developers and database administrators for data processing. Large commercial applications use SQL to query, manipulate, and visualize the data. However, massive data volumes, growing data diversity, and increasing information demands challenge the existing enterprise tools. The existing operational and analytical tools suffer from slow response time, lack of liveliness, impulsive workloads, and incapability to handle modern data types. As the data grows at terabyte size, even the most shared memory databases, such as MySQL, PostgreSQL, and SQL Server databases, encounter scaling issues [15]. Therefore, SQL for big data needs to be addressed with the following goals:

- To support SQL on distributed architectures for complete data storage and to compute across clusters of machines.
- To avoid data movement from the data hub to an external store for improved performance.
- To prevent investment on appliances that are extremely costly for massive parallel processing.
- To access the data directly as it is written and stored on the storage cluster.
- To sustain SQL queries on large datasets for several concurrent users.

■ To provide low latency and unstructured data processing.
■ To support existing SQL apps and business intelligence (BI) tools for immediate productivity.

Some of the SQL engines and products for a big data platform include:

■ Hive query language (HiveQL) HiveQL
■ CasandraQL
■ SparkSQL
■ Drill
■ Presto
■ Impala

11.2.3.1 HiveQL

Hive is a platform for reading, writing, and managing large datasets in distributed storage. Initially, Hive was developed by Facebook and was later picked up by Apache Foundation that developed it as an open-source tool. The HiveQL is an SQL engine used to access large datasets. HiveQL queries are converted into a series of jobs that execute on a Hadoop cluster through MapReduce or Apache Spark [16]. HiveQL allows the existing programming skills to be used for data preparation on top of the MapReduce interface. It supports both batch processing and interactive processing through Apache Impala or Apache Spark.

HiveQL includes SQL features such as CREATE tables, DROP tables, SELECT... FROM... WHERE clauses, Joins (inner, left outer, right outer and outer joins), Cartesian products, GROUP BY, SORT BY, aggregations, union, and many useful functions on primitive as well as complex data types [17]. Metadata browsing features such as list databases and tables are also supported. HiveQL has certain limitations compared with traditional Relational Database Management System (RDBMS) SQL. HiveQL allows creation of new tables that can have one or more partitions. Each partition can have one or more buckets. Insertion of data in single or multiple tables is allowed, but deletion or updating of data is not allowed. HiveQL is also extensible. The user-defined column transformation (UDF) and aggregation (UDAF) functions implemented in Java are also supported by HiveQL. Custom MapReduce scripts written by users in any language can be embedded for reading and writing row data in standard input and output, respectively [18].

11.2.3.2 CasandraQL

Apache Cassandra is an open-source, scalable, continuously available, fault-tolerant, distributed database designed to handle large amounts of data. Its design is based on Amazon's Dynamo and Google's Bigtable. Initially, Cassandra was developed by Facebook and later picked up by Apache Foundation.

According to Brewers Theorem (CAP theorem) [19], within a large-scale distributed data system, there are three requirements that have a relationship of sliding dependency: Consistency, availability, and partition tolerance. Cassandra primarily supports consistency and availability. Therefore, in case of a network or partition of network failure, the system blocks the partition in such a way that the database can only be limited to a single data center. This is appropriate for IoT applications that consume lots of fast incoming data from sensors and similar mechanisms present at different locations. Retail applications with exhaustive catalog searches, mobile apps and messaging service providers, media companies, and social media websites apply Cassandra to analyze data for better analysis and provide recommendations to their customers.

Cassandra Query Language (CQL) [20] is a query language for the Cassandra database. CQL shell, cqlsh, can be used to interact with Cassandra. Using CQL, users can create keyspaces and tables. They can also insert the data and query the tables. CQL has a flexible set of data types, comprising simple character and numeric types, collections, and user-defined types. CQL collection types include sets, lists, and maps. CQL also supports JSON, user-defined functions, user-defined aggregates, role-based access control, and native protocol. Without compromising on read efficiency, Cassandra system was intended to run on cheap commodity hardware and can handle high write throughput.

11.2.3.3 SparkSQL

Many big data applications require ETL (Extract, Transform, Load) operations to be performed on various data sources and need advanced analytics, such as machine learning and graph processing [21]. However, the existing systems force the users to choose ETL or advanced analytics. Spark SQL links the two models through two components, SparkSQL DataFrame API and Catalyst.

DataFrame in SparkSQLs API is a distributed collection of rows with a homogeneous schema. Using DataFrames, the relational operations performed on the schema can be done in a optimized manner. DataFrames can be built from external data sources or from existing RDDs of native Java/Python objects. Using Spark DataFrames, objects denote a logical plan to compute a dataset; however, execution occurs only when user performs a specific operation such as save. This facilitates rich optimization. But SparkSQL reports an error if the user types an invalid code before execution. DataFrames can be manipulated by all common relational operators, such as select, where, join, and groupBy clauses. There is a possibility that the user can register DataFrames as temporary tables in the system catalog and SQL can be used to query those tables. The DataFrames registered in the catalog can be accessed by programs applying JDBC/ODBC. The cache() function operated on a DataFrame provide in-memory caching that reduces memory by applying columnar compression techniques, such as dictionary encoding and run-length encoding. This feature enables interactive queries and is helpful for iterative algorithms in machine learning. UDFs can be defined easily as inline by passing Scala. Java or Python functions with Spark APIs. The registered UDFs can also be utilized through the JDBC/ODBC interface with BI tools. Catalyst is an extensible optimizer of SparkSQL that facilitates easy addition of data sources, optimization rules, and data types for machine learning. Catalyst supports both rule-based and cost-based optimization.

11.2.3.4 Drill

Drill is the open-source SQL engine specially designed for interactive ad-hoc analysis on large datasets [22]. It is capable of handling petabytes of data stored in thousands of servers. Drill doesn't need any preprocessing and [23] is easier for business users for the following reasons:

- Structuring the data for query processing is not needed.
- Creation and maintenance of metadata repository is not necessary.
- Easy to query historical data.

A JSON Data model in Drill can process data both from the plain text files or predefined data schemas. Irrespective of the data format, the given data is converted to a JSON structure before query processing. This is the main benefit of Drill over other SQL engines. The distributed architecture of Drill permits its Drillbit to run on any machine in a cluster. Moreover, data can be processed directly at its storage rather than moving it over the network. This leads to reduced latency, minimum data loss, and improved user experience and engine reliability. Drill can handle failure at the node level and reports the failed query. Additionally, it is extensible with well-defined APIs, query APIs, and user-defined functions. Drill supports ANSI SQL 2003 and JDBC/ODBC drivers, and can handle nested data.

11.2.3.5 Presto

Presto is an open-source distributed SQL query engine for running interactive analytic queries [24]. It can process data from multiple sources including HDFS, MySQL, Cassandra, Hive, among others. The size of the data source may range from gigabytes to petabytes. Presto was designed at Facebook. The main goal of developing Presto is to provide high performance with low latency while processing data at the resident without applying ETL operations. It can also process real-time data.

Presto supports many of the tasks that standard ANSI SQL engines can perform. It includes complex queries, aggregations, joins, left/right outer joins, and most of the common aggregate and scalar functions. In addition, sub-queries, window functions, approximate distinct counts, and approximate percentiles are performed by Presto [25]. Presto can work with BI tools, such as R, Tableau, MicroStrategy, Power BI, and Superset. It is best for both on-premise and cloud environments such as Amazon, Azure, and Google Cloud.

11.2.3.6 Impala

Impala is a general-purpose SQL query engine that processes both analytical and transactional workloads. Impala works on Apache Hadoop data stored in HDFS, HBase, or the Amazon's S3. Impala follows the format of Hive SQL for metadata, SQL syntax, and ODBC driver. The user interface of Impala (Hue) is the same as Apache Hive. With single users, Impala outperforms Hive [26]. In interactive mode, the speed up is between 25× and 68×, delivery of report at the speed of 6× to 56× and in deep analytical mode the speed up ranges from 6× to 55×. With regard to multiple user performance, query throughput is stable. Impala supports SELECT, joins, and aggregate functions of SQL-92 features of HiveQL. The HDFS file formats such as delimited text files, Avro, Parquet, SequenceFile, and RCFile are supported by Impala. Impala provides provision for code compression using snappy, GZIP, Deflate, and BZIP. For common data access interfaces such as JDBC, ODBC drivers are used by Impala. It supports Kerberos authentication, but does not permit UDFs.

11.2.4 Actor Model

Hewitt and Gul Agha defined the actor programming model for concurrent computation. Actor is the basic unit of computation in this model, that is, a message processing entity. The actor receives the incoming messages at a mailbox. When the message is processed, the actor's behavior responds to the message. The behavior of the actor is defined by the script. While processing the message, the actor can perform the following actions:

- Create a new actor.
- Send messages to other actors if it has their addresses.
- Decide its own successive behavior to process the next message from the actor's mailbox.

Identity, autonomy, communication, and coordination are some of the characteristics of actors. A system comprising actors is open, flexible, and adaptable as it is loosely integrated with peer entities. Concurrency occurs in the actor model through interactor and intra-actor concurrency [27]. Actor-based applications and systems are created by the developer for concurrent, parallel, and distributed programming on distributed-memory parallel processors, single workstations, and networks of workstations. Some of the tools that follow actor model are Akka, Storm, and S4.

11.2.4.1 Akka

Akka is a toolkit for designing distributed, concurrent, fault-tolerant, and scalable real-time applications. Investment and merchant banking, retail, social media, simulation, gaming and betting, automobile and traffic aystems, healthcare, and data analytics are areas where Akka is adopted [28]. Applications that are implemented with Akka benefit from high throughput and low latency. Akka actors handle service failures, load management, as well as both horizontal and vertical scalability. Akka applications are deployed as a library (as a regular JAR) or package (packaged with sbt-native-packager/Lightbend ConductR). The modules in Akka and their features are listed in Table 11.1.

Table 11.1   Overview of Akka Modules

Akka Module	Feature
Actor library	Used to design high-performance concurrent applications
Remoting	Enables the actors to work on different computers to exchange messages as on local computers
Cluster	Works on top of remoting to tie together all the computers using a membership protocol
Cluster sharding	Ensures that entities in the cluster are distributed to balance the load across the machines
Cluster singleton	Guarantees that the service is up even in case of system crashes or shutdown while scaling down
Cluster publish-subscribe	Used to broadcast messages to an interested set of parties in a cluster
Persistence	Restore the state of an actor when system restarts or crashes
Distributed data	Shares data between nodes in an Akka cluster and allows both reads and writes even in cluster partitions
Streams	Handle streams of events with high performance, utilizing concurrency and maintaining high resource utilization
HTTP	Expose services of a cluster to the external world using an HTTP API

11.2.4.2 Storm

Storm is an open-source programming model for processing real-time streaming data in a distributed environment. Nathan Marz developed Storm in 2010 [29]. Apache Storm can process data streams of any data type. Any programming language can be used with Storm to process data streams without any data loss. Storm has different types of components to perform specific tasks. Spout handles the input stream of a storm cluster. The data from spout is passed to another component called bolt. The bolt component transforms the stream and holds the data or passes it to another bolt. The storm cluster has two kinds of nodes, viz. master node and worker node. A daemon named Nimbus in master node is accountable for distributing code around the cluster, allocating tasks to each worker node, and supervising failures. Another daemon named Supervisor running in worker node executes a section of a topology. An advanced, embeddable networking library called zeromq is utilized by Storm giving it the following properties:

■ Socket library is used for concurrency
■ Messages are passed across IPC, TCP, and multcast
■ The multicore message passing apps utilize asynch I/O for scalability
■ N-to-N connection is offered through fanout, pubsub, pipeline, and request-reply
■ Compared to TCP, Zeromq is faster in clustered products and supercomputing

11.2.4.3 S4 (Simple Scalable Streaming System)

Introduced by Yahoo in 2008, S4 is a general-purpose distributed platform for processing unbounded data streams. S4 is easily scalable and therefore highly available. It is developed to solve real-world problems, especially search applications that apply data mining and machine learning algorithms. S4 is designed with the following objectives [30]:

■ Processing data stream is made easy by using simple programming interface.
■ Commodity hardware is used to design a cluster with high availability and scalability.
■ Each processing element uses the local memory and evades disk I/O bottlenecks for low latency.
■ The decentralized and symmetric architecture enable all nodes to share the same functionalities and responsibilities for simple deployment and maintenance.
■ Programming with S4 is easy and flexible.
■ The pluggable architecture of S4 helps programmers design generic and customizable applications.

S4 follows the actor programming model and has the processing element (PE) for computation. Communication between PEs happens by messages through data events. One PE can interact with other PEs by event emission and consumption. The framework also has the facility to direct event to appropriate PEs, as well as to create new instances of PEs. S4 supports PEs or standard tasks such as aggregate, count, join, etc. The definition of the standard tasks is provided in the configuration file. S4 has special software tools to program custom PEs. In some applications, unused PEs need to be removed. This is done through the time-to-live property of the events [30]. If a PE does not receive any event for a specified period of time, it is removed. Thus, the Quality of Service (QoS) is maximized and system performance is improved.

11.2.5 Statistical and Analytical Models

In this information era, there is tremendous amount of data production. The data produced is unavoidable, and businesses are looking for insights from their data for further development and revenue generation. Mckinsey conducted a global survey and found that the organizations that use the data, introduce new services, develop new business strategies, and sell the needed products and utilities [31]. The process of exploring the datasets (text, audio, or video) and inferring insights using software is called data analysis or analytics (DA). DA relies on statistics, computer science, applied mathematics, and economics. Some of the DA techniques are A/B testing, data fusing and data integration, data mining, machine learning, natural language processing, and statistics. Several tools have been developed for DA. They can be categorized as programming languages, statistical solutions, and visualization tools. This chapter discusses R (an open-source programming language for statistics and data science) and Mahout (an extensible machine learning framework).

11.2.5.1 R Programming

R is a resourceful open-source programming language for statistics and data science. It is modeled after S and S-Plus [32]. In the late 1980s, the S language was developed at AT&T labs. In 1995, the R project was initiated by Robert Gentleman and Ross Ihaka at the Statistics Department of the University of Auckland. It includes sophisticated statistical and machine learning packages, data wrangling and exploration tools, and graphics capabilities. R is applied in business, industry, government, medicine, academia, and so on. R has the following features [33]:

- It has a simple and easy to use syntax for data processing.
- Data can be stored in different formats, either locally or over the internet.
- In-memory processing of the user tasks with consistent syntax.
- Both built-in and open-source functions and packages are offered or data analysis.

- Statistical results can be represented in graphical form and stored on the disk.
- By creating new functions, analysis can be automated.
- The dataset is saved in the system between sessions to avoid the reloading of data.
- Can be executed on all platforms (Windows, Macintosh, and Linux).
- Free GUI options are also available in the form of RStudio, R Commander, StatET, ESS(Emacs Speaks Statistics), JGR Java GUI for R.
- Can be used for data extraction, data cleaning, data loading, data transformation, statistical analysis, data visualization, and predictive modeling.
- Supports linear and non-linear modeling, classic statistical tests, time-series analysis, classification, and clustering.

11.2.5.2 Mahout

In 2008, Mahout began as a sub-project of Apache Software Foundation. It is executed on top of Hadoop and uses MapReduce concepts. Mahout is a library for scalable machine learning. The sequential and parallel machine learning algorithms of Apache Mahout run on MapReduce, Spark, H2O, and Flink. The core themes of Mahout are clustering, classification, and collaborative filtering [33]. The machine learning algorithms of Mahout can be used in real world applications, such as e-commerce, email, videos, and photos. Some applications of Mahout include:

- Amazon.com, one of the most famous e-commerce site, applies collaborative filtering to deploy recommendations. The website keeps track of the purchases, site activity of the user, and recommends corresponding items that the user may be interested in.
- Google News uses clustering techniques to group news articles by topic, presenting news grouped by logical story, instead of offering a raw list of all articles.
- Yahoo! Mail utilizes classification techniques to identify the incoming spam messages based on earlier emails, spam reports from the users, and characteristics of the email.
- Google's Picasa, the photo-management application, employs classification techniques to create a human face from other regions of an image.

Other commercial applications include [34]:

- Mahout's clustering algorithms are consumed by Adobe AMP to increase video consumption by better user targeting.
- Mendeley offers recommendation services using collaborative filtering of Mahout to suggest a research article to the user from the area of interest.
- ResearchGate, a professional network for scientists and researchers, also uses collaborative filtering of Mahout.

- Twitter uses LDA implementation of Mahout for modeling user interest.
- Linked.In utilizes Mahout for model training.

Some of the academic applications include [34]:

- In Nagoya Institute of Technology, citizen participation platform project, funded by the Ministry of Interior of Japan, applies Mahout for research and data processing.
- The ROBUST project (co-funded by the European Commission), which concentrates on analyzing online community data, applies Mahout for processing.

11.2.6 Data Flow-Based Models

A dataflow model is a special case of Kahn Process Networks. The dataflow model represents a program as a set of concurrent processes that communicates with each other by FIFO channels. A set of firing rules called actors are related to each process. Actors are the functional units of the computation. In dataflow model, processing represents repeated firing of actors. When an actor is functional, firing doesn't have side effects. Hence, the actors are stateless. The output tokens are based on the functions of the input token. Stateful actors can also be modeled. There are two ways by which the dataflow models can be executed: Process-based and Scheduling-based [35]. In process-based model, each actor is denoted by a process and FIFO channels are used for communication. In the scheduling-based model (dynamic scheduling), the scheduler follows the input tokens for the actor and enables the execution of the actor. Oozie (a workflow scheduler for Hadoop) and Dryad (a general-purpose distributed execution engine for coarse-grain data-parallel applications) are discussed below.

11.2.6.1 Oozie

In 2008, Alejandro Abdelnur and a few engineers from Yahoo! developed the first version of Oozie. In 2011, Oozie become an Apache incubation project and various versions were released. Oozie is mainly designed to handle Hadoop components, such as MapReduce jobs and HDFS operations. Oozie can also coordinate other higher-level apache tools, such as pig, Sqoop, Hive, and DitCp. Though Oozie is designed for Hadoop, it can extend its support to custom Hadoop job written in any language and non-Hadoop jobs (java class/shell script). Oozie is developed with the following goals [36]:

- To facilitate simple programming and reduce developers' time.
- To easily address failures by troubleshooting and job recovery.

- To be extensible by giving provision for new types of jobs.
- To support scalability and reliability.
- To reduce the operational cost by multiuser service.

Oozie v3 is a server-based Bundle Engine that can start/stop/suspend/resume/rerun a set coordinator jobs in the bundle level for easy operational control. Oozie v2 is a server-based Coordinator Engine focused on executing workflow based on time and data availability. Oozie v1 is a server-based Workflow Engine dedicated for executing Hadoop Map/Reduce and Pig jobs [37]. A workflow in Oozie is a collection of Hadoop Map/Reduce jobs or Pig jobs (actions) arranged in a control dependency direct acyclic graph (DAG). Control dependency between action indicates that an action is executed only if its predecessor action is completed. hPDL (an XML process definition language) is a language used to define Oozie workflows. Oozie workflow actions can start the execution of the jobs from remote systems (i.e., Hadoop, Pig). Oozie notifies the remote system once an action is completed and proceeds to the next action in the workflow.

11.2.6.2 Dryad

Microsoft research team initiated a general-purpose data-parallel application execution engine called Dryad. Dryad can be installed on Windows HPC Server 2008 R2 Service Pack 1.

An application in Dryad is represented by a DAG where each vertex is a program and the edges denote data channels. The vertices can be executed concurrently on multiple computers or multicore within a computer. The communication between vertices happens through files, TCP pipes, and shared-memory FIFOs [38]. The graph may be dynamically modified as the computation progress to effectively utilize the available resources. Dryad is designed to support scalability. Dryad can create very large distributed, concurrent applications and schedule the available computing resources. During this process, it can recover the communication and computation failures [39]. It is used to implement image processing, time-series analysis, and various scientific computations. It can also be used to analyze log data and enormous collections of non-relational data.

11.2.7 Bulk Synchronous Parallel

Leslie Valiant of Harvard University developed the BSP model in the early 1990s [40]. A BSP computer comprises:

- A collection of processor, each with local memory for transaction processing and a distributed memory.
- A communication network for directing messages between the processors.
- A hardware capable of synchronizing all the components.

Algorithms designed for a BSP computer are portable. A BSP algorithm comprises a series of supersteps. A set of small steps (floating point operations, addition, subtraction, multiplication, or division) constitute computation superstep. The basic communication operations (transferring data in the form of real/integer) performed between processors constitute communication superstep. The BSP model is applied in solving problems such as Google pageranking, climate modeling, structural stability of skyscrapers, financial market pricing, and movie rendering. This section discusses Giraph, a iterative graph processing system, and Hama, a distributed computing framework for scientific computations based on BSP.

11.2.7.1 Giraph

Giraph system is an open-source graph-specific implementation of Google's Pregel [41]. Giraph is implemented in Java. Later, Facebook added multithreading and memory optimization to Giraph. It follows BSP model, and runs on standard Hadoop infrastructure. The computation of the graph vertices are executed in memory. It utilizes Apache ZooKeeper for synchronization. Giraph uses periodic checkpoints to avoid faults, as well as a set of workers (processors) to process large graph datasets. One processor acts as a master (coordinator) to direct other slave workers. The master takes care of global synchronization, assigning partitions to workers and handling errors. The features that are not supported by Pregel but included in Giraph are sharded aggregators, master computation, out-of-core computation, and edge-oriented input.

11.2.7.2 Hama

Hama, a distributer computing framework that adopts the BSP model established in 2012, is a project from the Apache Software Foundation. Other than the BSP programming model, Hama also provides vertex and neuron-centric programming models. It is used to perform diverse massive computational tasks on graphs, matrices, machine learning, deep learning, and network algorithms. It is implemented in Java and was installed on the HDFS. Some of the features of Hama include [42]:

- Programmers can operate at a lower level using BSP Primitives.
- Supports message passing explicitly.
- Hama APIs are simple, flexible, and small.
- Conflicts and deadlines during communication are overcome by BSP model.
- Though written in Java, supports C++ programs.
- Supports any distributed file system other than HDFS.
- Provides provision for general-purpose computing on graphics processing units (GPU).

11.2.8 High-Level Domain-Specific Language (DSL)

As the number of organizations grows, there is a need for innovation in collection and analysis of huge datasets. The enormous data size directs for the parallel systems. The existing solutions are low level and inflexible, requiring custom user codes, which are difficult to maintain and reuse. High-level DSLs are intended for this purpose. The DSLs combine the high-level querying similar to SQL and low-level procedural programming as that of MapReduce. This section presents a brief discussion on some of the DSLs, namely, Pig Latin, LINQ, Trident, Crunch, Cascading, Green Marl, AQL, and Jaql.

11.2.8.1 Pig Latin

Pig is an open-source project in the Apache incubator. It is used by Yahoo! programmers. Pig Latin is a simple SQL-like scripting language. It invokes user-defined code written in JRuby, Jython, and Java [43]. Pig Latin can function over plain input files without any schema information and files in HDFS. Its debugging environment is especially useful when dealing with enormous datasets. A Pig Latin program is a series of steps, similar to a programming language. Each step performs a single data transformation (filtering, grouping, and aggregation), which is of interest to programmers. Pig Latin is used in web log processing and web search platforms. It supports ad-hoc querying and modeling of algorithms in processing large datasets.

11.2.8.2 Crunch

Crunch is build on top of Apache Hadoop to process data. It is a framework for writing, testing, and running MapReduce pipeline programs in Java [44]. Crunch is designed based on Google's FlumeJava. It uses simple primitive operations and light-weight, user-defined functions to perform complex, multistage pipelines. Crunch compiles the pipeline into a sequence of MapReduce jobs at runtime and manages their execution. Java developers use Crunch comfortably as it enables them to write functions to manage pipeline execution and dynamically construct new pipelines. Crunch supports Hadoop's writable format in reading and writing data. Craft libraries using Crunch's data model can be designed by experts in machine learning, text mining, and ETL. These libraries can be used to build custom pipelines that converts raw data into a structured input for a machine learning algorithm.

11.2.8.3 Cascading

The Cascading framework is a collection of applications, languages, and APIs for developing data-intensive applications [45]. Cascading is the core Java API in this framework to design complex data flows and connecting the flows with backend systems. It has a query planner for mapping and carrying out logical flows on a computing platform. Cascading has the following advantages:

- Developers can build robust, consistent, data-oriented applications in Java.
- Cascading applications can be integrated with existing legacy systems.
- New data processing code and algorithms can be tested and reused in Cascading.
- Applications written with Cascading are portable to any fabric that Cascading framework supports.

11.2.8.4 LINQ

LINQ is an acronym for Language Integrated Query. LINQ is integrated, unitive, extensible, declarative, hierarchical, composable, and transformative [46]. It can easily integrate its query syntax in C# language. The LINQ query is shorter, easier to read, color-coded, fully type-checked, and IntelliSense-aware. The result set is converted in an object-oriented format. LINQ exploits the power of C# debugger while writing and maintaining queries. LINQ provides a single, unified method for querying diverse types of data, which enables developers to learn a new technology. LINQ allows developers to simply define what they intended to do (declarative), rather than worrying about how it is done (imperative). LINQ follows hierarchical data model, which is more flexible than the SQL query that returns data in a grid format. LINQ queries are composable implying that queries can be combined in many ways. One query can form a base for another query. LINQ transforms the result of a query in one format into another format.

11.2.8.5 Trident

Trident is a high-level abstraction for performing real-time computing on top of Storm. It allows performing high-throughput stateful stream processing with low-latency distributed querying. Using Trident, operations such as joins, grouping, aggregations, functions, and filters can be performed. Trident semantics are fully fault-tolerant and are processed exactly once. This feature is vital for real-time processing. Trident has primitives to perform stateful, incremental processing on top of any database or persistence store.

11.2.8.6 Green Marl

Green Marl [47] is a high-level DSL intended for graph data processing programs. Green Marl specially proposed to utilize modern parallel computing environments such as multicore and heterogeneous computers. The programmer describes their algorithm using the high-level DSL, Green Marl constructs. The compiler transforms it to the equivalent low-level source code for the target execution environment. The machine code is generated from the low-level source code using the existing low-level compiler. Some of the features of Green Marl include [48]:

- Green Marl follows an imperative programming.
- Green Marl uses random memory access.
- In Green Marl, data access is immediate, so the programmer need not plan for data to be required in the next timestep.
- As Green Marl programs are natural description of graph algorithms, it is easy to define global computation, reverse edge iteration, random vertex access, and breadth-first-order traversal in graphs.

11.2.8.7 Asterix Query Language (AQL)

Started in 2009, the NSF-sponsored Asterix project [49] has been concentrating on the development of new technologies for ingesting, managing, storing, indexing, querying, and analyzing vast quantities of semi-structured information at UC Irvine. Asterix has a more affluent set of data types, which are implemented on top of the Algebricks API. Algebricks is a model, algebraic layer for parallel query processing and optimization. Algebricks comprises a set of logical operators, physical operators, rewrite rule framework, metadata provider API, and a mapping of physical operators to the runtime operators in Hyracks. Asterix is well-suited to handle rigid, relation-like data collections to flexible and potentially more complex data in data collections, which are highly variant and self-describing.

11.2.8.8 Jaql

Jaql is a functional data processing and query language used for JSON query processing on big data [50]. It was initiated as an open-source project at Google and was taken over by IBM as primary data processing language for Hadoop software package, BigInsights. Design features of Jaql are: flexible data model, reusability, varying levels of abstraction, and scalability. Jaql's data model is based on JSON. It is used to represent different types of datasets such as flat, relational tables, and collections of semi-structured documents. A Jaql script can process data with no schema or only a partial schema. It supports higher-order functions and packaging of related function into modules for reusability. Jaql uses higher-order functions, which deals with both composition and encapsulation. This feature supports reusability and physical transparency.

11.3 Conclusion

This chapter discusses big data programming models that are suitable for processing voluminous IoT data. The various programming models explored in this chapter are MapReduce, functional models for programming, SQL-based models for querying, actor models for real-time transaction processing, statistical and analytical models to draw insights from the data, scheduling models to control data flow, computing framework for massive scientific computation and large-scale graph processing, models for complex data transformation, and high-level DSL.

References

1. https://en.wikipedia.org/wiki/Programming_paradigm (accessed May 9, 2019).
2. Dean, Jeffrey, and Sanjay Ghemawat. "MapReduce: Simplified data processing on large clusters." *Communications of the ACM* 51, no. 1 (2008): 107–113.
3. Kaushik Pal. www.tutorialspoint.com/articles/advantages-of-hadoop-mapreduce-programming (accessed April 8, 2019).
4. Johnson, Anumol, P. H. Havinash, Vince Paul, and P.N. Sankaranarayanan. "Big data processing using Hadoop MapReduce programming model." *International Journal of Computer Science and Information Technologies* 6, no. 1 (2015): 127–132.
5. Harrison, John. *Introduction to Functional Programming, Course Notes*. Cambridge: University of Cambridge, 1997.
6. www.geeksforgeeks.org/functional-programming-paradigm/ (accessed April 9, 2019).
7. Scott, James A. *Getting Started with Apache Spark*. Santa Clara, CA: MapR Technologies Inc., 2015.
8. Zaharia, Matei, Mosharaf Chowdhury, Tathagata Das, Ankur Dave, Justin Ma, Murphy McCauley, Michael J. Franklin, Scott Shenker, and Ion Stoica. "Resilient distributed datasets: A fault-tolerant abstraction for in-memory cluster computing." In *Proceedings of the 9th USENIX Conference on Networked Systems Design and Implementation*, p. 2. USENIX Association, San Jose, CA, 2012.
9. Zaharia, Matei, Mosharaf Chowdhury, Michael J. Franklin, Scott Shenker, and Ion Stoica. "Spark: Cluster computing with working sets." *HotCloud* 10, no. 10-10 (2010): 95.
10. https://spark.apache.org/ docs/latest/rdd-programming-guide.html (accessed April 10, 2019).
11. https://data-flair.training/blogs/spark-rdd-operations-transformations-actions/ (accessed April 12, 2019).
12. https://blog.newrelic.com/engineering/what-is-apache-flink/ (accessed April 13, 2019).
13. https://flink.apache.org/flink-architecture.html (accessed April 12, 2019).
14. Carbone, Paris, Asterios Katsifodimos, Stephan Ewen, Volker Markl, Seif Haridi, and Kostas Tzoumas. "Apache Flink: Stream and batch processing in a single engine." *Bulletin of the IEEE Computer Society Technical Committee on Data Engineering* 36, no. 4 (2015): 28–38.
15. Pal, Sumit. *SQL on Big Data Technology, Architecture, and Innovation*. Wilmington, MA, 2016. ISBN-13 (pbk): 978-1-4842-2246-1, ISBN-13 (electronic): 978-1-4842-2247-8, doi:10.1007/978-1-4842-2247-8.
16. *Apache Hive Guide – Cloudera*. Cloudera Enterprise 5.8.x, December 12, 2018. www.cloudera.com/documentation/enterprise/5-8-x/PDF/cloudera-hive.pdf (accessed April 17, 2019).

17. Kumar, Rakesh, Neha Gupta, Shilpi Charu, Somya Bansal, and Kusum Yadav. "Comparison of SQL with HiveQL." *International Journal for Research in Technological Studies* 1, no. 9 (2014): 1439–2348.

18. Thusoo, Ashish, Joydeep Sen Sarma, Namit Jain, Zheng Shao, Prasad Chakka, Suresh Anthony, Hao Liu, Pete Wyckoff, and Raghotham Murthy. "Hive: A warehousing solution over a map-reduce framework." *Proceedings of the VLDB Endowment* 2, no. 2 (2009): 1626–1629.

19. https://intellipaat.com/tutorial/cassandra-tutorial/cassandra-overview/ (accessed April 19, 2019).

20. *CQL for Apache Cassandra 3.0 (Earlier version)*. DataStax, 2018. https://docs.datastax.com/en/pdf/cql33.pdf.

21. Armbrust, Michael, Reynold S. Xin, Cheng Lian, Yin Huai, Davies Liu, Joseph K. Bradley, Xiangrui Meng, Tomer Kaftan, Michael J. Franklin, Ali Ghodsi, and Matei Zaharia. "Spark SQL: Relational data processing in spark." In *Proceedings of the 2015 ACM SIGMOD International Conference on Management of Data*, pp. 1383–1394. ACM, New York, 2015.

22. Hausenblas, Michael, and Jacques Nadeau. "Apache drill: Interactive ad-hoc analysis at scale." *Big Data* 1, no. 2 (2013): 100–104.

23. Agapova, Elena. "SQL engines for big data analytics: Comparison and its usage in business field." Czech Technical University in Prague Faculty of Information Technology, Department of Software Engineering, Bachelor's Thesis, 2018.

24. https://prestodb.github.io/docs/current/overview/concepts.html (accessed April 22, 2019).

25. Chen, Yueguo, Xiongpai Qin, Haoqiong Bian, Jun Chen, Zhaoan Dong, Xiaoyong Du, Yanjie Gao, Dehai Liu, Jiaheng Lu, and Huijie Zhang. "A study of SQL-on-Hadoop systems." In *Workshop on Big Data Benchmarks, Performance Optimization, and Emerging Hardware*, pp. 154–166. Springer, Cham, 2014.

26. Kornacker, Marcel, Alexander Behm, Victor Bittorf, Taras Bobrovytsky, Casey Ching, Alan Choi, Justin Erickson, Martin Grund, Daniel Hecht, Matthew Jacobs, Ishaan Joshi, Lenni Kuff, Dileep Kumar, Alex Leblang, Nong Li, Ippokratis Pandis, Henry Robinson, David Rorke, Silvius Rus, John Russell, Dimitris Tsirogiannis, Skye Wanderman-Milne, and Michael Yoder. "Impala: A modern, Open-Source SQL engine for Hadoop." In *CIDR*, vol. 1, p. 9. Asilomar, CA, 2015.

27. Kafura, Dennis, and Jean-Pierre Briot. "Actors and agents." *IEEE Concurrency* 2 (1998): 24–28.

28. https://doc.akka.io/docs/akka/current/guide/modules.html#remoting (accessed May 5, 2019).

29. Leibiusky, Jonathan, Gabriel Eisbruch, and Dario Simonassi. *Getting Started with Storm*. Sebastopol, CA: O'Reilly Media, Inc., 2012.

30. Neumeyer, Leonardo, Bruce Robbins, Anish Nair, and Anand Kesari. "S4: Distributed stream computing platform." In *2010 IEEE International Conference on Data Mining Workshops*, pp. 170–177. IEEE, Sydney, 2010.

31. https://searchbusinessanalytics.techtarget.com/definition/big-data-analytics (accessed May 5, 2019).

32. Matloff, Norman. *The Art of R Programming: A Tour of Statistical Software Design*. San Francisco, CA: No Starch Press, 2011.

33. Owen, Sean, and Sean Owen. *Mahout in Action*. Shelter Island, NY: Manning, 2012.

34. https://mahout.apache.org/general/powered-by-mahout.html (accessed May 5, 2019).

35. Misale, Claudia, Maurizio Drocco, Marco Aldinucci, and Guy Tremblay. "A comparison of big data frameworks on a layered dataflow model." *Parallel Processing Letters* 27, no. 1 (2017): 1740003.
36. Islam, Mohammad Kamrul, and Aravind Srinivasan. *Apache Oozie: The Workflow Scheduler for Hadoop.* Sebastopol, CA: O'Reilly Media, Inc., 2015.
37. https://oozie.apache.org/docs/4.0.1/DG_Overview.html (accessed May 5, 2019).
38. Isard, Michael, Mihai Budiu, Yuan Yu, Andrew Birrell, and Dennis Fetterly. "Dryad: Distributed data-parallel programs from sequential building blocks." *ACM SIGOPS Operating Systems Review* 41, no. 3 (2007): 59–72.
39. https://en.wikipedia.org/wiki/Dryad (programming) (accessed May 7, 2019).
40. https://en.wikipedia.org/wiki/Bulk_synchronous_parallel (accessed May 7, 2019).
41. Sakr, Sherif, Faisal Moeen Orakzai, Ibrahim Abdelaziz, and Zuhair Khayyat. *Large-Scale Graph Processing Using Apache Giraph.* Cham: Springer International Publishing, 2016.
42. Siddique, Kamran, Zahid Akhtar, Edward J. Yoon, Young-Sik Jeong, Dipankar Dasgupta, and Yangwoo Kim. "Apache Hama: An emerging bulk synchronous parallel computing framework for big data applications." *IEEE Access* 4 (2016): 8879–8887.
43. Olston, Christopher, Benjamin Reed, Utkarsh Srivastava, Ravi Kumar, and Andrew Tomkins. "Pig Latin: A not-so-foreign language for data processing." In *Proceedings of the 2008 ACM SIGMOD International Conference on Management of Data*, pp. 1099–1110. ACM, New York, 2008.
44. https://www.baeldung.com/apache-crunch (accessed May 8, 2019).
45. https://www.cascading.org/projects/cascading (accessed May 8, 2019).
46. Calvert, Charlie, and Dinesh Kulkarni. *Essential LINQ.* Upper Saddle River, NJ: Addison-Wesley Professional, 2009.
47. Hong, Sungpack, Hassan Chafi, Edic Sedlar, and Kunle Olukotun. "Green-Marl: A DSL for easy and efficient graph analysis." *ACM SIGARCH Computer Architecture News* 40, no. 1 (2012): 349–362.
48. Hong, Sungpack, Semih Salihoglu, Jennifer Widom, and Kunle Olukotun. *Tech Report: Compiling Green-Marl into GPS*, semanticscholar.org, 2012.
49. http://asterix.ics.uci.edu/ (accessed May 9, 2019).
50. Beyer, Kevin S., Vuk Ercegovac, Rainer Gemulla, Andrey Balmin, Mohamed Eltabakh, Carl-Christian Kanne, Fatma Ozcan, and Eugene J. Shekita. "Jaql: A scripting language for large scale semi-structured data analysis." In *Proceedings of VLDB Conference*, Seattle, WA, 2011.

Chapter 12

IoTBDs Applications: Smart Transportation, Smart Healthcare, Smart Grid, Smart Inventory System, Smart Cities, Smart Manufacturing, Smart Retail, Smart Agriculture, Etc.

R. Sujatha, E. P. Ephzibah, and S. Sree Dharinya
Vellore Institute of Technology

Contents

275

12.1 Introduction

International Data Corporation (IDC) made exotic analysis on data that is copied and created to be growing by 40%. Characteristics of big data such as volume, variety, velocity, and veracity make it a highly challenging field along with data generated from Internet of Things (IoT). In view of this, IoT and big data technologies are getting amalgamated for applications in various fields, including transportation, healthcare, inventory, agriculture, among others. The keyword that rocks this entire concept is "smart." Based on the domain selection of features, collecting data and analyzing the versatile data to gain knowledge makes this application extremely interesting and informative. Data derived from the past helps in fine-tuning the architecture of the system to the optimal level. Human standard of living is being shaped by incorporating smartness along with high transparency with the invent of putting together device-generated massive data in big data analytics. Scope of the research is more prominent to reach a higher horizon by working with algorithms and the architecture involved in them.

12.2 Smart Transportation

The motorcar was first patented by German inventor Karl Friedrich Benz in 1885 (Kennedy, 2015). Since then, many inventors have been continuously seeking to build better, faster, safer, and more convenient automobiles. The inventions of modern cruise control in 1948, adaptive cruise control in the late 1990s, and systems in mid-2000s were major steps toward automating driving. Reaching technological feats were once possible only in science fiction films. Nowadays, people own personal computing devices small enough to fit in their pockets and yet many times more powerful than the computer systems that sent man to the moon. As technology advances and integrates with our lives, it is also advancing and integrating into vehicles and transportation systems, improving our quality of life. Connected and autonomous vehicles with automated systems can safely operate vehicles whether the driver is in the car or not. These new technologies on the road aim to proactively plan and build for future transportation systems, in which the connected systems are fully automated (Jadaan et al. 2017). The implementation of connected vehicle technology will change the way we travel and the very roads we travel on. This technology is capable of sensing and quickly reacting to the environment through external sensors, global positioning system (GPS), Internet connectivity, and their connection to other vehicles and infrastructure. Radar and Lidar technology along with ultrasonic sensors and video cameras create a 360° visual of the automobile surroundings. These sensors detect lane lines, other vehicles, curves in the road-ways, pedestrians, buildings, and any other obstacles. All this data comes together and is processed at the vehicle central processing units, much like our brains control our bodies (Elliott et al. 2019). To change lanes or even slam on the brakes to avoid collisions, computer-controlled technology will be much quicker than a human driver, and a computer will never get distracted or tired.

12.3 Connected Automated Vehicles (CAVs)

When CAV makes up most of the vehicles on the road, accidents caused by human errors will be virtually eliminated, which has consistently accounted for over 90% of all accidents over the last 30 years. CAV traveling on connected highways will be able to do so more safely and efficiently by having the first vehicle communicate and lead the following vehicles (Zhang et al. 2019). Trucks benefit from this connected vehicle technology by allowing them to travel in small groups, known as truck platooning. The amount of space between the platooning trucks or passenger cars known as a head way can be safely reduced, which allows for more consistent traffic flow. Platooning reduces congestion as vehicles travel at a more constant speed with fewer stops, resulting in fuel saving, safer driving, and reduced CO_2 omissions. The same roadway in the future will accommodate more vehicles and will operate more efficiently (Yang et al. 2019).

Internets of Things (IoT)-based transport systems are intelligent systems that use communications technologies to link people, roads, and vehicles. To observe traffic-related issues, there are various IoT-based companies that have been under-taking initiatives to create vehicle-centered, safe environment-friendly and comfortable transport through the use of intelligent transport system, an integrated approach that encompasses people, vehicles, and the traffic environment (Mfenjou et al. 2018). Research is being actively conducted by these companies on road-to-vehicle, vehicle-to-vehicle, and pedestrian-to-vehicle communication systems that provide direct communication among vehicles, vehicle, and road-side infra-structure and between vehicles and pedestrians. Signals at 700 mega Hz are easily diffracted and can be used for communications over a wide area, making them effective for communication with vehicles at intersections with poor visibility (Amanatiadis et al. 2019).

Research and development of environmental systems that intend to improve fuel efficiency are also being accelerated at the ITS (Intelligent Transport System) proving ground. Toyota is researching and developing a system to help drivers from overseeing or missing red lights. This system is installed at intersections and uses a transmitter to transmit traffic signal information to vehicles by warning the driver about the red light, which can potentially reduce accidents caused by traffic signal violations. The transmitter sends the traffic signal information for the direction in which the vehicle is traveling. In cases where the vehicle determines that the traffic signal is red and the vehicle speed is not reduced, voice guidance and display warning are given to the driver about the stop signal in the vehicle's travel direction (Malygin et al. 2018). Installed at intersections and vehicles, the right turn collision prevention system exchanges intermediate information along with road-side infrastructure to support safe driving by reducing collisions when it is hard to see the vehicle coming close, as well as to help prevent collisions with pedestrians crossing the road. When large oncoming vehicles obstruct visibility and make it difficult to confirm nearby conditions, the vehicle detection center detects oncoming vehicles transmitting data to the vehicle. If the driver attempts to turn even though an oncoming vehicle is approaching, a warning about the oncoming vehicle is provided (Sun et al. 2016).

In addition, the pedestrian detection sensor detects the presence of a pedestrian on the crosswalk where the vehicle is turning. If the driver attempts to turn even though there is a pedestrian on the crosswalk, a warning about the pedestrian is provided (Mateus et al. 2019). The safe driving support system uses intervehicle communications to help detect surrounding vehicles. This helps reduce collisions between vehicles at intersections with poor visibility due to obstructions caused by buildings and walls. Vehicles driving in urban areas use radiowaves to exchange information concerning their driving status such as their position. At intersections where buildings or walls obstruct visibility and the driver cannot directly confirm the presence of the approaching vehicle, the vehicles engage in direct communication, and voice guidance and a displayed warning alerts the driver about other approaching vehicles at the intersection (Janušová & Čičmancová 2016).

The transport industry is one of the most technologically challenging industry. These industries are literally always on the move; transportation work demands increased levels of communication to navigate in this congested world and to stay safe on the road and manage to run wherever to airport or harbor. This has resulted in constantly evolving communication and access needs. IoT is now playing a key role in driving the world on roads, rails, sea, or in the air. IoT devices are making travel more safe, performance more efficient, and can even help to find a parking space and park the vehicle. This is a powerful change in transportation and is becoming more sophisticated each day. These advancements need to create an environment that allows travelers to keep moving easily and safely (Matthias Weber et al. 2016).

Intelligent travel will enhance all forms of transportation, whether by car, rail, or air. People on the move can continue to impeccably link every means of transport. The objective of smart transport is that the vehicle be equipped with navigation, communication, entertainment, safe, and efficient travel devices. The vehicle becomes an extension of the digital lifestyle. Downloading music, videos, TV shows from a cloud, as well as asking for directions and getting broad direction-finding data with valid maps and digital imaginary. When fuel level or battery level gets low, the nearby fuel filling station or a battery recharging station will be automatically searched for. Sensors both inside and outside the vehicle will provide safe and secured travel. Inside the vehicle, cameras can identify the driver and provide adapted seating, monitor the temperature of the vehicle, and give amusement preferences to match. Outside, sensors will detect lane departures, and the sensor will respond to dangers, such as not slowing down for a forthcoming halt-side and continuously recognizing visible vehicles appearing before, sideways, or behind to avoid collisions. A parking system will allow maintaining a safe space from a car in front of the vehicle (Alrawi 2017).

Connected intelligence will extend beyond the vehicle. Existing and evolving wireless signal transmissions will enable automobiles and their corresponding devices across the moving arrangement of vehicles to communicate with each other, permitting computerized, smart, real-time decisions to enhance travel experience. For example, deliberately employed cameras will identify blocking of vehicles or accidents or automatically alert emergency personal, as well as providing a warning for upcoming vehicles and informing through neighboring digital road-side signs. Smart traffic lights will be kept more prominent for identifying traffic movement from each path and spontaneously changing signs to increase flow of vehicles. Distributed intelligence that is safe and dependable is an important aspect in transforming the complete traffic setup from passive and uninformed to a practical intelligent linked sensor response system that improves travel. Building that arrangement on the present standards-built design is the principal to making this transportation visualization a reality (Ashokkumar et al. 2015).

With respect to weather-oriented traffic system and secured system, connected vehicle technology can help in handling these concerns with more efficiency, especially when the roads are greasy. Data compiled from many linked vehicles can regulate during possible risks caused by frozen roads, informing or alerting drivers before they face them. The current status of weather data from automobiles can be sent to traffic management centers (TMC) so that real-time information can help observe and cope with the transportation system performance. The centers can then take immediate efforts to adjust the traffic signs and the allowable speed limits, notifying maintenance crews, providing repair works on the road, and broadcasting warnings for drivers. Drivers can get real-time road weather information by paying attention to highway wireless communication posts. They can also have easy access to road weather data on their individual mobile phones before departing from their residence (Yang & Pun-Cheng 2018).

Reducing carbon emissions by vehicles can be accomplished with the help of connected vehicle technology. Ecolanes can help drivers accommodate environment-friendly automobiles that drive at a speed that preserves fuel. The dynamic message sign boards that appear to the drivers can alert them regarding the proper and correct speed of the vehicle they drive. This application can provide information to the drivers regarding unnecessary stops to reduce idling with the help of smart traffic signals. Transportation signs announcement data about the existing sign and timing can inform the arrangements inside the vehicles to use the data to regulate speed assistance for motorists. Motorists could then correct their vehicle speed to move through the next traffic signal or stop at the signal in the most environment-friendly manner, saving fuel, reducing emissions, as well as saving money (Grant-Muller & Usher 2014).

Smart transportation system can enhance alertness of unpredicted wayside occurrences like deactivated vehicles, vehicle clashes, and first responders caring for crash victims. Incidents on cautions will alert drivers on forthcoming events and alert them to reduce the speed of the vehicle or switch over lanes. Notifications can also be directed to immediate neighbors on the road at the same time to warn them about the dangers of the approaching vehicles. This technology could aid in controlling traffic movements and decrease the resulting collisions and accidents beforehand. With millions of vehicles, the ability to share robust data with each other can be improved. Smart setup can help increase traffic movements and enhance management with fellow travelers (Sumalee & Ho 2018).

Dynamic ride-sharing applications with the logistic ride-sharing will aid reliability and make communication easier by connecting vehicles and hand-held devices. Applications will do the matching for us authenticating users and connecting riders with drivers. The cooperative adaptive cruise control application helps drivers avoid starts and stops, which can also help conserve fuel and improve traffic flow. Queue warning application monitors traffic data to detect stretches of slow-moving traffic and warn motorists to reduce speed to avoid potential collisions (Linares et al. 2017).

The potential benefits of connected transportation system are that they enable safety and mobility and address environmental impacts. It would enhance livability of the communities and will ultimately make our transportation safer and smarter.

12.4 Smart Healthcare

IoT makes our world a smarter place to live. Even though we have devices to aid a comfortable living in the traditional setup, we have to keep instructing machines for the task to be accomplished every now and then. With the help of IoT technology, human interaction has been limited and devices can start to interact, collaborate, and learn from each other to accomplish the task just like human beings. This can ultimately reduce human intervention in a machine cycle. Machines are instructed to keep in touch with each other and to complete the task at a particular time. Machines can also modify their functionalities based on the need and requirement. Thus, IoT is a platform where everyday devices are connected to the Internet so that they can interact and exchange data with each other (Ray 2018).

The growth of smart technology can be possibly applied in healthcare engineering by gathering reliable and robust data from equipment connected with the patients along their bedside, observing patient data and identifying them in a real-life situation. The complete setup of patient attention could be enhanced. This can be considered not as a disturbance to the patient but to make it a comfortable experience. By 2020, around 87% of all healthcare administrations will have employed IoT machinery. But today, many healthcare devices operate in silence. Over one-third of healthcare organizations in the world attempt to smear data from associated devices to the different commercial developments with a machine that creates incompetence, potential for data loss, and mistakes in analysis (Mutlag et al. 2019). A good healthcare system depends on the speed and correctness of the diagnosis. A wide range of equipment is becoming associated with the emergence of IoT. Almost half of the devices available in the healthcare sector would completely depend on IoT technology in the next 2 years. From hand-held devices to health archives to medical equipment, the production of devices is agreeing with the world of connected things. The impending use of IoT becomes limitless when there is a common language and a single platform for these devices to operate. Time consumption on rigorous monitoring and health management of the patient's health everyday can be considerably reduced as the entire system comes under this technology. Experts need not visit the patient in-person but can monitor the patient's health condition from a remote location and give advice using a remote diagnosis system. With advanced sensors and Wi-Fi connectivity, complete and quality care can be given more quickly and efficiently. Nearly three-quarters of healthcare leaders who have adopted IoT leave its key benefit to be to monitor and control medical devices and sensors. Tasks involving patient's heart monitoring, checking temperature using temperature gauges, and many more become easier with the help of real-time data collecting devices that already exist in healthcare. Currently, this setup can be used to create a harmless and more operative atmosphere. Several applications in hand-held devices enhance the capabilities of the staff and even the patients to manage IoT data. IoT refers to an easier and more efficient patient care experience allowing staff to do their jobs better, which is why 76% of healthcare leaders project that it is going to transform their industry (Sodhro et al. 2019, Zamanifar & Nazemi 2019).

IoT equips a multitude of domains and millions of devices with connectivity every day. A smart medicine dispenser is a smart appliance that stores, dispenses and manages the medicine. The healthcare and the general practice of medicine majorly face issues in one or more of these three areas: research, devices, and care (Minaam & Abd-ELfattah 2018). Medical research has to rely on leftover data in controlled settings for medical examination. It lacks real-world data that can solve critical conditions. IoT could be the answer to all these problems. It opens the road to a wealth of valuable data through analysis and real-time testing. IoT empowers healthcare professionals and improves the quality of care. Finally, it ultimately reduces the unsustainably high costs of medical devices. One such example is a care device. A care device has certain parameters that are considered safe. Once one of them is breeched the sensor immediately relays this message via a secured gateway to the cloud. It is vital for the gateway to be secure as it holds all the valuable medical records. The cloud then passes the remote signal to a smart device that is monitored either by a nurse or a caretaker at home. The beauty of remote patient monitoring is that the patients can now replace a long wait at the doctor's office with a quick check-in, data share, and instructions on how to proceed. IoT bridges the gap between reading devices and delivering healthcare by creating systems rather than just equipment (El Zouka & Hosni 2019, Qiu et al. 2017).

12.5 The Continuous Glucose Monitoring (CGM) System

A CGM system consists of sensors that last up to 3 months, a transmitter with on-body wearable, and a smart phone app instead of a separate receiver; data is sent directly to the smart phone. This system consists of a small transmitter worn on the arm and a tiny sensor that is just inserted under the skin. The sensor stays in place and measures glucose in the interstitial fluid for up to 3 months. The transmitter wirelessly powers the sensor every few minutes; this power stimulates the device that sparks an LED light source. This LED light excites a polymer coating available outside the sensor. The quantity of light produced by the polymer coating increases or decreases along with the body's glucose concentration as the glucose level from the body is bound to the coating. Produced light is read by photodetectors available in the sensor. Special circuitry digitizes the light signal and relays it back to the transmitter. The body-worn transmitter receives this data and calculates the glucose concentration. The transmitter the sends glucose data via Bluetooth to a smart phone. This eliminates the need to carry an extra receiver device. The transmitter is smart and provides on-body wearable even when the smart phone is inside the bag. The smart phone application can wirelessly send the sensor glucose history to an email or a cloud-based application or the data can be downloaded from the transmitter to a personal computer via USB. The sensor glucose data may be shared with a family member or doctor so that they too can view the sensor glucose history (Bruttomesso et al. 2019, El Zouka & Hosni 2019, Khowaja et al. 2018).

In United States, every 20 minutes, a senior citizen falls and every second in the world one elderly person falls. Most of the falls prove to be fatal and are the major cause for any sort of hip injuries or spinal injuries. Moreover, most of these cases are fatal, and there is a shocking report that says that in most of the cases, the one who has fallen is detected only after 3–4 hours. There is no clue as to when they fell, and by the time anyone has reached them, they have already either passed away or are in a critical state requiring an operation. A system using IoT and sensors to detect the fall not before the fall, but immediately after the fall, has been created. It has a wearable kind of environment setup, a couple of wearable be worn in the right shoulder and in the left shoulder that will detect the fall. When old people fall, both of their hands will also generally fall at tremendous speed. When they move a single hand, it is understood that it is not a fall, and when they move both the hands faster, it is obviously because of a fall. Whenever the sensory data is received, it will be sent to the server, which will process the data. Following data processing, through the GSM module, a call to the person will made who is registered as the caretaker of that particular person. As there are sensors connected to the wearable, when there is a fall the data is immediately recorded. That data is taken to the microcontroller and is then transmitted or sent to Bluetooth.

According to the second approach, when an old person goes to the restroom, they tend to remove whatever wearable they have, so a sensor and receiver (infrared, IR, transmitter and receiver) is kept at the entry of the restroom. The moment someone enters the restroom the IR transmitting to the receiver will be interrupted, signaling that there is a person in the restroom. Inside the restroom, piezo plates are pasted over the tiles. If someone falls inside the toilet, they tend to cover five to six tiles at least, indicating that the person has fallen. From there, an alert message is sent to the concerned person or the caretaker. Through the transmitter part of the Bluetooth module, the data goes to the server. Analytics will be done and the GPS module will help the patient in calling the caregiver using a GSM call. It's all about collecting the fall data, analyzing if it is fall data, and then sending it to the corresponding GPS module. The GPS module will then call the corresponding person and the data will be recorded in the cloud. It is a complete IoT application wearable technology plus bathroom fall detection system (Makhlouf et al. 2017, Koo et al. 2016).

Big data can help create personalized medical plans for individuals based on their genetic makeup. Clinical trials today have higher success rates as researchers are able to make more informed decisions. Today, organizations across the world access tremendous amount of data. Take social networks, for example. Every day, around 315 millions of new entries are uploaded in Facebook. On Twitter, 6,000 tweets are published every second. Similarly, healthcare generates a large amount of data measured in terabytes. Technically, this large, complex, and voluminous data cannot be processed by traditional database processing applications. Early disease detection, personalized medicine, clinical trials, and increased profitability via detection of high-cost patients are some of the applications of big data in healthcare (Mehta & Pandit 2018, Pashazadeh & Navimipour 2018). Big data analytics for carrier movements was utilized to understand the spread of the Ebola virus in Africa to the world. This provided the World Health Organization (WHO) crucial information using which they could create strategies to negate the spread of this disease. Healthcare organizations are analyzing the genetic makeup, body composition, and lifestyle habits of individuals to predict the onset of diseases. Today, efforts are being made to create personalized medical treatments on a probation basis. The success rate of clinical trials has improved as researchers can make more informed decisions using sample set selection. Big data enables real-time exhaustive tracking and reporting, which was not possible in traditional databases. Increased profitability to the hospitals via big data is possible by identifying the spending patterns of patients. Merely 5% of U.S. patients account for more than half of their healthcare spending. Hospitals can shortlist these patients and ensure a high standard of healthcare and customer service (Saheb & Izadi 2019, Sahoo et al. 2018).

Big data can be used to revolutionize healthcare by creating algorithms to detect and treat diseases. The impact of big data on the practice of medicine is fundamentally going to transform the physician's ability to personalize care directly for the patients. It can be with the help of a hand-held device that has amazing capability in Bluetooth-enabled inhalers for asthma patients, blood pressure monitors, and other devices. The data will be checked against the genetic profile of the patients. Individualized models for each person that maps out their health course trajectory. It will be something that patients are engaged in on a daily basis but not necessarily actively triggered, but the algorithm will alert users with the intimation of the disease well in advance so that they can approach their doctor before contracting the disease. To benefit from big data, patients have to give up some privacy. There is a shift in culture that says you are being more open in sharing your medical data (Kobusińska et al. 2018).

12.6 Smart Grids

The smart grid is an evolving and vital area that was initiated in 2007 by the U.S. Congress and approved by President George W. Bush. The need for electricity grows exponentially, and deployment of electricity grid also increases, which is expensive and throws the burden on the consumer. The innovative ingredient with this generic electricity grid and renewable energy sources makes research more interesting and worthwhile. Across the nation, planning is ongoing for providing electricity by incorporating the concept of information technology for security, reliability, and efficiency. Popularly coined as "electricity with a brain" (nist.gov).

The influence of the smart grid is increasing, irrespective of the sector. The benefit of using smart grid in business, market, manufacturing, customer relationship management, distribution, and transmission is manifold. Fast response, risk management, quick decision making, standardization, increased efficiency are some of these benefits. Features of smart grid such as resiliency, supervision, sustainability, marketization, and flexibility make it unique. The smart grid framework shown in Figure 12.1 was proposed by P. Acharjee in his work on strategy and implementation of smart grids in India, providing insights that all the components are interdependent and correlated in nature. A service provider has a link with the consumer alone. Considering the requirement of developing the nation and its social, political, economic, and climatic condition, the strategy move is required to incorporate smart grid for efficient working of various sectors in a profitable manner along with user friendliness (Acharjee, 2013).

With the advent of putting together a renewable source of energy with electricity makes the system very challenging in a smart grid perspective. Simulation of the proposed system throws light on things to be enhanced for better system design. Delamare and his researchers using AnyLogic simulation created an environment with versatile energy sources like batteries, renewable sources with weather, solar, and price module along with demand. Based on the requirement and framework, the provisions of electricity is fine-tuned for different types of houses and has conveyed that by introducing the stationery electricity and still more other resources provide scalable and flexible environment (Delamare et al. 2015).

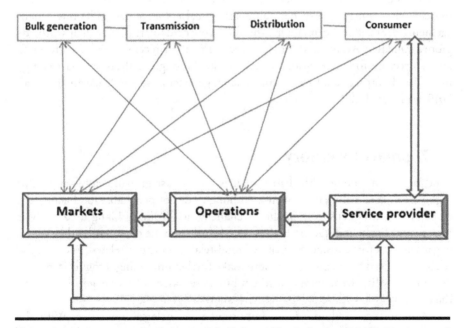

Figure 12.1 Framework of smart grid. (Adapted by Acharjee (2013). Strategy and implementation of smart grids in India.)

The amount of data generated via smart grid requires the usage of the cloud. The variant of this is proposed by Demir and his co-workers entitled as the hybrid hierarchical cloud concept. The ultimate objective of this cloud-based smart grid architecture is to tackle scalability along with security. Port Hopping Spread Spectrum is integrated that shows dafaulting clients shortly and minimizes distributed denial of service. Its three-layered architecture handles time-sensitive data. The primary layer is broken bundle as broker servers. The second layer possesses application servers dedicated to processing data in batch and visualization in specific. The third layer is made up of public cloud infrastructure that acts as intermediate with third parties. The communication of the smart grid happens through layer 1, and other layers rely on broker servers. Availability and throughput performance analysis have shown its good design for further process (Bera et al. 2015, Demir et al. 2018).

In a recent development, Baum and his team extensively researched the way of utilizing the resource from a smart grid for various household products. Energy from hydro, solar, wind, and other renewable sources are devised as variable energy resources. Demand response is the buzzword that illustrates the need for consumers by joining the two terms such as dynamic and active demand. Monte Carlo simulation is used to study system performance and forecast that this method acts as providing energy in an economical manner based on individual user's requirement (Baum et al. 2019).

To tackle the electric power requirement of the forthcoming generation, the need for smart grids is mandatory. Smart meters along with renewable energy sources with contemporary communication technologies will aid power management in an effective manner. The data collected in real time helps provide proper remedies. Avancini and his researchers in their recent work have proposed an architecture for smart grid. In their work, thorough analysis of smart energy meters with various application and challenges facing research (Avancini et al. 2019, Fadel et al. 2015).

12.7 Smart Inventory

Food processing along with distribution is a very fast growing industry in this highly fast-paced competitive world. Although sales of perishable food across the globe are trending, ensuring quality is challenging. Work by Liang used analytic hierarchy process, and questionnaires were framed to take decisions by the process of gauging. Factors considered included food-related, operator-related, and process-related, followed by assigning weight to make further processing. From this, to take decisions, quality, frequency, and recent purchase-based rules were generated with the process along with sequential pattern analysis (Liang 2013).

Maintaining warehouse is an important task in large industries. With the advent of information communication and technology, the deployment of computers in maintenance reduces risk to a large extent. The radiofrequency identification tagging is used in effective tracking, and its implementation is easier and cost-effective. The tag has a unique identification number with an address as a reader. The evolution of IoT makes this smart inventory very interesting. Figure 12.2 shows the roadmap of IoT given by SRI consulting business intelligence. In this work, open-source IoT named NodeMcu was deployed. With this combination, the system finds data in a dynamic manner and updation occurs in a timely manner (Tejesh & Neeraja 2018). The system is designed for a refrigerator to work in a responding manner with the concept of integrating transponders, IBM security directory integrator, and sensors (Khan et al. 2016).

IoT enabled with cloud computing provides high visibility and traceability by utilizing laser scanner at shop floors. In the enterprise resource planning process, all departments work in a correlated manner by utilizing a centralized huge dataset setup. M. Mehdizadeh conducted extensive work pertaining to spare parts distribution with inventory management as an important module to take a decision about purchase strategies. ABC analysis is performed to get a preview about new order placements. Patterns and rules are derived from uncertain information received via ABC analysis (Mehdizadeh 2019).

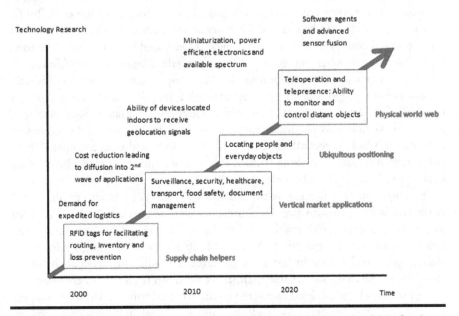

Figure 12.2 IoT technology roadmap. (Adapted by SRI consulting business intelligence.)

12.8 Smart City

By 2050, 70% of the world's population is expected to be living in cities covering less than 2% of the earth's surface (Brock et al. 2019). Never have cities been so challenged, and the trend continues to grow. This raises many issues like pollution, infrastructure access, traffic congestion, mobility, as well as safety and health of its residents. The development and combination of new technologies, such as the IoT, artificial intelligence, and big data analytics, offer a multifaceted solution, that is, the smart city. Smart cities are hyperconnected cities that are technologically equipped to improve the lives of their residents. Smart cities provide solutions for most of the existing problems in our daily lives using technologies.

There are some areas where people are still struggling to get permanent access to electricity. Sensors can be installed in those places to analyze the use of electricity in various sectors to optimize energy across the grid. This results in less frequent power cuts and distributed energy. In the UK, the city of Bristol created a data dome, a public platform where information on traffic, air quality, noise, as well as governance can be shared. The status of the city is determined by exploiting the data collected so that maintenance activity can follow based on the need in each and every location (Reed & Keech 2019).

The world is changing fast. Cities are growing and urban population is rising. The need for transportation of people is increasing but so are congestion, air pollution, road accidents, and climate change. Though we need more mobility, it needs to be done in a smarter way. This is the demand for the future (Gohar et al. 2018).

Electric vehicles can be charged when goods are loaded. A driver enters to lead the connected convoy onto the public roads. A dedicated bus line should be used if possible. Autonomous connected trailers create safe margins and flexible vehicle convoys to adapt to transportation needs. Adjusting to schedule updates, flexible convoy switching goods along the way through a mobile consolidation center is possible. The transport system is enabled through an integrated cloud platform, connecting vehicles, people, infrastructure, and logistic. In the city, the sensors on autonomous trucks detect all movements in the vicinity and react automatically to any potential incidents, making citizens safe and preventing accidents before they happen (Aujla et al. 2019, Heidrich et al. 2017).

Bus platooning will improve the efficiency and capacity in city public transportation. With silent emission-free buses, public transport can be brought closer to people and even drive inside the buildings. This opens up completely new opportunities for city planning. A fast and efficient way of charging from the electric grid can be done in just a few minutes. To build the city and the infrastructure in the more sustainable manner we need electricity. Zero emission and low noise give electric vehicles access to environmental zones in the city. Imagine a silent and machine-free city, a cleaner and safer and more resource-efficient world without compromising our every life and health in a smart city (Haas & Friedrich 2017).

Street lights can become a central point of technology for other IoT solutions. Each street light in the system is digitally connected to a network with features like on-board analytics, which monitor usage and self-report to the system. Locally, on-board controllers with LEDs save energy costs and significantly reduce maintenance expenses. Intelligent lighting gives a cloud-based platform that allows wireless control to turn lights in the system on and off or to dim them. Energy analytics help manage usage, event-driven outage notifications, speed service, and maintenance (Chen et al. 2017). This increases efficiencies and control costs for the community, neighborhoods, shopping centers, and schools, while enabling fewer outages resulting in greater visibility and safety. With smart digital banners, audio speakers, street signs, sensors, and small sounds, user experiences can be enhanced. Events can be promoted, alerts can be delivered, and public safety can be improved. Highly energy-efficient quality lights enable various city services. They also act as an information highway. Connected street lights transmit data between millions of devices. Autonomous vehicles navigate the road safely with the help of sensors, and street lights that scan the road and transmit information augment vehicles with on-board sensors (Petritoli et al. 2019).

A smart city is a digitally advanced urban ecosystem that uses electronic data collection and IoT to ensure sustainable development of institutional factors, physical factor, social factors, and economic infrastructure. Smart cities work by infusing technology into city operations with sensors, networks, and communication. The need for a smart city is that the global population is expected to live in urban areas. These cities are important to the economy as the top 600 urban centers generate 60% of global GDP. According to frost and Sullivan, the smart city market will be worth 1.5 trillion dollars (Brock et al. 2019).

Smart cities adopt smart technology to improve our environment and daily living. Smart technology is a combination of information and communication technology and IoT, harnessing the power of data. A smart city should be livable, efficient, sustainable, and safe. It requires smart planning, smart environment, smart services, and smart living.

12.9 Smart Manufacturing

12.9.1 Paradigm Shift-Industry 4.0

Developing countries have re-emphasized producing with national aggressive procedures, for example, Industry 4.0. Nonetheless, a large portion of developing nations may not be prepared for Industry 4.0. This investigation aims to propose an applied system of "Industry 3.5" as a half-breed procedure between Industry 3.0 and to-be Industry 4.0, to address a portion of the requirements for adaptable choices and shrewd generation in Industry 4.0. The view of the entire world is on developing new products and frameworks using IoT and big data. Successful organizations are combating overwhelming positions in this recently developed field by offering novel strategies and additionally utilizing new advances to upgrade to Industry 4.0. The concept of big data, however, has significant problems such as storing materials, capacity constraints for processing, and maintaining the security and privacy of data of the emerging industry (Brugo et al. 2016). Big data can support activities by providing constant answers for difficulties in each industry. Future industries are striving to execute the proposed Industry 3.5 to encourage the relocation of Industry 4.0.

Furthermore, smart factories with the paradigm shift to Industry 4.0 will focus on the factory to have decision-making systems, which in turn will enhance the digitization, automation, and upgradation of manufacturing systems in terms of hardware, mainly focusing on software integration (Atzori et al. 2010). The development of the web into a system of interconnected items is described with the jargon as the IoT. Also, the selection of IoT for Industry 4.0 empowers the change of conventional fabricating frameworks into digitalized ones, creating noteworthy opportunities through reforming enterprises (Renu et al. 2013).

IoT enables cutting-edge organizations to receive new information-driven systems and handle the global need for industry reformation more effectively. Be that as it may, the selection of IoT expands the overall volume of the produced information, changing the modern information into mechanical big data (Kim et al. 2002). IoT applications are used for genuine mechanical information which can be produced prompting industrial big data for effectively shaping the industry. It turns into a pivotal issue for nations to develop a reasonable procedure to fit in the tempest of assembling knowledge (Li et al. 2008).

12.10 Digital Manufacturing

The natural and digital environment forms a society. Mass customization of items and administrations is favored over large-scale manufacturing. Organizations request assisting a specific client on a focused price toward the large-scale manufacturing price through brief conceivable improvement time and creation time (Hashem et al. 2015). Additionally, data innovation has significantly impacted conventional businesses. Digital manufacturing is system-driven, necessitating innovation-based ways to deal with assembling, information examination, production, inventory network, and different procedures by an advanced connection to characterize and creating an advanced manufacturing technique (Rostamzadeh et al. 2015). Virtual manufacturing, e-manufacturing, includes advanced techniques which apparently increase the productivity for industries, involving digital manufacturing.

Digital manufacturing is applied to various sectors such as automotive, defense, food, chemical compounds, and medicine (Zhang et al. 2015). Cloud-based plan and assembling, an advanced administration technique, is an arranged

and organized advancement model, which is considered as another rising innovation that will enhance the computerized assembling and structure development, under the guidance of digital physical frameworks, IoT, and big data
(Maksimovic et al. 2015).

12.11 Data Analytics in Large-Scale Manufacturing

Large-scale manufacturing poses a severe challenge for industries as they face severe
process complexity and require innovative manufacturing techniques. One area of
concern is insufficient data. Usage of scalable structures and early prototypes are a
solution to support technology.

The need for automation is difficult when multiple databases are used
(Kao et al. 2015).

Sometimes the data is also reduced which is a big challenge for methods
involved in data analytics. In the current IT infrastructure, the data is applicable
only to small-scale industries, which is a limitation.

Prioritization and applying data analytics to technological development phases
involve adaptive prioritization, and scalable methods of data prioritization are the
road to successful usage of data analytics in large-scale industries (Xiang & Hu
2012). The firmly related Industry 4.0 involves the use of the non-exclusive idea of
cyber-physical frameworks.

Involving strategic prioritizations and evaluating use-cases provide typical optimization plans. Techniques of data analytics influence the cost involved in each
use-case, which makes it more beneficial and extends a larger solution. Adaptive
data availability, which involves the specific use-cases based on the benefit and
effort, gives a strategic prioritization technique. Scalable data analytics provide
feedback based on evaluations to have better adaptive data.

Strategic planning helps cluster use-cases based on effort and benefit. The prototype based on historic data works in a series production technique, which deploys
production lines to roll out scalable data analytics.

12.12 Industrial Big Data

IoT applications involve industrial data to transform into industrial big data. More
devices with sensors and tools for manufacturing with enabled data can be used for
providing data as industrial big data. The various cyber protection systems generate
various raw data using various sensors (Sundmaeker et al. 2010). Using IoT, data
acquisition occurs which, in turn, is preprocessed. Data packets are then organized
and stored in big data cloud as industrial big data. Digital manufacturing is similar
to additive manufacturing, and big data analytics constitute the scope for customized market needs. Critical systems data need to be evaluated and validated before

authentic considerations, such as healthcare data. Large datasets involve large repositories and different manufacturing stages. Systems with embedded information devices have their data stored for the entire lifecycle (Zhang et al. 2010). The IoT worldview changes businesses into digital frameworks equipped to be adaptable and versatile and completely mindful to developing conditions. Few better approaches for separating and preparing the information ought to be considered to decrease the developed and transmitted information. The involvement of IoT and various sensors can thereby produce large industrial data for new paradigm shift in the industries.

12.13 Smart Retail

12.13.1 Need for Smart Retailing

Smart technologies involve several actors for a better urban society. The growing technologies that focus on smart cities make smart retailing pivotal. Smart retailing also focuses on smart organizational structures.

The use of smart technology similar to RFID helps build a novel idea of smart retail assisted through contemporary skills.

12.13.2 Types of Smart Retailing

Smart selling involves activities at the organizational level and selling activities. The major features involve the method of developing capabilities based on demand. The relation between the consumer and salespersons for different product consumption build a relation and a service (Hollands, 2008).

Smart usage of technology in transaction calls for modifications in organizational methods and marketing actions. At the structural level, these techniques need determination for figuring out, choosing, and presenting the excellent technology, even for improving the method to produce, accumulate, accomplish, and switch information starting from purchasers corporations, in addition to developing smart partnership among customer and seller for in-shop acceptance. In actuality, merchants want to recognize the ecological alternative and perform accordingly, which thrusts in the direction of the advent of a growing generation (Anthopoulos & Vakali 2012). Hereafter, they need to increase functionality toward understanding the new aggressive situations, allowing modernization and the connected movement approach by assimilating and reconfiguring inner and peripheral structural capabilities and assets (Samuelsson 1991).

Smart technology is also capable of alternate actions with respect to purchasers' gaining admission to the production, associations through dealers, and product service intake (Nam & Pardo 2011). For the process to have an entry to the technology, consumers can access the creation/carrier via smart skills, which conquer old-fashioned obstacles of existing factors of sale by permitting direct entry from home, from personal phones, from storefront home windows, and many others (Capalbo et al. 2017). Consequently, customers can engage by the creation and can earn the facility, which is at their hand that interactively reacts to customers' variable needs (Anttiroiko et al. 2013).

The access is similarly supported with big existence of plans, which includes user-interactive presentations, cellular components, among others. Accordingly, even as adapting the position of a physical purchasing assistant, these skills variation pave the way for constructing and retaining sturdy associations with consumers. Moreover, they provide new methods for filing requirements to shops on behalf of stores to answer to consumers, with the aid of actively involving each actor within the salesperson (Cai & Xu 2006). These technologies guide communications among customers, outlets, and inventions. Consequently, they need an instantaneous impact on vendors' process by imparting sustenance for the implementation in their duties. For example, they offer up-to-date records of existing merchandise, which workers may practice for responding to purchasers' requirements (Crissman et al. 1998).

In old retail situations, customers sell and deal with the purchasers at the same time. In the new smart surroundings, the procurement may be offered in hoard and brought at once to home (Schaffers et al. 2011). Consequently, the primary features symbolizing smart generation for transactions are as follows: evolving competences based on demand, variations in information control and the advent of smart partnership, and modifications in salesperson job.

12.13.3 Consumers in Smart Retailing

Consumer expectancies are described as the goals or wants of customers. Client expectations are crucial indicators of consumer notion and satisfaction, and accordingly why retailers are looking to manipulate customers' expectancies. For stores, it can be said that expectancies are what customers believe before they make a buy related to their products or services. But, consumer expectations in a smart retailing environment are varied as the current generations generally tend to have unique beliefs about new technology (Kim et al. 2007). The primary motive why conventional retailing equipment are unobservable in online markets is because in the previous couple of years retailing has changed intensely due to the advent of online channels and ongoing digitalization A smart retail setting has been advanced that can be a useful way for a firm to generate more purchaser and enterprise value (Pantano & Timmermans, 2011). Smart retailing has sought to provide higher know-how of technology as well as consumer's interactions concerning future innovations in retail settings. Therefore, an enhanced smart retailing may be essential, or it may exceed consumer expectations (Xu & Wu 2012). New apps and new equipment must be used to take into account the effects of new technology on human relationships and transaction protection.

12.14 Smart Agriculture

The need for food is increasing exponentially across the globe. The strengthening and usage of modern techniques help in getting better outputs in the form of quality and quantity. In the modern era, usage of IoT greatly adds weightage in the field of agriculture. IoT basically incorporates sensing, data transfer, followed by data storage and manipulation as three layers. Each layer works based on Internet connectivity with RFID and WSN technologies. Utilizing the various sensors and other hardware components helps in monitoring and controlling agriculture, as well as supply chain management in the food sector. Challenges based on hardware, software, and network security need to be taken into consideration (Tzounis et al. 2017).

Climate smart agriculture is interesting in the field of agriculture to increase yield. Three pillars considered in this are a sustainable increase in the productivity of agriculture and livestock, familiarization to climate alteration, and working effectively to reduce the greenhouse emissions. Various approaches including simulation modeling, optimization methods, cost–benefit analysis, econometrics, ranking, meta-analysis, spatial analysis, and integrated assessing modeling are used to set the priorities that boost productivity (Thornton et al. 2018).

Deep learning is a booming technology in agriculture for early detection of leaf diseases, tracing weed, classifying lands, recognizing plants, and fruit calculation. By utilizing the deep learning concepts, visualization for various datasets with greater clarity is retrieved. It provides better output for performance metrics compared to other traditional methods. Therefore, data is required for preprocessing and for other steps to be incorporated (Kamilaris & Prenafeta-Boldú 2018). Big data analytics work with a versatile and large dataset. A smart farming framework includes data chain, farm management, farm processes, along with network management to carry out analysis and take decisions. Data chain comprises data capture, storage, transfer, transformation, analytics, and marketing. Tasks and attaining them falls under farm process and management. The hardware, software, and peripherals working in a coordinated manner comprise network management (Wolfert et al. 2017).

Internet of underground thing is the latest in the smart agriculture era for precision-based cultivation. The sensors used in this helps to find moisture of soil, physical attributes of soil, soil macronutrients that help obtain the best yields (Vuran et al. 2018). Opinion mining is deployed in the governance of sustainable agriculture. The framework consists of the data collection phase, preprocessing of the same by removing duplication, stemming, selection of attributes, special characters removal, followed by opinion classification via naïve Bayesian, support vector machine, multilayer perceptron, k-Nearest neighbor, decision tree, as well as evaluation measures such as precision, recall, and accuracy (Kumar & Sharma 2018).

12.15 Conclusion

Smart city is the ultimate goal of many developing nations and its the matter of integrating various services in a unified manner. Economic and social development of people is possible if all sectors work in an indigenous manner to achieve this goal. Internet usage is having a greater impact on the lifestyle of individuals. All fields ranging from transportation, agriculture, healthcare, inventory system, to manufacturing system are experiencing exponential growth. Large amounts of data are being generated with electronic technologies, and analyzing the same has immense potential in providing smart city features on the whole.

References

Acharjee, P. (2013). Strategy and implementation of smart grids in India. *Energy Strategy Reviews*, 1(3), 193–204.

Alrawi, F. (2017). The importance of intelligent transport systems in the preservation of the environment and reduction of harmful gases. *Transportation Research Procedia*, 24, 197–203.

Amanatiadis, A., Karakasis, E., Bampis, L., Ploumpis, S., & Gasteratos, A. (2019). ViPED: On-road vehicle passenger detection for autonomous vehicles. *Robotics and Autonomous Systems*, 112, 282–290.

Anthopoulos, L. G., & Vakali, A. (2012). Urban planning and smart cities: Interrelations and reciprocities. *Lecture Notes in Computer Science*, 7281, 178–189.

Anttiroiko, A.-V., Valkama, P., & Bailey, S. J. (2013). Smart cities in the new service economy: Building platforms for smart services. *Artificial Intelligence & Society*, 29, 323–334.

Ashokkumar, K., Sam, B., Arshadprabhu, R., & Britto. (2015). Cloud based intelligent transport system. *Procedia Computer Science*, 50, 58–63.

Atzori, L., Iera, A., & Morabito, G. (2010). The Internet of Things: A survey. *Computer Networks*, 54(15), 2787–2805.

Aujla, G. S., Kumar, N., Singh, M., & Zomaya, A. Y. (2019). Energy trading with dynamic pricing for electric vehicles in a smart city environment. *Journal of Parallel and Distributed Computing*, 127, 169–183.

Avancini, D. B., Rodrigues, J. J., Martins, S. G., Rabêlo, R. A., Al-Muhtadi, J., & Solic, P. (2019). Energy meters evolution in smart grids: A review. *Journal of Cleaner Production*, 217, 702–715.

Baum, Z., Palatnik, R. R., Ayalon, O., Elmakis, D., & Frant, S. (2019). Harnessing households to mitigate renewables intermittency in the smart grid. *Renewable Energy*, 132, 1216–1229.

Bera, S., Misra, S., & Rodrigues, J. J. (2015). Cloud computing applications for smart grid: A survey. *IEEE Transactions on Parallel and Distributed Systems*, 26(5), 1477–1494.

Brock, K., den Ouden, E., van der Klauw, K., & Podoynitsyna, K., & Langerak, F. (2019). Light the way for smart cities: Lessons from Philips lighting. *Technological Forecasting and Social Change*, 142, 194–209.

Brugo, T., Palazzetti, R., Ciric-Kostic, S., Yan, X. T., Minak, G., & Zucchelli, A. (2016). Fracture mechanics of laser sintered cracked polyamide for a new method to induce cracks by additive manufacturing. *Polymer Testing*, 50, 301–308. doi:10.1016/j.polymertesting.2016.01.024.

Bruttomesso, D., Laviola, L., Avogaro, A., & Bonora, E. of the Italian Diabetes Society (SID). (2019). The use of real time continuous glucose monitoring or flash glucose monitoring in the management of diabetes: A consensus view of Italian diabetes experts using the Delphi method. *Nutrition, Metabolism and Cardiovascular Diseases*, 29(5), 421–431.

Cai, S., & Xu, Y. (2006). Effects of outcome, process and shopping enjoyment on online consumer behavior. *Electronic Research and Applications*, 5(4), 272–281.

Capalbo S.M., Seavert C., Antle J.M., Way J., Houston L. (2018). Understanding Tradeoffs in the Context of Farm-Scale Impacts: An Application of Decision-Support Tools for Assessing Climate Smart Agriculture. In: Lipper L., McCarthy N., Zilberman D., Asfaw S., Branca G. (eds) *Climate Smart Agriculture. Natural Resource Management and Policy*, 52, Springer, Cham, pp. 173-197.

Chen, Y., Ardila-Gomez, A., & Frame, G. (2017). Achieving energy savings by intelligent transportation systems investments in the context of smart cities. *Transportation Research Part D: Transport and Environment*, 54, 381–396.

Crissman, C. C., Antle, J. M., & Capalbo, S. M. (Eds.). (1998). *Economic, Environmental and Health Tradeoffs in Agriculture: Pesticides and the Sustainability of Andean Potato Production* (281 pp.). Dordrecht: Kluwer Academic Publishers.

Delamare, J., Bitachon, B., Peng, Z., Wang, Y., Haverkort, B. R., & Jongerden, M. R. (2015). Development of a smart grid simulation environment. *Electronic Notes in Theoretical Computer Science*, 318, 19–29.

Demir, K., Ismail, H., Vateva-Gurova, T., & Suri, N. (2018). Securing the cloud-assisted smart grid. *International Journal of Critical Infrastructure Protection*, 23, 100–111.

Elliott, D., Keen, W., & Miao, L. (2019). Recent advances in connected and automated vehicles. *Journal of Traffic and Transportation Engineering (English Edition)*, 6(2), 109–131.

El Zouka, H. A., & Hosni, M. M. (2019). Secure IoT communications for smart healthcare monitoring system. *Internet of Things*. doi:10.1016/j.iot.2019.01.003.

Fadel, E., Gungor, V. C., Nassef, L., Akkari, N., Malik, M. A., Almasri, S., & Akyildiz, I. F. (2015). A survey on wireless sensor networks for smart grid. *Computer Communications*, 71, 22–33.

Gohar, M., Muzammal, M., & Rahman, A. U. (2018). SMART TSS: Defining transportation system behavior using big data analytics in smart cities. *Sustainable Cities and Society*, 41, 114–119.

Grant-Muller, S., & Usher, M. (2014). Intelligent transport systems: The propensity for environmental and economic benefits. *Technological Forecasting and Social Change*, 82, 149–166.

Haas, I., & Friedrich, B. (2017). Developing a micro-simulation tool for autonomous connected vehicle platoons used in city logistics. *Transportation Research Procedia*, 27, 1203–1210.

Hashem, I. A. T., Yaqoob, I., Anuar, N. B., Mokhtar, S., Gani, A., & Khan, S. U. (2015). The rise of "big data" on cloud computing: Review and open research issues. *Information Systems*, 47, 98–115.

Heidrich, O., Hill, G. A., Neaimeh, M., Huebner, Y., & Dawson, R. J. (2017). How do cities support electric vehicles and what difference does it make? *Technological Forecasting and Social Change*, 123, 17–23.

Hollands, R. G. (2008). Will the real smart city please stand up? Intelligent, progressive or entrepreneurial. *City*, 12(3), 303–320.

Jadaan, K., Zeater, S., & Abukhalil, Y. (2017). Connected vehicles: An innovative transport technology. *Procedia Engineering*, 187, 641–648.

Janušová, L., & Čičmancová, S. (2016). Improving safety of transportation by using intelligent transport systems. *Procedia Engineering*, 134, 14–22.

Kamilaris, A., & Prenafeta-Boldú, F. X. (2018). Deep learning in agriculture: A survey. *Computers and Electronics in Agriculture*, 147, 70–90.

Kao, H-A., Jin, W., Siegel, D., & Lee, J. (2015). A cyber physical interface for automation systems – Methodology and examples. *Machines*, 3, 93–106.

Kennedy, R. (2015). Looking back to move forward: The Dymaxion revisited. *Procedia Technology*, 20, 46–53.

Khan, A. M., Khaparde, A., & Savanur, V. P. (2016, August). Self-aware inventory system based on RFID, sensors and IBM security directory integrator. In *2016 International Conference on Inventive Computation Technologies (ICICT)* (Vol. 3, pp. 1–4). Coimbatore: IEEE.

Khowaja, S. A., Prabono, A. G., Setiawan, F., Yahya, B. N., & Lee, S.-L. (2018). Contextual activity based healthcare Internet of Things, Services, and People (HIoTSP): An architectural framework for healthcare monitoring using wearable sensors. *Computer Networks*, 145, 190–206.

Kim, J., Fiore, A. M., & Lee, H. H. (2007). Influences of online store perception, shopping enjoyment, and shopping involvement on consumer patronage behavior towards an online retailer. *Journal of Retailing and Consumer Services*, 14(2), 95–107.

Kim, H., Lee, J.-K., Park, J.-H., Park, B.-J., & Jang, D.-S. (2002). Applying digital manufacturing technology to ship production and the maritime environment. *Integrated Manufacturing Systems*, 13(5), 295–305.

Kobusińska, A., Leung, C., Hsu, C.-H., Raghavendra, S., & Chang, V. (2018). Emerging trends, issues and challenges in Internet of Things, big data and cloud computing. *Future Generation Computer Systems*, 87, 416–419.

Koo, D. D., Lee, J. J., Sebastiani, A., & Kim, J. (2016). An Internet-of-Things (IoT) system development and implementation for bathroom safety enhancement. *Procedia Engineering*, 145, 396–403.

Kumar, A., & Sharma, A. (2018). Socio-sentic framework for sustainable agricultural governance. *Sustainable Computing: Informatics and Systems*, 10.1016/j. suscom.2018.08.006.

Li, Y., Thai, M. T., & Wu, W. (2008). *Wireless Sensor Networks and Applications*. New York: Springer.

Liang, C. C. (2013). Smart inventory management system of food-processing-and-distribution industry. *Procedia Computer Science*, 17, 373–378.

Linares, M. P., Barceló, J., Carmona, C., & Montero, L. (2017). Analysis and operational challenges of dynamic ride sharing demand responsive transportation models. *Transportation Research Procedia*, 21, 110–129.

Makhlouf, A., Nedjai, I., Saadia, N., & Ramdane-Cherif, A. (2017). Multimodal system for fall detection and location of person in an intelligent habitat. *Procedia Computer Science*, 109, 969–974.

Maksimovic, M., Vujovic, V., & Perisic, B. (2015, June). A custom Internet of Things health-care system. In *2015 10th Iberian Conference on Information Systems and Technologies (CISTI)* (pp. 1–6). Aviero: IEEE.

Malygin, I., Komashinskiy, V., & Korolev, O. (2018). Cognitive technologies for providing road traffic safety in intelligent transport systems. *Transportation Research Procedia*, 36, 487–492.

Mateus, A., Ribeiro, D., Miraldo, P., & Nascimento, J. C. (2019). Efficient and robust pedestrian detection using deep learning for human-aware navigation. *Robotics and Autonomous Systems*, 113, 23–37.

Matthias Weber, K., Heller-Schuh, B., Godoe, H., & Roeste, R. (2016). ICT-enabled system innovations in public services: Experiences from intelligent transport systems. *Telecommunications Policy*, 38(5–6), 539–557.

Mehdizadeh, M. (2019). Integrating ABC analysis and rough set theory to control the inventories of distributor in the supply chain of auto spare parts. *Computers & Industrial Engineering*, 139, 105673.

Mehta, N., & Pandit, A. (2018). Concurrence of big data analytics and healthcare: A systematic review. *International Journal of Medical Informatics*, 114, 57–65.

Mfenjou, M. L., Ari, A. A. A., Abdou, W., & Spies, F. (2018). Methodology and trends for an intelligent transport system in developing countries. *Sustainable Computing: Informatics and Systems*, 19, 96–111.

Minaam, D. S. A., & Abd-ELfattah, M. (2018). Smart drugs: Improving healthcare using smart pill box for medicine reminder and monitoring system. *Future Computing and Informatics Journal*, 3(2), 443–456.

Mutlag, A. A., Ghani, M. K. A., Arunkumar, N., Mohammed, M. A., & Mohd, O. (2019). Enabling technologies for fog computing in healthcare IoT systems. *Future Generation Computer Systems*, 90, 62–78.

Nam, T., & Pardo, T. A. (2011). Smart city as urban innovation: Focusing on management, policy and context. In *Proceedings of ICEGOV Conference* (pp. 185–194). New York: ACM.

Pantano, E., & Timmermans, H. J. P. (2011). *Advanced Technologies Management for Retailing: Frameworks and Cases*. Hersey, PA: IGI Global.

Pashazadeh, A., & Navimipour, N. J. (2018). Big data handling mechanisms in the healthcare applications: A comprehensive and systematic literature review. *Journal of Biomedical Informatics*, 82, 47–62.

Petritoli, E., Leccese, F., Pizzuti, S., & Pieroni, F. (2019). Smart lighting as basic building block of smart city: An energy performance comparative case study. *Measurement*, 136, 466–477.

Qiu, T., Liu, X., Han, M., Li, M., & Zhang, Y. (2017). SRTS: A self-recoverable time synchronization for sensor networks of healthcare IoT. *Computer Networks*, 129(24 Part 2), 481–492.

Ray, P. P. (2018). A survey on Internet of Things architectures. *Journal of King Saud University – Computer and Information Sciences*, 30(3), 291–319.

Reed, M., & Keech, D. (2019). Making the city smart from the grassroots up: The sustainable food networks of Bristol city. *Culture and Society*, 16, 45–51.

Renu, R. S., Mocko, G., & Koneru, A. (2013). Use of big data and knowledge discovery to create data backbones for decision support systems. *Procedia Computer Science*, 20, 446–453.

Rostamzadeh, K., Nicanfar, H., Torabi, N., Gopalakrishnan, S., & Leung, V. C. M. (2015). A context-aware trust-based information dissemination framework for vehicular networks. *IEEE Internet Things Journal*, 2(2), 121–132.

Saheb, T., & Izadi, L. (2019). Paradigm of IoT big data analytics in the healthcare industry: A review of scientific literature and mapping of research trends. *Telematics Informatics*, 41, 70-85.

Sahoo, P. K., Mohapatra, S. K., & Wu, S.-L. (2018). SLA based healthcare big data analysis and computing in cloud network. *Journal of Parallel and Distributed Computing*, 119, 121–135.

Samuelsson, M. (1991). Advanced intelligent network products bring new services faster. *AT&Technology*, 6(2), 2–7.

Schaffers, H., Komninos, N., Pallot, M., Trousse, B., Nilsson, M., & Oliveira, A. (2011). Smart cities and the future Internet: Towards cooperation frameworks for open innovation. *Lecture Notes in Computer Science*, 6656, 431–446.

Sodhro, A. H., Luo, Z., Sangaiah, A. K., & Baik, S. W. (2019). Mobile edge computing based QoS optimization in medical healthcare applications. *International Journal of Information Management*, 45, 308–318.

Sumalee, A., & Ho, H. W. (2018). Smarter and more connected: Future intelligent transportation system. *IATSS Research*, 42(2), 67–71.

Sun, L., Li, Y., & Gao, J. (2016). Architecture and application research of cooperative intelligent transport systems. *Procedia Engineering*, 137, 747–753.

Sundmaeker, H., Guillemin, P., Friess, P., & Woelfflé, S. (2010). Vision and challenges for realising the Internet of Things. *Cluster of European Research Projects on the Internet of Things*, 3(3), 34–36.

Tejesh, B. S. S., & Neeraja, S. (2018). Warehouse inventory management system using IoT and open source framework. *Alexandria Engineering Journal*, 57(4), 3817–3823.

Thornton, P. K., Whitbread, A., Baedeker, T., Cairns, J., Claessens, L., Baethgen, W., & Howden, M. (2018). A framework for priority-setting in climate smart agriculture research. *Agricultural Systems*, 167, 161–175.

Tzounis, A., Katsoulas, N., Bartzanas, T., & Kittas, C. (2017). Internet of Things in agriculture, recent advances and future challenges. *Biosystems Engineering*, 164, 31–48.

Vuran, M. C., Salam, A., Wong, R., & Irmak, S. (2018). Internet of underground things in precision agriculture: Architecture and technology aspects. *Ad Hoc Networks*, 81, 160–173.

Wolfert, S., Ge, L., Verdouw, C., & Bogaardt, M. J. (2017). Big data in smart farming – A review. *Agricultural Systems*, 153, 69–80.

www.nist.gov/engineering-laboratory/smart-grid. Accessed 7 May 2019.

Xiang, F., & Hu, Y. F. (2012, January). Cloud manufacturing resource access system based on Internet of Things. *Applied Mechanics and Materials*, 121, 2421–2425.

Xu, Q., & Wu, Z. (2012). A study on strategy schema for smart cities based on the innovation driven. In *Proceedings of ISMOT Conference* (pp. 313–315). Hangzhou: IEEE.

Yang, D., Kuijpers, A., Dane, G., & van der Sande, T. (2019). Impacts of large-scale truck platooning on Dutch highways. *Transportation Research Procedia*, 37, 425–432.

Yang, Z., & Pun-Cheng, L. S. C. (2018). Vehicle detection in intelligent transportation systems and its applications under varying environments: A review. *Image and Vision Computing*, 69, 143–154.

Zamanifar, A., & Nazemi, E. (2019). An approach for predicting health status in IoT health care. *Journal of Network and Computer Applications*, 134, 100–113.

Zhang, Y, Chen, K. B., Liu, X., & Sun, Y. (2010). Autonomous robotic pick-and-place of microobjects. *IEEE Transactions on Robotics*, 26, 200–207.

Zhang, Y., Wang, W., Wu, N., Member, S., & Qian, C. (2015). IoT – Enabled real-time production performance analysis and exception diagnosis model. *IEEE Transactions on Automation Science and Engineering*, 13, 1318–1332.

Zhang, Y., Wu, C., Qiao, C., & Hou, Y. (2019). The effects of warning characteristics on driver behavior in connected vehicles systems with missed warnings. *Accident Analysis & Prevention*, 124, 138–145.

Chapter 13

Big Data Management Solutions for IoT: Case Study – Connected Car

T. Lucia Agnes Beena
St. Josephs College

D. Sumathi
VIT-AP University

Rajalakshmi Krishnamurthi
Jaypee Institute of Information Technology

Prabha Selvaraj
VIT-AP University

Contents

13.1 Introduction

The most important technology that is expected to rule the future world is the IoT (Internet of Things). It is gaining momentum and grabbing the attention of a wide range of industries. It is a new technology visualized as an international network of machines and devices, competent in interacting with each other. Currently, about 10 billion IoT devices are in use. This will increase to more than 64 billion by 2025 [1]. Over several thousands of exabytes of data are generated through sensors built into the IoT devices which are connected to the Internet. The continued growth of the IoT industry influences all the organizations across the world. It is expected that the IoT market will grow to over $3 trillion annually by 2026 if all the organizations exploit the power of the IoT and Internet effectively. Goldman Sachs Global Investment Research [2] revealed that key IoT attributes (sensing, efficient, networked, specialized, everywhere) can change the direction of the development of tech companies toward new product cycles with cost and energy efficiency.

By definition, the IoT, which connects machines and devices, can send data and interact with other things and people connected to it. These devices can be connected with the digital world to

- Enhance customer service
- Build new products and services for revenue generation
- Streamline the operations and infrastructure
- Reduce system downtime by identifying and resolving the bottlenecks
- Make decisions concerning future infrastructure investments intelligently
- Predict and rectify the mean time to failure for machinery.

The things in IoT generate massive volumes of structured, semi-structured, and unstructured data. It is a complex task to collect, prepare, and analyze these data. Gaining insights from voluminous and different types (structured, semi-structured or unstructured) of data is beyond the scope of the traditional enterprise data warehouses (EDWs) and business intelligence (BI) software. In this context, harnessing a big data platform that can assist in collecting, preparing, and analyzing diverse data sources becomes essential [3]. Nowadays, various analytical techniques including incremental approaches, granular computing, machine learning, and deep learning are applied to face big data challenges and for stream processing [4]. According to Goldman Sachs [2], the most recent areas of applications with the IoT are wearables, connected homes, connected cities, the industrial Internet, and connected cars.

According to a report published by Allied Market Research [5], the global autonomous vehicle market is anticipated to rise from $54.23 billion in 2019 to $556.67 billion by 2026. Recently, the automotive digital technology is focusing on enhancing the in-car experience. The connected car is one such initiative. A car that is equipped with Internet connectivity and able to communicate and share the Internet access with other devices, both inside as well as outside the vehicle, is a connected car. Currently the leaders in the connected car market are Google, Delphi Automotive, General Motors, Audi AG, Ford Motor Company, AT&T, NXP Semiconductors, Alcatel-Lucent, BMW, and Apple [6]. This chapter elaborates on the connected car, its architecture, the leveraging technologies, and solutions for it.

13.2 Connected Car

A connected car is a car that is equipped with Internet access that allows the car to share data through Internet access, with other devices both inside and outside the vehicle [6]. Earlier in 2011, Kleberger et al. [7] outlined that a connected car consists of three domains: the vehicle, the automotive company portal to deliver services, and a communication link between the vehicle and the portal. These cars focus mainly on the in-vehicle wireless network that connects all the electronic components of the vehicle to control the car.

The picture of a connected car is shown in Figure 13.1. In 2014, the Future of Privacy Forum [8] elucidated that the car which has in-car telematics with connectivity through the Internet or via dedicated short-range communication (DSRC) for better diagnostics and to offer protection, convenience, and communication services is referred to as a connected car. A connected car has the potential to reduce traffic blockage. It also assists in reducing both vehicular emissions and energy consumption.

Currently, 20% of cars worldwide have Wi-Fi capabilities. It is expected to increase to 50% by 2023 [9]. These Wi-Fi capabilities lead to a variety of applications that can be categorized into infotainment (in-car applications) and telematics (external Wi-Fi applications). These capabilities have changed the car from being a mode of transport to a place for work and entertainment.

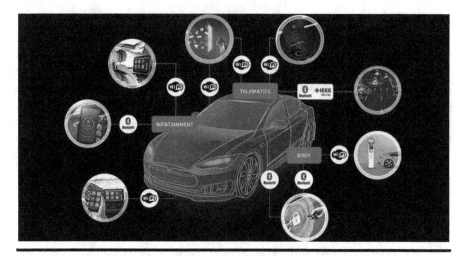

Figure 13.1 Connected car [45].

13.3 Different Modes of Connections

The Internet connectivity in a connected car is made possible by a Wi-Fi connection through a built-in embedded modem on board called a telematics control unit (TCU) inside the car [10]. With the aid of the Internet, the car can support onboard vehicle-to-sensor on board (V2S), vehicle-to-vehicle (V2V), vehicle-to-road infrastructure (V2I), and vehicle-to-Internet (V2I) interactions. Based on the type of interaction, the car has to apply a form of technology linked with that respective connection. The connectivity can be classified as intra-vehicle connectivity, inter-vehicle connectivity, and V2I connectivity [11].

13.3.1 Intra-Vehicle Communication

Connected cars are furnished with lots of sensors for better service in detecting road conditions and monitoring tire pressure and temperature of water in the cooling system [11]. These sensors interact with the electrical control units (ECUs) through event-driven or time-driven messages for better control. To enable these V2S interactions, an intra-vehicle communication network is designed using either wired technologies (controller area network (CAN) protocol, TTEthernet, and FlexRay that require cable connections between ECU and sensors) or wireless sensor communication and network technologies. The various wireless technologies that can be used for intra-vehicle wireless sensor network are discussed in this section.

Bluetooth: The Bluetooth wireless technology is a low-cost, user-friendly air interface with a short-range connectivity solution based on the IEEE 802.15.1 (IEEE: Institute of Electrical and Electronics Engineers) standard for personal, portable, and handheld electronic devices [12]. It allows 1 Mbps data rate communication between portable devices with an operating frequency of 2.4 GHz industrial, scientific, and medical (ISM) band. With regard to multiple access capacity, it can support eight nodes (one node as master with seven slave nodes) [13]. The present-day automobiles use Bluetooth for headset and rearview mirror.

ZigBee: The ZigBee networking stack is built based upon the IEEE 802.15.4 standard. It has physical (PHY) and medium access control (MAC) layers for a low-data-rate low-power network (NWK) and application (APL) layer specifications based on 802.15.4. This full-layered structure is called ZigBee stack [14]. ZigBee modules along with the security system can be used by a user to monitor their car from being stolen by somebody [15]. Hsin-Mu Tsai et al. [16] used the ZigBee sensor nodes in their study to perform packet transmission in the intra-car experiments and reported its effectiveness using various parameters.

Ultra-Wideband: Ultra-wideband (UWB) refers to radio systems that have been considered a revolutionary technology for transmitting large amounts of digital data over a broad frequency spectrum (3.1–10.6 GHz) using short-pulse communications at data rates up to 480 Mbps with low-power radio signals [13]. Niu et al. [17] designed an intra-vehicle UWB wireless sensor network consisting of ABS motor control simulating system, wheel speed sensors, UWB transmitting nodes, and the UWB network coordinator interfacing with electronic control unit (ECU) to transmit automotive speed data from four wheel speed sensors to the ECU. The result shows that at most 20,000 wheel speed sensor data of size 32 bps could safely reach the UWB receiver without message loss. Low-cost and low-complexity transceivers with UWB technology can be designed to receive high data signals from hundreds of wireless sensors for automotive vehicles in future [18].

Radio Frequency Identification (RFID) System: RFID is a wireless communication technology. It uses electromagnetic fields to automatically identify and track tags attached to objects, which contain electronically stored information [19]. Examples of RFID technologies are RFID readers, RFID writers, RFID smart sensors, RFID controllers, and RFID barcode scanners [20]. This technology helps in communication between cars, parking [21], and traffic management. Also, RFID technology can be used to reduce the fuel consumption of a car, make the car eco-friendly by reducing the pollution, and improve its efficiency [20].

60 GHz Millimeter Wave: The carrier frequencies between 30 and 300 GHz for communication are referred to as millimeter-wave (mmWave) communication. Modern vehicles are equipped with radars (radio detection and ranging) for object detection, lidars (light detection and ranging) for generating high-resolution depth-associated range maps, and visual cameras as virtual mirrors to improve the safety and efficiency of driving [22]. These equipments have sensors that generate data at high rates. mmWave communication is the only feasible approach for high-bandwidth-connected vehicles. mmWave allows the exchange of sensor data by expanding their sensing range for better automated driving functions. Multiple mmWave transceivers should be fitted in a vehicle to relieve blockage and have better spatial wadding in vehicular environments [23].

13.3.2 Inter-Vehicle Communication

Connected cars and V2V communications with IoT contribute to intelligent transportation and smart cities [26]. Inter-vehicle communication involves vehicle-to-vehicle (V2V), vehicle-to-infrastructure (V2I), vehicle-to-human (V2H), and vehicle-to-cloud (V2C) interactions. Smart devices in vehicles and cloud/fog infrastructures are connected using vehicular ad-hoc networks (VANETs). A user will get a convenient transportation experience by the smart decisions provided by the various sensors in a connected car that talk to each other [24]. This section discusses some of the wireless technologies such as DSRC, dynamic spectrum access (DSA), and continuous air interface for long and medium range (CALM) used in VANETS.

DSRC: DSRC is a short to medium range communication services that maintain public safety and private operations in V2I and V2V communication environments. The U.S. Federal Communications Commission (FCC) has allocated 75 MHz bandwidth at 5.9 GHz spectrum band for DSRC [11]. To support safety and non-safety services simultaneously, the dedicated bandwidth is split up into seven channels. The IEEE 802.11p for PHY and MAC layers and the IEEE 1609 family for upper layers represent the specifications of DSRC in the IEEE Standard for Wireless Access in Vehicular Environments (WAVE). There is a positive response from Information and Communication Technologies (ICT) manufacturers, automobile industry, academia, and governments for this technology. DSRC PHY layer is sufficient to support safety message delivery. Safety messages, either time driven or event driven, are mostly distributed to all the nodes within the communication range that requires low latency and high reliability. Many MAC protocols were proposed based on the time-division multiple access (TDMA) method that is capable of controlling channel access more precisely. Using this technique, a vehicle listens to the channel and broadcasts a message during the acquired time slot; thereby the quality of service (QoS) of safety in real-time applications is maintained in high-vehicular-density scenarios.

DSA: High-quality video streaming applications require a large amount of spectrum resources that forces difficulty in providing the QoS with the dedicated bandwidth, and the spectrum scarcity is more severe in high vehicular density areas of urban environments. The alternative technology that can be used for this scenario is DSA [11]. The unused television spectrum between 54 and 698 MHz, referred to as TV white space, offers superior propagation and building penetration compared to the DSRC frequency band. The IEEE has standardized the IEEE 802.11af and the IEEE 802.22 based on DSA over TV white space for wireless local area networks (WLANs) and wireless regional area networks (WRANs), respectively.

The effective use of DSA over TV white space to solve the expected spectrum shortage was experimented and found successful [25].

Communication Access for Land Mobile (CALM): CALM stood for continuous air interface for long and medium range until 2007, Since 2007, CALM stands for communication access for land mobile. The purpose of CALM is to extend a standardized networking terminal for connecting vehicles and roadside systems continuously using cellular WLANs and short-range-microwave (DSRC) or infra-red technology [27, 28]. CALM can be utilized in V2I non-IPv6, V2V local IPv6, V2I MIPv6, V2I NEMO, and V2V non-Ipv6 communication scenarios. The CALM architecture guards critical in-vehicle communication using a firewall controlled by the vehicle. This architecture also supports parental controls.

13.3.3 V2I Communication

Internet services are provided to the vehicle users through wireless access technologies such as cellular and Wi-Fi. The 3G and 4G-LTE cellular networks can provide reliable and ubiquitous access services [11]. Due to the rapid growth in wireless communication, 5G networks are expected to boost the communication requirements of future intelligent transportation systems (ITSs). A new hierarchical 5G next-generation VANET architecture is proposed [29] to offer flexible network management and control and high resource utilization. The software-defined networking (SDN) and cloud-RAN (CRAN), with 5G communication technologies, are integrated in this architecture for flexibility. For effective communication between the vehicle and road side units (RSUs), a fog computing framework was utilized. The results of this architecture indicate reduced transmission delay, minimized control overhead on controllers, and improved throughput.

Renault, Toyota, Kapsch TrafficCom, NXP, and Autotalks all support Wi-Fi as the standard for connected cars, while Daimler, Ford, Deutsche Telekom, Ericsson, PSA Group, Huawei, Samsung, Intel, and Qualcomm all support 5G [30]. Some of the features, such as extra speed, low latency, and ability to connect to more devices simultaneously, made 5G suitable for the connected car.

13.3.4 Cloud-Assisted Vehicular Internet of Things

The combination of VANETs and cloud computing is referred to as vehicular cloud (VC). The VC is proposed to overcome limitations such as storage, computation, and network services [31]. The basic goal of VC is to provide low-cost services to drivers and reduce accidents and congestion of traffic. The onboard resources of cars and infrastructure are utilized by the VC to offer the capabilities of "cloud on the fly" to users. Depending on the traffic scenarios, different forms of VCs, such as stationary VC, VC linked with a fixed infrastructure, or dynamic VC, were proposed in literature. The visualization of smart city and intelligent transportation covers connected cars and vehicular IoT as a significant component. The eventual goal of the Internet of Vehicles (IoV) is the incorporation of vehicles, infrastructure, smart things, homes, or anything to promote efficient transportation, accidental safety, and fuel efficiency for a pleasant travel experience to the driver. The technology requires communication between V2V, V2H, V2C, V2I, etc. to exchange vehicle telematics and gather information about the environment to offer services to the users.

The basic safety messages (BSMs) (vehicle position, heading, and speed w.r.t vehicle and path) are to be exchanged among smart entities in safety applications of IoV. These interactions can occur using DSRC technology which allows rapid communication (up to ten times per second) between elements of IoV network required for end-user applications.

13.4 Architecture of the Connected Car

13.4.1 Introduction

A revolution in the digital world creates a great impact in the automotive industry that provides boundless potential to gain a pleasant travelling experience by driving in a safe mode. Pioneers in the automotive industry join together with software developers to bring out a far-reaching transformation in the automotive industry by taming and replacing the existing technologies with the state-of-the-art concepts such as artificial intelligence. A connected car refers to an autonomous car with an amalgamation of IoT and telematics. It could be designated as a group of physical objects that are in a network and have sensors or actuators implanted on them. Intelligence and sensing capabilities are embedded in vehicles with the help of several technologies such as cloud computing; wired and wireless connectivity; low-power, low-cost sensors; and high-capacity processors. Thus, this results in the generation of data, greater interaction, and efficient connectivity.

Framework behind the Scenario: The framework of a connected car is depicted as shown in Figure 13.2. The nature of a connected vehicle is to interact with the environment. Vehicles communicate, and they are capable of transmitting data. In addition to that, the data is shared among other vehicles, external infrastructure, and other devices.

V2V: One vehicle communicates with another in a wireless network [32]. The speed and location details of the vehicles in the network are transmitted to the vehicles nearby in order to prevent accidents, and thus the safety of the travelers could be improved significantly [33]. Messages are being transmitted to nearby vehicles in a continuous fashion. The communication technology preferred for vehicular communication is DSRC [34]. The network that vehicles rely on for exchanging data is VANET [35–36].

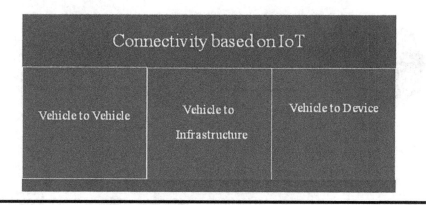

Figure 13.2   Framework of connected car.

V2I: Information about the roadside infrastructure has to be transmitted to avoid accidents so that safety, mobility, and environmental benefits could be ensured. Moreover, drivers also would be able to know about the status of the traffic, diversions in the road, and various weather conditions. Due to this, the number of accidents and causalities could be reduced. Emergency vehicles would be able to reach the destination with the help of the information.

V2D: Cars get connected to several external receiving devices to which they transmit information about traffic and road diversions that could be passed on to other vehicles so that they can drive accordingly. In particular, in emergency vehicles, DRSC technology is used for communication and for transmitting alerts about the traffic.

13.4.2 Architecture

The architecture of a connected car is shown in Figure 13.3. It encompasses hardware modules which enable interactions. Hardware modules mentioned in the figure are described as follows [37–38].

- *TCU/Embedded Modem*: Using a 2G, 3G, or 4G network, a TCU /embedded modem provides Internet connection to the car.
- *Infotainment Module*: It transmits information along with the entertainment content [39].
- *V2X/DSRC*: A vehicle is connected to the infrastructure, and it is estimated that they operate with DSRC technology.

Certain technologies such as DSRC, cellular network (3G, 4G), Wi-Fi, Bluetooth, and Near Field Communication (NFC) are used.

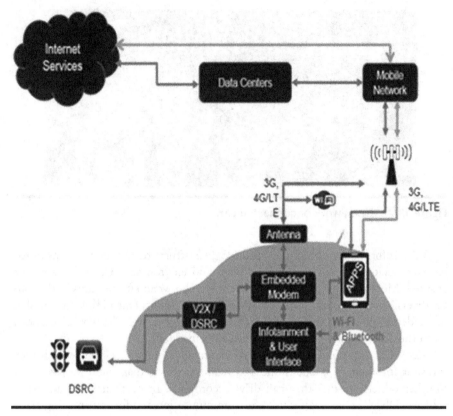

Figure 13.3   Architecture of connected car.

13.5 Services

13.5.1 Traffic Safety and Efficiency

The use of cars has increased tremendously and resulted in traffic congestion all over the world. To overcome this problem, many big data analytics and IoT techniques are used to gather information from CCTV cameras and other vehicle-related data that will help to improve traffic management. A better traffic management system will help to regulate the traffic, utilize natural resources properly, and reduce pollution. The main benefits of an automated car are safety and comfort. Energy saving could be done with this technology. A car can crash due to the drowsiness of the driver. Sensors and certain computer vision applications implanted could determine the state of the driver, i.e., whether they are distracted or exhausted, through their eye movement. The time intervals for the closing of eyes could be fixed. Other factors such as rubbing of the eye, yawning, and stress patterns in the driver could be determined. The stress of the driver could be identified by measuring the heart rate variation or by steering the wheel speed sensors. Breath and touch sensors could be implanted to determine if the driver is drunk.

Smart traffic management considers many factors like organized and congestion-free parking, proper streetlights, accident assistance, and highway monitoring. Traffic lights can be used for multiple purposes with the help of IoT technologies; for example, they can be used to regulate traffic density and record information about areas with high traffic density. Smart traffic management using big data analytics also helps in finding an alternative route to divert the traffic. Based on the weather condition, turning on, dimming, or turning off the headlight can be done with the help of sensors. Smart parking is another important factor that needs to be considered, and it uses IoT-based sensors to detect a free lot and allocate the space to a vehicle instead of the vehicle going around and searching. Accident assistance also needs to be considered, that too in highways, for which information from road sensors and CCTVs is used to alert nearby emergency facilities about an accident.

The challenges for safety and efficiency in traffic management are the lack of adequate infrastructure support in implementing the IoT technology, requirement of speedy data transfer with a faster Internet connection, and need for security to prevent the devices from being hacked.

13.5.2 Infotainment

Today infotainment for vehicle attracts the user of the vehicle so manufacturers add more firmware devices to the vehicles which is said to be infotainment of vehicle. The vehicle has FM radio and multimedia devices that support audio/video, USB, SD card, iPod, and AUX. It also has wireless connectivity like Internet, accessing phone app, and Bluetooth. It also has the telematics like rear-seat entertainment, GPS, and modem.

The automation of infotainment techniques reduces the distraction of drivers for more seconds. With the invent of in-vehicle infotainment (IVI) techniques, the traffic safety is improved. The voice-command function helps the drivers to concentrate and keep their attention on roads. Even though the development in technology reduces the distraction of drivers for two seconds, it will increase the risk for accident. If an in-vehicle technology is not designed properly, then it is going to complicate the task and distract the drivers to take more time to complete the task, which is considered to be an important challenge.

13.5.3 Location-Based Services

The location-based services are navigation, searching infotainment, tracking, etc. IoT is used for gathering data and performing analysis over the data attached with the vehicles. Location-based services are supported by augmented reality, smart phones, etc. Augmented reality connects the physical location coordinate with the environment for processing data to provide details about the real-world landmark.

It helps the pedestrian for navigating and reducing the time of travel. The use of IoT provides a map for guiding the travel to give information about the location and the message service. The smart phone is tracked using GPS or RFID technology to find the location based on the mobility. The automobile industry is disrupted and reshaped with the growth of technology. The development right from the connection, sensors, maps, artificial intelligence (AI), machine learning and augmented reality (AR), neural network, audio-based UI, etc. has changed the level of car deployment. The driverless car has given a new direction for smart mobility.

13.6 Connected Car and Big Data

The advanced technologies to enable the vehicle operation involve gathering of huge information from various sensors installed on vehicles, processing these data, and also storing them for further analysis. It is noted that, in case of connected car, about 40 TB of vehicle status information and engine conditions is accumulated per year [40]. Basically, the connected car provides a platform for information exchange between vehicle machines and drivers, various sensor operations implanted in vehicle, vehicle logistics, and monitoring road and traffic conditions [41].

The major challenges in the connected car concept are collecting huge volume of vehicle functioning data for different customer services, providing efficient mechanism for vehicle monitoring, and performing efficient data analytics on information about these vehicles. In addition, the accuracy of information, usefulness of gathered knowledge, and precise cognitive mechanism are key for efficient connected car ecosystem.

Apache sqoop: It is a software tool designed by Apache. The primary objectives of sqoop are to (1) transfer data efficiently, (2) establish the connection between existing database systems, and (3) provide data unification for business or predictive analytics. First apache sqoop provides command line interfaces to transfer huge volume of data from relational databases or enterprise resource data into distributed file systems. That is, structured databases stored in MySQL, Oracle, or MongoDB are efficiently transferred into Apache Hadoop. This way, the parallel processing of voluminous data is carried out at Hadoop and it provides quick availability of data to various workloads and database users. Second, apache sqoop provides prebuilt interfaces to integrate different database systems, including Oracle, MongoDB, MySQL, and PostgreSQL. These connectors facilitate Hadoop to perform offline workload and to provide several deeper insight of data. Third, the sqoop provides data unification by combining unstructured, semi-structured, and structured data into a single tangible platform, in order to enhance data analytics, apply machine learning models, and optimize data processing.

In case of connected car ecosystem, there exists huge volume of structured, unstructured, and semi-structured data about vehicle functioning. These data are generally stored in conventional relational databases such MySQL and Oracle. Hence, these data need to be transferred into parallel and distributed file systems of Apache Hadoop Ecosystem. The apache sqoop provides import and export connectors through command line interpreter. The connectors facilitate the data exchange between HDFS and RDBM.

Hive and HiveQL: The vehicle data gathered in different tables need efficient querying mechanism for data analysis [42]. In connected car concept, the query model is associated with different events of the vehicle, such as journey plan, location-based services, speed limits, fuel mileage, and engine diagnostic information. Further, in enhanced version, the driver activities and behaviors, accelerometer, and engine condition of the cars are monitored. In order to meet these purposes, the Hive data warehouse and Hive SQL querying model are incorporated.

Hadoop HDFS and Map Reduce Functions: The various vehicle events are recorded and stored in Hadoop distributed file system (HDFS) [43]. The Hadoop platform performs parallel processing of data by splitting the various input data into several chunks of data. Each data chunk is then assigned to data node of Hadoop to carry out the parallel execution. The Hadoop framework utilizes the map reduce functionality where each input is mapped to a key-value pair. These key-value pair is then shuffled and sorted for further reduction tasks, and finally, the results are grouped to provide the desired output. The map reduce function reduces the computation time by parallel processing of different tasks [44].

13.7 Solution for Connected Cars

13.7.1 Microsoft-Connected Vehicle Platform

It provides connected car solutions for the different automobile manufacturers this way, the automakers' brand identity is maintained, and also, the customer's service requirements are addressed. Further, through several differentiated applications, they generate profitable revenues [45].

The Microsoft-connected vehicle platform includes three basic layers, namely, common services layer, Microsoft-connected vehicle platform layer, and purpose-built layer. This architecture is shown in Figure 13.4.

Common Services Layer: This layer provides Microsoft-based productivity suite based on Azure platform utilizing the platform as a service (PaaS). This suite includes Cortana software as voice-based personal assistant, Azure IoT suite, machine learning models and data analytic packages, artificial intelligence, geolocation and map facilities, search models and enterprise modes through graphs, human-to-human interaction through Skype business solutions, and Office 365. Along with these features, this common service layer provides additional services of Azure such as storage facility, computing capability, and networking features.

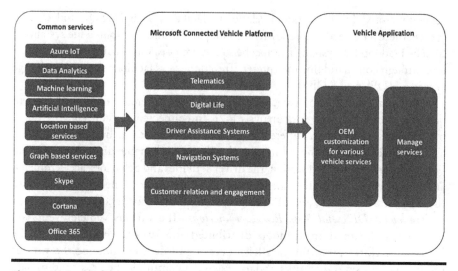

Figure 13.4 Architecture of Microsoft-connected vehicle platform.

Microsoft-Connected Vehicle Platform layer: The objective of this layer is to provide support for the entire common customer-based use cases of connected cars. The platform spans in-car as well as on to the cloud platform through networking. Various functionalities of this layer include telematics services, predictive analytic, enhanced digital life style, advanced assistance system of car drives, and advanced navigation systems, and finally provide insight and engagement of customers.

Purpose-Built Layer: This layer comprises several managed services that can be customized according to the original equipment manufacturer (OEM) requirements and specifications.

13.7.2 Google Android Automotive Operating System

IVI and interconnection among various subsystems of cars is the leading objective of Google Androids Automotive Operating Systems. For this purpose, the bus topologies are preferred by auto manufactures [45]. Various bus topology-based architectures include CAN, Media Oriented Systems Transport (MOST), and TCP/IP-based Ethernet bus for Automotive, Local Interconnect Network (LIN) bus. The main feature of Android Automotive Operating Systems is to provide hardware abstraction layer (HAL) that involves transparent human–machine interfaces (HMI) regardless of the underlying physical transport protocols and services, which is shown in Figure 13.5. In this aspect, the HAL is the primary interface for any application developed for Android Automotive.

The implementation of HAL involves two important interfaces to be interconnected. These interface modules are HAL interface with function-specific

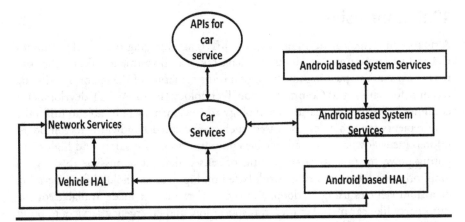

Figure 13.5 Architecture of Android Automotive and Vehicle HAL.

operations and the network interface with specific networking operations. The HAL layers comprise microcontroller-based CPU unit, a real-time operating system, CAN-based bus system, and serial communication for accessing CPU and the Android Automotive Operating System. In case of distributed environment, the dedicated central processing unit is replaced by the cloud-based virtualized processing units. The Automotive manufacture can easily customize the HAL as per the requirements and specifications suitable for their fulfillment.

The Android Automotive architecture consists of application protocol interfaces, namely Car API, CarService, VehicleNetworkService, and VehicleHAL. The Car API basically constitutes the CarHVAC Manager interfaces and CarSensorManager interfaces. The CarService API provides detailed services of the car. Next, the VehicleNetworkService provides control over the security system within the HAL. Access-based control system and OEM access mechanism are well defined within this VehicleNetworkService API. Finally, VehicleHAL provides all the interfaces necessary for the implementation of OEM properties of the vehicle. The data types of each vehicle property are defined through metadata.

Further, the HAL of Android Automotive operating system provides three important levels of security features for data accessing, namely, system-only access, permission-based application access, and permission-less access of car services. The Android system provides direct access to various metadata properties of vehicles through system components. In this case, vehicle network service API will act as the gatekeeper for monitoring various data access-level permissions.

Next, the validation of HAL for Android Automotive includes command line tool to load and do operations on the vehicle HAL. This mechanism adds advantage by accessing the system stages during the development of application services. Next, the testing mechanism for various car services is available in HAL. These tests target to monitor the behavior of various car services and observe the behavior while deploying these service modules.

13.8 Conclusion

A smart connected car in union with the IoT is an emerging theme. The automotive and telecommunication industries have taken an investment stake on the connected car market, pushing for the digital transformation of the sector by utilizing recent Information and Communication Technology (ICT). As ICT developments continue, it is expected that the technology advancements will be able to fulfill the requirements for vehicular use cases, such as increased bandwidth for on-board infotainment, low latency, and reliable communications for safety and high computing power to process large amount of sensed data. It is possible to design a monitoring and analytics framework based on big data technology for processing data from vehicles using Hadoop, and the final results are made available for the third party like car manufacturer, transportation, and emergency services to build useful applications.

This chapter also explains the connected car solutions like Microsoft-connected vehicle platform and Google Androids Automotive Operating Systems. The reader will be inspired about connected car and technologies that leverage the connected car, after reading this chapter.

References

1. www.businessinsider.com/internet-of-things-definition?IR=T. Accessed August 18, 2019.
2. www.goldmansachs.com/insights/pages/internet-of-things/iot-report.pdf. Accessed August 19, 2019.
3. Oussous, Ahmed, Fatima-Zahra Benjelloun, Ayoub Ait Lahcen, and Samir Belfkih. "Big data technologies: A survey." *Journal of King Saud University-Computer and Information Sciences* 30, no. 4 (2018): 431–448.
4. www.globenewswire.com/news-release/2019/07/03/1877861. Accessed August 20, 2019.
5. https://en.wikipedia.org/wiki/Connected_car. Accessed August 20, 2019.
6. Kleberger, Pierre, Tomas Olovsson, and Erland Jonsson. "Security aspects of the in-vehicle network in the connected car." In *2011 IEEE Intelligent Vehicles Symposium (IV)*, pp. 528–533. IEEE, Baden-Baden, 2011.
7. Jerome, J. The connected car and privacy: Navigating new data issues. 2014, https://fpf.org/2014/11/13/new-fpf-paper-the-connected-car-and-privacy-navigating-new-data-issues/ Accessed on August 20, 2019.
8. www.cypress.com/blog/corporate/driving-connected-car-revolution. Accessed August 21, 2019.
9. Dakroub, Husein, Adnan Shaout, and Arafat Awajan. "Connected car architecture and virtualization." *SAE International Journal of Passenger Cars-Electronic and Electrical Systems* 9, no. 2016-01-0081 (2016): 153–159.
10. Lu, Ning, Nan Cheng, Ning Zhang, Xuemin Shen, and Jon W. Mark. "Connected vehicles: Solutions and challenges." *IEEE Internet of Things Journal* 1, no. 4 (2014): 289–299.

11. Bisdikian, Chatschik. "An overview of the Bluetooth wireless technology." *IEEE Communications Magazine* 39, no. 12 (2001): 86–94.

12. Qu, Fengzhong, Fei-Yue Wang, and Liuqing Yang. "Intelligent transportation spaces: Vehicles, traffic, communications, and beyond." *IEEE Communications Magazine* 48, no. 11 (2010): 136–142.

13. Chakravarty, Suhas, Varun Jain, Nakul Midha, and Prashant Bhargava. "Low-cost driver assistance using ZigBee/IEEE 802.15. 4." *Freescale Beyond Bits* 4 (2009): 78–82.

14. Hashim, Nik Mohd Zarifie, M. H. A. Halim, H. Bakri, S. H. Husin, and M. M. Said. "Vehicle security system using Zigbee." *International Journal of Scientific and Research Publications* 3, no. 9 (2013): 3–9.

15. Tsai, Hsin-Mu, Ozan K. Tonguz, Cem Saraydar, Timothy Talty, Michael Ames, and Andrew Macdonald. "Zigbee-based intra-car wireless sensor networks: A case study." *IEEE Wireless Communications* 14, no. 6 (2007): 67–77.

16. Niu, Weihong, Jia Li, Shaojun Liu, and Timothy Talty. "Intra-vehicle ultra-wideband communication testbed." In *MILCOM 2007 – IEEE Military Communications Conference*, pp. 1–6. IEEE, Orlando, FL, 2007.

17. Li, Jia, and Timothy Talty. "Channel characterization for ultra-wideband intra-vehicle sensor networks." In *MILCOM 2006 – 2006 IEEE Military Communications Conference*, pp. 1–5. IEEE, Washington, DC, 2006.

18. Nath, Badri, Franklin Reynolds, and Roy Want. "RFID technology and applications." *IEEE Pervasive Computing* 5, no. 1 (2006): 22–24.

19. Gaba, Gurjot Singh, Nancy Gupta, Gaurav Sharma, and Harsimranjit Singh Gill. "Intelligent cars using RFID technology." *International Journal of Scientific & Engineering Research* 3, no. 7 (2012): 1.

20. Pala, Zeydin, and Nihat Inanc. "Smart parking applications using RFID technology." In *2007 1st Annual RFID Eurasia*, pp. 1–3. IEEE, Istanbul, 2007.

21. Va, Vutha, Takayuki Shimizu, Gaurav Bansal, and Robert W. Heath Jr. "Millimeter wave vehicular communications: A survey." *Foundations and Trends® in Networking* 10, no. 1 (2016): 1–113.

22. Choi, Junil, Vutha Va, Nuria Gonzalez-Prelcic, Robert Daniels, Chandra R. Bhat, and Robert W. Heath. "Millimeter-wave vehicular communication to support massive automotive sensing." *IEEE Communications Magazine* 54, no. 12 (2016): 160–167.

23. Gupta, Maanak, and Ravi Sandhu. "Authorization framework for secure cloud assisted connected cars and vehicular Internet of Things." In *Proceedings of the 23rd ACM on Symposium on Access Control Models and Technologies*, pp. 193–204. ACM, Indianapolis, IN, 2018.

24. Ihara, Yutaka, Haris Kremo, Onur Altintas, Hideaki Tanaka, Masaaki Ohtake, Takeo Fujii, Chikara Yoshimura, Keisuke Ando, Kazuya Tsukamoto, Masato Tsuru, and Yuji Oie. "Distributed autonomous multi-hop vehicle-to-vehicle communications over TV white space." In *2013 IEEE 10th Consumer Communications and Networking Conference (CCNC)*, pp. 336–344. IEEE, Las Vegas, NV, 2013.

25. https://en.wikipedia.org/wiki/Communications_Access_for_Land_Mobiles. Accessed August 26 2019.

26. www.cse.wustl.edu/~jain/cse574-06/vehicular_wireless.htm.

27. Yoon, Jaewoo, and Byeongwoo Kim. "Designing control software for vehicle-to-vehicle communication device applied to model-based design technique." *International Journal of Control and Automation* 11, no. 7 (2018): 25–34.

28. Khan, Ammara Anjum, Mehran Abolhasan, and Wei Ni. "5G next generation VANETs using SDN and fog computing framework." In 2018 *15th IEEE Annual Consumer Communications & Networking Conference (CCNC)*, pp. 1–6. IEEE, Las Vegas, NV, 2018.

29. www.pymnts.com/innovation/2019/connected-vehicle-5g/. Accessed August 27 2019.

30. Ahmed, Zeinab E., Rashid A. Saeed, and Amitava Mukherjee. "Challenges and opportunities in vehicular cloud computing." In *Cloud Security: Concepts, Methodologies, Tools, and Applications*, pp. 2168–2185. IGI Global, Hershey, USA, 2019.

31. Whaiduzzaman, Md., Mehdi Sookhak, Abdullah Gani, and Rajkumar Buyya. "A survey on vehicular cloud computing." *Journal of Network and Computer Applications* 40 (2014): 325–344.

32. Whitepaper – "Transforming the automotive industry with connected cars – An Internet of Things perspective." IGATE Global Solution, Madhusudhan Reddy Nukala, Shreyas Bhargave, Bipin Patwardhan, April 2014.

33. Whitepaper – "The connected car and privacy navigating new data issues." *Future of Privacy Forum*, November 13, 2014.

34. Buddhika R. Maitipe, U. Ibrahim, M. I. Hayee, and Eil Kwon, "Vehicle-to-infrastructure and vehicle-to-vehicle information system in work zones dedicated short-range communications." *Transportation Research Board of the National Academies* (2012): 125–132. doi:10.3141/2324-15.

35. Labiod, Houda, ed. "Vehicle-to-vehicle communications: Applications and perspectives." In Ch 12: *Wireless Ad Hoc and Sensor Networks*, pp. 285–308. doi:10.1002/9780470610893.

36. "Federal Communications Commission. News Release, October 1999." *FCC*. Accessed January 12, https://www.fcc.gov/, 2016.

37. "Cellular network." https://en.wikipedia.org/wiki/Cellular_network. Accessed January 4 2016.

38. Whitepaper – "2025 every car connected: Forecasting the growth and opportunity." GSMA-SBD February 2012.

39. Michigan Department of Transportation and Center for Automotive Research. "Connected vehicle technology Industry Delphi study." pp. 1–22, 2012. www.cargroup.org/assets/files/mdot/mdot_industry_delphi.pdf.

40. Johanson, Pål Dahle, and Andreas Soderberg. "Remote vehicle diagnostics over the Internet using the DoIP protocol." In *ICSNC 2011: The Sixth International Conference on Systems and Networks Communications*, 2011, pp. 22623, Barcelona.

41. Nkenyereye, Lionel, and Jong-Wook Jang. "Integration of big data for querying CAN bus data from connected car." In *2017 Ninth International Conference on Ubiquitous and Future Networks (ICUFN)*, pp. 946–950. IEEE, Milan, 2017.

42. "Traffic management centers in a connected vehicle environment." *Future of TMCs in a Connected Vehicle Final Report*, TMC03, pp. 1–27, 2013.

43. Analytics, Customer. "The art of possibility: Connected vehicles and big data analytics." (2014): 1–10. http://blogs.sas.com/content/customeranalytics/2014/12/29/the-art-of-possibility-connected-vehicles-and-big-dataanalytics.

44. McQueen, Bob. *Big Data Analytics for Connected Vehicles and Smart Cities*, Cloud Publish, London, 2017.

45. www.cypress.com/blog/corporate/driving-connected-car-revolution. Accessed on August 29, 2019.

Index